JESUS AS HEALER

Jesus as Healer

A Gospel for the Body

Jan-Olav Henriksen *&* Karl Olav Sandnes

WILLIAM B. EERDMANS PUBLISHING COMPANY
GRAND RAPIDS, MICHIGAN

Published 2016 by
Wm. B. Eerdmans Publishing Co.
2140 Oak Industrial Drive N.E., Grand Rapids, Michigan 49505

Printed in the United States of America

22 21 20 19 18 17 16   7 6 5 4 3 2 1

Library of Congress Cataloging-in-Publication Data

Names: Henriksen, Jan-Olav, author.
Title: Jesus as healer: a gospel for the body / Jan-Olav Henriksen & Karl Olav Sandnes.
Description: Grand Rapids, Michigan: Eerdmans Publishing Company, 2016. |
    Includes bibliographical references and index.
Identifiers: LCCN 2015046914 | ISBN 9780802873316 (pbk.: alk. paper)
Subjects: LCSH: Bible. Gospels — Criticism, interpretation, etc. | Healing in the Bible. |
    Healing — Biblical teaching. | Miracles — Biblical teaching. | Jesus Christ.
Classification: LCC BS2555.6.H4 H46 2016 | DDC 226/.066—dc23
    LC record available at http://lccn.loc.gov/2015046914

www.eerdmans.com

Contents

Acknowledgments

There are several people we would like to thank as we finalize this book. First of all, we would like to thank (MF) Norwegian School of Theology, which has offered us the chance to do the research necessary for completion. Furthermore, all the people with whom we have had formal and not so formal conversations: The members of the research groups in New Testament and systematic theology at our school, and other colleagues who have provided input in different ways and helped us develop the following arguments.

Henriksen would like to thank his wife, Hilde Marie, for long conversations on the topics here dealt with, and for offering valuable contributions to how the different arguments should be shaped.

Sandnes thanks Dr. Sigurd Kaiser (Nanjing Union Theological Seminary, China) who kindly commented on a draft of this manuscript while we were colleagues there. Also, my former colleague Associate Professor em. Martin Synnes (MF Norwegian School of Theology, Oslo) offered constructive criticism.

We would both like to thank PhD student Christine H. Aarflot for improving the English of the manuscript considerably, and our assistant Åsulv W. Eikaas for a thorough working over of references and literature. We are deeply grateful for their meticulous efforts.

Let us finally say that although this work is for the most part building on the work of separate disciplines of theology, we hope that the reader will be able to detect that we have benefited from engaging with each other's material and modes of working. Thus the present book is a testimony to the fact that our theological disciplines are not uninformed by each other, and that further cooperation in the field is possible. Hence, we have enjoyed doing this together.

JAN-OLAV HENRIKSEN & KARL OLAV SANDNES

Abbreviations

ANF   *The Ante-Nicene Fathers.* Edited by Alexander Roberts and James
       Donaldson. 1885–1887. 10 vols. Repr., Peabody, MA: Hendrickson,
       1994.

ANRW   *Aufstieg und Niedergang der römischen Welt: Geschichte und Kultur*
       Roms im Spiegel der neueren Forschung. Part 2, Principat. Edited by
       Hildegard Temporini and Wolfgang Haase. Berlin: De Gruyter, 1972–

Ant.   Josephus, *Antiquities of the Jews*

BDAG   Frederick W. Danker, Walter Bauer, William F. Arndt, and F. Wilbur
       Gingrich. *Greek-English Lexicon of the New Testament and Other Early*
       Christian Literature. 3rd ed. Chicago: University of Chicago Press,
       2000

Cels.   Origen, *Contra Celsum*

Doctr. chr.   *De doctrina christiana*

Eph.   Ignatius of Antioch, *Epistle to the Ephesians*

Haer.   Irenaeus, *Adversus haereses*

Hist. eccl.   Eusebius of Caesarea, *Historia ecclesiastica*

LSJ   Henry George Liddell, Robert Scott, and Henry Stuart Jones.
       A Greek-English Lexicon. 9th ed. with revised supplement. Oxford:
       Clarendon, 1996

Orat.   Tatian, *Oration to the Greeks*

TDNT   *Theological Dictionary of the New Testament.* Edited by Gerhard Kittel
       and Gerhard Friedrich. Translated by Geoffrey W. Bromiley. 10 vols.
       Grand Rapids: Eerdmans, 1964–1976

WUNT   Wissenschaftliche Untersuchungen zum Neuen Testament

ZNW   *Zeitschrift für die neutestamentliche Wissenschaft und die Kunde der*
       älteren Kirche

Introduction

If you ask what people care about today, religion and health are both high on the list of possible answers. Healing and health concern everybody — and increasingly more so, it seems. Health is one of the most central cultural values of contemporary Western societies, and one that determines policies, public services, and budgets, as well as influences discussions about both private and public priorities. As a consequence, some speak of "healthism" as a new ideology or religion.[1] Although health is not religion, the interest in it seems to take on almost religious character sometimes.

Health and religion have always been closely related. In the phenomenon we call religious or spiritual healing, people sometimes claim to have been healed, often rather unexpectedly, in ways that cannot be explained in medical terms. In Christianity, however, the relationship between health and healing has been somewhat ambiguous. Throughout the history of Western Christianity, health matters have traditionally been taken care of within the hospital tradition. As a result, practices of healing in a more spiritual and nonmedical sense have often been placed in the background. There are many possible reasons why this is the case, and we will touch on some of them in the following pages.

Healers receive attention. Jesus of Nazareth was no exception in this regard. The stories of the New Testament make that clear. But the fact that Jesus was a healer does not seem to have been emphasized to the same degree or to have played a similar role in early Christianity, or in the development of Christian theology throughout the centuries, as it did in the New

1. See Robert Crawford, "A Cultural Account of Health: Control, Release and the Social Body," in *Issues in the Political Economy of Health Care,* ed. John B. McKinley (New York: Tavistock, 1984), pp. 60–103.

1

•

Testament. Given the amount of stories in the New Testament about Jesus' work as a healer, this seems somewhat surprising, and gives rise to a number of questions. In this book, we will look into possible reasons for this lack of focus on Jesus' activity as a healer in the Western Christian tradition. We will also consider, from a more constructive point of view, potential sources for reflection about what it can mean for Christian theology today to understand Jesus as a healer.

In much of recent Western Christianity, religion and health seem to be clearly differentiated.[2] We will return to the reasons behind this in a later chapter. However, there are exceptions to this clearly delineated separation between religion and health: we find concerns for health and healing, for example, in versions of evangelical theology, in the charismatic movement, and in the different versions of so-called alternative spiritualities that have emerged in the West since the 1960s. But with few exceptions, the topics of Jesus as a healer (a topic that can help us discuss basic and important elements in Christianity) on the one hand and health and healing on the other hand are mostly missing when we look for more detailed examinations and contributions in academic theological literature.[3]

We will argue that there are good reasons for considering the topic of Jesus as a healer from the perspectives of both New Testament scholarship and contemporary and constructive systematic theology. The present book should be seen as an attempt to add to and even open up venues related to the discussion of the significance of Jesus' healing ministry. Not only will this be a possible contribution to, and development of, the cooperation between historical and contemporary theology, but it will also be an approach that allows for these disciplines to take into account knowledge from other sources, like anthropology, ethnology, and religious studies in general. Furthermore, we maintain that such an approach may help us to address the topic of Jesus as healer in a way that makes it possible to interpret his healing ministry and its significance as more than an illustration of Jesus as someone in possession of divine powers. It may also contribute to the picture of him as a human being who stands alongside other humans

2. Some of the reasons why this may be the case are analyzed in a book by sociologist of religion Meredith McGuire. See Meredith B. McGuire, *Lived Religion: Faith and Practice in Everyday Life* (Oxford: Oxford University Press, 2008).

3. Warrants for this claim will be given in detail later. A notable example is how Wolfhart Pannenberg's *Systematic Theology,* which is among the most thorough treatises of dogmatic subjects published in recent decades, has no section devoted to the topic. There are, however, also exceptions, which will be discussed below.

in carrying out this type of ministry. This does not, however, exclude the fact that Jesus' work as a healer is integrated in a wider web of practices that makes him stand out as distinct, or even unique, compared to his contemporaries.

In the following parts of this book, we will accordingly consider what it means for contemporary Christian theology that Jesus was a healer. He was not medically trained, and was nevertheless able to heal those who sought his help. For many years this dimension of his ministry has been neglected or looked on with some suspicion, perhaps because Jesus' healings have so often been attributed to his ability to "perform miracles." The present academic scene offers some fortunate conditions for embarking on such a project. First, New Testament scholarship has presently left behind much of historical criticism's rationalistic approach to texts, which tended to dismiss the healing stories of the New Testament as historically inadequate.[4] Furthermore, the growing interaction of New Testament studies with other anthropological studies of the Mediterranean and Near Eastern areas provides good opportunities for seeing the healing practices of Jesus in relation to the religious context of his time — a context where we also find other healers (as is indicated already in the Gospels and the book of Acts).

Systematic theology today also seems more open to both empirical studies and to the field of religious studies than was the case some decades ago. To write theology informed by empirical disciplines allows contemporary theology to weave the concerns of normative theology into a web of human experience and human conditions. This approach may in turn help people realize what may be the contemporary relevance of the Christian message, in a way that allows it to be interpreted in light of other and richer sources of knowledge than what can be found in the theological tradition. We hope thereby to counter the perceived isolation or irrelevance that many today experience when presented with theological reflection.

Against this wider scholarly backdrop, we find it plausible to affirm that Jesus was a healer, and that he healed many people. It is not the intention of this book to provide an extensive or apologetic argument that it was in fact possible for Jesus to perform such acts — recent anthropological and ethnographic studies provide us with sufficient reasons for asserting Jesus' healing ministry. There are, however, a number of other concerns that have informed and influenced the writing of this book:

---

4. See, e.g., the theology of Rudolf Bultmann, which may nevertheless also offer some important reflections for us to work with in a contemporary context. See part II below.

3

- We believe the topic "Jesus as healer" helps us to address the *embodied* character of Christian faith in a way that underscores how one can experience God's care and compassion as something related to more than human spiritual welfare. In this, we agree with those who see healing as more than good medical health, but as something that has to do with all realms of human life, whether physical, spiritual, social and cultural, or psychological.
- We are accordingly hesitant to view Jesus as healer as a topic that is mainly about some kind of "supernatural" reality. Such a perspective seems to add little to the understanding of the facts in question. Instead, we find that this topic opens up to a fuller theological understanding of the created, experienced world in which God has placed humans. This reality is embodied, relational, and divinely recognized as worthy of care, concern, and mercy, and not only as a gateway to "a spiritual" or supernatural realm.
- Following from the above concerns, we also suggest that one does not see Jesus as healer mainly within a framework that addresses his ministry as an expression of the miraculous. There is, admittedly, an extraordinary character to his healing ministry, but as we shall see, this is not adequately addressed simply by interpreting it in a category that places it outside of what is possible in this world.

Furthermore, and in a wider context, we believe it is important that Christian theology has something to say about the connection between God, Jesus, health, and healing. Much contemporary spirituality that does not have a distinctively Christian mark strongly underscores the relation between spirituality and healing. But there are no good reasons why Christian theology should leave the relation between healing and spirituality to be addressed only by the representatives of alternative forms of spirituality. As a consequence, we want to investigate in what ways a contemporary established understanding of Jesus as healer, which also takes the historical sources into account, may have something to offer in that regard. We remain convinced that the best way to do so is by approaching the theme of Jesus as healer. Leaving the understanding of healers to the alternative scene or New Age or to Christian charismatic groups that strongly emphasize the proclamation of Jesus as healer, but without equally strong theological warrants for this claim, seems to us not to be a good option for a firmly and scholarly based Christian theology.

There are also more theological, and even christological, concerns behind the present project: Jesus is, no matter how we understand his life and work, a human being in the human world. Whereas one previously saw Jesus' miraculous healings as a testimony to his divine power, there is reason to question whether this should still be taken for granted as the only acceptable view. In fact, it may prove fruitful to see Jesus' healing ministry as parallel to other healers' ministries, although one should be careful from the outset neither to conflate Jesus as healer with nor separate him from these other healing practitioners. To view him against the backdrop of such analogies requires no preestablished assumption of a "supernatural intervention." Contemporary *christological* reflection cannot and accordingly should not immediately assume that it can attribute everything that is not easy to explain in Jesus' ministry to his divine nature, which traditional dogmatic Christology has seen as conjoined with the human person Jesus of Nazareth. Such an approach rests on several debatable assumptions, which we will address more in detail throughout the book.

What do we hope to achieve in this book? First, we aim to develop a contemporary account of how Christians have remembered and may still viably understand the healing ministry of Jesus. Second, we hope to help people recognize in what ways God may be seen to have a healing presence in the world. There is a gospel for the body. The latter point cannot be realized without also offering some hermeneutical tools for how to relate to and interpret a world that still seems to be full of healers, and accordingly, of different accounts about what their ministry is all about. Christians, as well as others, need to face that world, because they believe in a God who is not only the God of life but also the creator of all that is.

This book is divided into two main parts: The first part discusses contributions from contemporary New Testament scholarship to an understanding of Jesus as healer. The main focus here is on discussing how and why Jesus was remembered as a healer. This part also discusses witnesses about Jesus as healer in relation to other ancient reports on healers in order to more clearly bring to the fore the specific and extraordinary in Jesus' ministry as healer. The perspective employed here implies that we primarily focus on the therapeutic dimension of Jesus' work, and therefore leave out stories with no or only weak analogies to the contemporary material (including reports of bringing dead people to life). This does not mean that we reject these other events as unhistorical; but we find that there is hardly sufficient evidence for interpreting them in the same manner as we do past and present healing events. Accordingly, when we leave out this dimension of how Jesus' ministry was remembered, it is more a result of methodological than of ontological or theological decisions.

The second part presents and discusses different material that can situate the understanding of Jesus as healer within a wider contemporary context of theological interpretation. In addition to presenting recent studies related to spiritual healing, material for the understanding of "miracles," and some interpretations of Jesus as healer in modern theology, this part also formulates some basic principles for a viable understanding of Jesus as healer. These principles may in turn also shed some light on the church's continuous ministry of healing.

This book is not intended to be the final word on Jesus as healer. However, we do hope to open up a discussion that moves away from the debate of whether healing takes place or not, to a more fruitful conversation about how Christian theology can interpret the fact that healing seems to be an important element in the spiritual practices of many religious traditions, Christianity included. Neither healing nor Jesus as healer is a unique phenomenon. For those who believe in him, it is precisely this situation that calls for a theological understanding of what it means that Jesus was a healer.

PART I

Remembering Jesus as Healer:
Perspectives from New Testament Scholarship

Karl Olav Sandnes

Introductory Remarks to the New Testament Part

We start this part of the book by stating a fact: Jesus was remembered as a healer. This remembrance is to be found almost exclusively in stories. Jesus' healings were recounted and passed on. Storytelling always serves the present in one way or the other. From the very outset we can therefore point out that Jesus was remembered as a healer in a way relevant for posterity. Outside the narrative genre, Jesus as healer is a topic that plays no significant role in early Christianity. It is, for example, entirely absent in the Apostles' Creed, as well as in creed-like texts in the New Testament, which are building blocks towards later formulations of what Christian faith is about (Rom 1:3–4; Phil 2:6–11; Col 1:15–20; 1 Tim 3:16; Heb 1:2–4). In a way that became formative for the church, these texts encapsulate the pivotal elements in the ministry of Jesus. Strikingly, the wonder traditions[1] are absent. This is, however, not the case in the book of Acts (see later), and it is also worth noticing that Justin Martyr (c. 160 CE) at times includes Jesus' healings and exorcisms in his creedal statements on the life of Jesus: "In these books, then, of the prophets we found Jesus our Christ foretold as coming, born of a virgin, growing up to man's estate, and healing every disease and every sickness, and raising the dead, and being hated, and unrecognized, and crucified, and dying, and rising again, and ascending into heaven, and being called the Son of God" (*1 Apology* 31, cf. 48). To Justin, Jesus' healing sickness is a fulfillment of prophecy; it is part of his proof-from-prophecy argument. The Christians

1. English "wonder" is synonymous with "miracle," and here refers to all such acts performed by Jesus. Whenever possible I prefer "wonder" to "miracle" for two reasons. First, it picks up on how these acts were perceived by people who witnessed them as something amazing and unexpected. Furthermore, "miracle" is more conducive to entail ontology, as referring to something supernatural or divine. That particular issue will become a topic especially in the second part of this volume.

did tell and pass on stories about Jesus as healer, and also about his disciples who continued this ministry, albeit more randomly.

As Craig S. Keener points out, "Miracle stories compose nearly one-third of Mark's Gospel."[2] The evidence for Jesus as a wonderworker is overwhelming in the relevant sources. It is found explicitly in Q, Mark, Matthew, Luke, John, Acts, as well as polemically in Jewish as well as pagan sources. The latter sources, for example, rabbinic texts and Celsus, make sense of this activity of Jesus' differently from how the Gospels present it. They say that Jesus owed his healing power to sorcery, a hostile interpretation echoed also in Mark 3:22 and parallels and some other passages. The polemics make no attempt, however, to deny that Jesus really performed wonders. It is the explanations that differ, and greatly so, not the fact that Jesus performed healings.

Apparently the first-century Jewish historian Josephus attests that Jesus was seen as a wonderworker. In his so-called *Testimonium Flavianum* (*Ant.* 18.63), he says that Jesus was a wise man who "worked startling deeds" (*paradoxa erga*). The Greek adjective *paradoxos* refers to something contrary to all expectations, or what is incredible;[3] it refers to things perceived as miraculous. The fact that the wonders are labeled *ta paradoxa* is worth noticing, since it gives reason to question the commonly held view that people in the ancient world were exceedingly credulous.[4] We need to be reminded that a common reaction to Jesus' healings was the following: "We have never seen anything like this" (Mark 2:12 par.).[5] However, the reliability of this piece of information in Josephus is debatable. No doubt, the testimony has been shaped by Christians; but whether it is a Christian addition throughout or only partly remains an issue. It is probable that Josephus included some information about Jesus of Nazareth at this point in his story, and that Chris-

---

2. Craig S. Keener, *Miracles: The Credibility of the New Testament Accounts*, 2 vols. (Grand Rapids: Baker Academic, 2011), p. 5.

3. LSJ s.v. According to Luke's version of how the bystanders react to the healing of the crippled, they witnessed *paradoxa* (NRSV "strange things") (Luke 5:26). This term is also used by Josephus for the miracles worked by Elijah and Elisha (*Ant.* 9.182; cf. 2.267, 285; 10.28, 235; 13.282; 15.379).

4. Graham H. Twelftree, *Jesus the Miracle Worker: A Historical and Theological Study* (Downers Grove, IL: InterVarsity Press, 1999), p. 254; Ruben Zimmermann, "Grundfragen zu den frühchristlichen Wundererzählungen," in *Kompendium der frühchristlichen Wundererzählungen*, vol. 1, *Die Wunder Jesu*, ed. Ruben Zimmermann et al. (Gütersloh: Gütersloher Verlagshaus, 2013), p. 19.

5. This is a case in which the plural *paradoxa* appears in Luke as a reaction of the bystanders (Luke 5:26).

tians then expanded on it, but also shaped what might have been there already. To be sure, some of the concepts conveyed about Jesus in this passage find little compliance with how Christians commonly talked about Jesus, thus suggesting that it is not a Christian invention throughout.[6] Furthermore, the fact that Josephus mentions "the brother of Jesus" (*Ant.* 20.200) assumes that the readers have already been introduced to Jesus; most likely this is where the *Testimonium Flavianum* is now found. If the *Testimonium Flavianum* is removed, this piece of information about "the brother of Jesus" is left hanging in the air. Hence, it seems justified to assume that the wonders of Jesus had already been mentioned by Josephus.[7] The Greek magical papyri (PGM) give witness to the fact that even outsiders considered the name of Jesus to be able to perform miraculous things.[8] Although this is worth noticing, PGM attest to the repute of Jesus only.

This source-critical situation complies with the principle of multiple attestation in historical Jesus research. Again, in the words of Craig S. Keener: "The evidence is stronger for this claim than for most other historical claims that we could make about Jesus or earliest Christianity."[9] This means that the general picture is authentic, but it can nevertheless not be applied to every single instance. What matters in the present context is to point out that Jesus was clearly and broadly remembered as a healer. It is the memories of this activity, not a secured minimum of historically authentic material, that eventually come into play for present-day theology.

It is here worth rehearsing briefly what Chris Keith has called "the Jesus-memory approach" in historical Jesus research.[10] Its point of departure is the fundamental insight of recent memory studies, which has been picked up

6. Jesus is called "a wise man [*sophos anēr*]," who performed "amazing deeds [*paradoxa*]"; he was "a teacher of people who accept truth with pleasure [*hēdonē*]." This portrayal is indicative of an outsider perspective, albeit some overlap with New Testament passages may occur. Furthermore, the Christians are called "a tribe [*phylon*]."

7. This is suggested by the detailed investigation made by Robert E. Van Voorst, *Jesus outside the New Testament: An Introduction to the Ancient Evidence* (Grand Rapids: Eerdmans, 2000), pp. 81–104.

8. Hans Dieter Betz, ed., *The Greek Magical Papyri in Translation, including the Demotic Spells* (Chicago: University of Chicago Press, 1992).

9. Keener, *Miracles*, p. 23. Likewise Justin Meggitt, "The Historical Jesus and Healing: Jesus' Miracles in Psychosocial Context," in *Spiritual Healing: Scientific and Religious Perspectives,* ed. Fraser Watts (Cambridge: Cambridge University Press, 2011), pp. 17–20.

10. Chris Keith, "Memory and Authenticity: Jesus Tradition and What Really Happened," *ZNW* 102, no. 2 (2011): 155–77. See also Anthony Le Donne, *Historical Jesus: What Can We Know and How Can We Know It?* (Grand Rapids: Eerdmans, 2011).

on in New Testament studies: Remembering is not simply an act of recalling the past, but the past is reconstructed in the light of present needs. In other words, memory is formed or shaped by the present. Applying this to the Gospels and considering them as "receptions of Jesus-memory" has significance not only for historical Jesus research but also for the present project. This way of thinking assumes that both past and present have conditioned the memories about Jesus.

These memories were not made without any basis in what happened; certainly the past provided stories to be told and remembered. However, the past would not be remembered and told if it did not bring anything to the present, and the present provided parameters for how to remember and how to make sense of the remembrances. By implication, the present has made it into the stories about the past. This way of thinking is a blow against the traditional aim of separating authentic from nonauthentic material in the Jesus tradition. In the memory approach the two are inextricably interwoven. The central role occupied by healing activity in the memories about Jesus is likely to mirror the need of those who remembered him in this way. The focus is therefore on the remembered or reported Jesus: in practice how he is portrayed in the Gospels — rather than on making a narrow search for authenticity throughout.

In this context I will therefore limit myself to concentrating on Jesus as healer and how he was remembered as such in early tradition. The historical part serves a hermeneutical and present-day perspective. Part I of the present study will therefore have a threefold structure. First, we will look at the emphasis given to the tradition of Jesus as healer. Because of limitations in scope, I will not proceed with each Gospel, but will view them together, and where necessary pay due attention to their differences. Second, we proceed to see how Jesus' ministry is continued in the mission of his disciples. And third, we will look into the role assigned to the tradition of Jesus as healer in other early Christian literature, with a particular focus on how Christians came to make use of this tradition. Like everybody else, early Christians fell sick and suffered from bodily weaknesses. What did they do to find a cure? They venerated narrative traditions in which healing miracles held pride of place. Furthermore, their surroundings provided various ways to help the sick. How did they then react, and how did they conceive of the means provided through magic spells, the god of medicine Asclepius, and various other healing practices? What bearing did their faith in Jesus and the stories about him have on the question of their health? Some of these questions broaden the perspective beyond Jesus as healer and also include later disciples.

How is "healing" to be defined then? For now, this term refers to restoring people to health in all possible ways, that is, physically, psychologically, and socially.[11] As we will see in the next chapters, the definition of healing is a matter of dispute in medical anthropological studies, on which many New Testament scholars rely in their understanding of the healing stories. What was Jesus actually doing when he restored people to health? What aspects of health were involved? At the moment, a more precise definition than the one given above would be to anticipate unduly. In the canonical Gospels, the healings of Jesus belong within his activity as wonderworker, which include three different kinds of activities: therapeutic,[12] nontherapeutic,[13] and exorcisms. Healing applies, for obvious reasons, to the therapeutic wonders, while the nontherapeutic will be left out in the present work. As for exorcisms, they cannot be left out. Exorcisms and healings are not identical, although there is clearly some overlap between them. This is so partly because some of the exorcisms are simply referred to as healings. Among the thirteen healing stories in Mark's Gospel, four are stories of exorcism. Some texts, such as Luke 8:2–3 and Acts 10:38, consider healing to liberate from the shackles of the evil, and thus favor the view that healing and exorcism cannot be entirely separated. Stylistically and to some extent also terminologically, the exorcisms appear as distinct, albeit not always equally clearly so, from healing stories. Regarding the content of the miracles themselves or what is at stake in our understanding of healing, however, this distinction is difficult to uphold. Furthermore, all exorcisms involve a return to fellowship for a person who was marginalized and made an outcast because of his or her demon. Jesus' casting out the demon thus implies healing at various levels. Finally, including exorcisms in our study will enhance our possibility of reaching an adequate understanding of Jesus as healer generally, even as it enhances the strangeness of Jesus' wonders for present-day readers. This will become apparent below.

11. For a detailed presentation of how to define "healing," see pp. 136–51 in the present volume.

12. Instances of raising the dead are here considered as ultimate healing stories; see Jesus' response to John the Baptist according to the Q tradition (Matt. 11:2–6//Luke 7:18–23).

13. Such as feeding the hungry, walking on the sea, etc.

The Evidence of the Canonical Gospels: A Survey

This chapter provides an overview of the relevant healing material in the Gospels, which is of two kinds, stories and summaries. The table below sorts the texts according to sickness or diagnostics and the healing method used by Jesus. Doing diagnostics across centuries is, of course, risky business at best (see below). A present-day example is the way homosexuality is now seen compared to only some decades ago. Sickness may also come in a cultural garb, particularly if the disease is psychosomatic. The diagnostic below will keep strictly to what the New Testament passages say themselves, and refrain from any attempt to transfer this into the medical terminology of our time. The relevant passages are not very forthcoming in offering information for a precise diagnosis. The overview includes only healing *stories,* and is followed by a separate section on summaries.

Healing Stories

Texts	Sickness/Diagnosis	Healing Method	Outcome
Mark 1:23–28// Luke 4:33–37	Unclean spirit	Words	The spirit left
Mark 1:29–31// Matt. 8:14–15// Luke 4:38–39	Fever	Touching	Fever left
Mark 1:40–45// Matt. 8:1–4// Luke 5:12–16	Leper (*lepros/lepra*)	Touching and words	Cleansed; according to Matthew and Luke: "Show yourself to the priest."

Texts	Sickness/Diagnosis	Healing Method	Outcome
Mark 2:1–12// Matt. 9:1–8// Luke 5:17–25	Paralytic *(paralytikos)* who is carried	Words	Stood up, carried his mat, and walked away
Mark 3:1–6// Matt. 12:9–14// Luke 6:6–11	A withered hand	The man is asked to stretch out his hand; Unclear healing method	Mark: hand restored *(apekatestathē)*. Matthew: restored *(apekatestathē hygiēs)*. Luke: restored *(apekatestathē)*.
Mark 5:1–20// Matt. 8:28–34// Luke 8:26–39	Mark: unclean spirit. Uncontrollable. Matthew: two persons; both are fierce *(chalepoi)*, frightening to people. Luke: the man wore no clothes, unable to live among people.	Command/ words.	Mark: the spirit came out; man calmed *(sōphronein)* and clothed; returns home. Matthew: the spirit came out. Luke: the spirit came out; the man clothed and in his right mind *(sōphronein)*; returned home; Healed *(esōthē)*
Mark 5:21–24, 35–43// Matt. 9:18–19, 23–26//Luke 8:41–42, 49–56	Mark: at the point of dying *(eschatōs echei)*, then dead. Matthew: dead. Luke: dying, then dead	Mark: touching, withdrawal from the crowd; command *(talitha koum)*. Matthew: touching. Luke: touching; command	Mark: got up and walked around; told to eat. Matthew: got up. Luke: started breathing *(epestrepsen to pneuma autēs)*
Mark 5:25–34// Matt. 9:20–22// Luke 8:43–48	All: suffering from hemorrhages for twelve years. Mark and Luke: spent all her money on physicians unable to help (Luke's reading uncertain)	All: she touched Jesus. Mark and Luke: A power went out from Jesus	Mark: her bleeding stopped immediately *(euthys)*; healed *(iatai, sōzein, hygiēs)*. Matthew: healed *(esōthē)*. Luke: healed instantly *(iathē parachrēma; sōzein)*; went in peace

Texts	Sickness/Diagnosis	Healing Method	Outcome
Mark 6:54–56// Matt. 14:34–36	Mark: sick *(hoi kakōs echontes* and *hoi asthenountes)* carried on their beds. Matthew: *hoi kakōs echontes*	People touching Jesus, even the fringe of his cloak	Healed *(esōzonto)*
Mark 7:24–30// Matt. 15:21–28	Mark: little girl *(thygatrion)* with an unclean spirit. Matthew: daughter (age not mentioned)	Words (distance)	Mark: the spirit left her. Matthew: healed *(iathē)*
Mark 7:31–37// Matt. 15:29–31	Mark: man deaf with an impediment in his speech *(mogilalon)*. Matthew turns this into a summary: lame, maimed, blind, mute, and many others	Mark: touching; withdrawal from the crowd; putting finger in his ear; spitting and touching his tongue; command: *ephphatha*	Mark: able to hear and spoke plainly *(orthōs)*. Matthew: cured *(etherapeusen);* mute speaking; maimed whole *(hygieis);* lame walking; blind seeing
Mark 8:22–26	Blind	Touching twice; withdrawal from the crowd; saliva on the eyes	Sight restored; returned home
Mark 9:14–27//Matt. 17:14–18//Luke 9:37–43	Mark: a spirit making a boy unable to speak *(pneuma alalon);* the spirit seizes him, dashes him down; he foams and grinds his teeth and becomes rigid; convulsed by the spirit, casting him into fire and water; from childhood. Matthew: Moonstruck *(selēniazetai);* suffers terribly; falling into fire and water. Luke: a spirit seizes him and he shrieks; it convulses him until he foams at the mouth; it mauls him and will scarcely leave him	All: command	Mark: the spirit that kept the boy from speaking and hearing left. Matthew: the spirit left; healed at once *(etherapeuthē)*. Luke: healed *(iasato)* and given to his father

Texts	Sickness/Diagnosis	Healing Method	Outcome
Mark 10:46–52//Matt. 9:27–31//20:29–34// Luke 18:35–43	Mark: blind beggar (Bartimaeus). Matthew: two blind men. Luke: blind beggar	Mark: word or command; Matthew: (1) touching and words; (2) touching. Luke: word or command	Mark: healed *(sōzein);* regained sight at once *(euthys).* Matthew: (1) the eyes were opened; followed Jesus; (2) regained sight at once *(eutheōs);* followed Jesus. Luke: regained sight immediately *(parachrēma);* healed *(sōzein)*
Matt. 8:5–13// Luke 7:1–10// cf. John 4:46–54	Matthew: paralytic *(paralytikos)* servant; in terrible distress. Luke: ill *(kakōs echōn)* and dying. John: sick *(ēsthenei)* and about to die	Matthew: words. Luke: words. John: words	Matthew: healed *(iathē)* at once *(en tē hōra ekeinē).* Luke: good health *(hygianonta).* John: fever left and the boy recovered from the moment Jesus told it would
Matt. 9:32–34//12:22–24// Luke 11:14–15	Matthew: (1) a demoniac who was mute; (2) demoniac who was blind and mute. Luke: demoniac who was mute		Matthew: (1) demon cast out; the mute spoke; (2) healed him *(etherapeusen)* so he could speak and see. Luke: demon cast out and the mute spoke
Matt. 21:14–17	Blind and lame		Healed *(etherapeusen)* them
Luke 7:11–17	Dead; the only son of a widow	Touching; command	The young boy rose and started to speak; gave him to his mother
Luke 13:10–17	A spirit of sickness *(astheneia)* that has crippled a woman for eighteen years; bent over and unable to stand up straight	Words. touching	Set free *(apolelysai)* from her ailment; immediately *(parachrēma)* she stood up straight
Luke 14:2–6	Dropsy *(hydrōpikos)*	Touching *(epilabomenos)*	Healed *(iasato)* him and sent him away

Texts	Sickness/Diagnosis	Healing Method	Outcome
Luke 17:12–19	Ten lepers *(leproi)*	Words (show yourself to the priests)	Cleansed *(ekatharisthēsan)*. Healed *(iathē* and *sesōken)*
Luke 22:50–51	No illness, but an ear acutely cut off	Touching	Healed *(iasato)*
John 5:2–18	Man sick for thirty-eight years	Words	Made well *(hygiēs)* immediately *(eutheōs);* took his mat and walked away; healed *(iatheis)*
John 9:1–7	Born blind	Spat on the ground and made mud with the saliva and spread the mud on the man's eyes; command: wash yourself in the Pool of Siloam	Regained his sight
John 11:1–57	Illness that caused death four days ago (smells already)	Command	The dead man came out bound with strips of cloth; Jesus has him unbound and lets him go

Summaries

In addition to the stories included above, the Gospels include summary statements on Jesus' ministry. In these summaries, his healings are recurrent. Summaries are, according to their nature, general; they briefly list events and condense information. Little can therefore be gleaned from them with regard to what the beneficiaries of Jesus' healings suffered from. They are still highly relevant texts in depicting how Jesus was remembered as a healer.

Mark 1:32–34//Matthew 8:16–17//Luke 4:40–41: Mark speaks of the sick *(kakōs echontes)*; it is worth noticing that they were carried or brought to Jesus. Some were demoniacs. A reference is also made to different kinds of diseases *(poikilais nosois)*. Matthew gives much of the same picture, but adds "infirmities" *(astheneiai),* which also occurs next to *nosoi* in the citation he uses from Isaiah 53:4. Luke alters the picture slightly, speaking about those who were sick from different diseases *(asthenountes nosois poikilois)* being led to Jesus. Demoniacs are included since they appear in the "outcome" in his summary. As for healing method, Mark does not mention any at all; Matthew simply says, "in words" *(logō)*, while Luke has touching. According to Luke, Jesus also orders the demons not to tell who he is. As for the outcome, the three unanimously say that Jesus healed *(etherapeusen)* and cast out the demons.

Mark 3:7–12: Jesus healed *(etherapeusen)* many suffering from diseases *(mastiges)*. Unclean spirits are ordered not to announce his identity.

Matthew 4:23–25: Jesus healed *(therapeuōn/etherapeusen)* every disease and sickness *(pasa nosos kai pasa malakia)*. They carried to him all the sick *(kakōs echontes)*, those afflicted with various diseases and pains *(basanoi)*, demoniacs, epileptics *(selēniazomenoi)*, and paralytics.

Matthew 9:35: Jesus healed *(therapeuōn)* every disease and sickness *(pasa nosos kai pasa malakia)*.

Luke 6:17–19: Those who had diseases *(nosoi)* were cured *(iathēnai)*. Those troubled *(enochloumenoi)* by unclean spirits were healed *(etherapeuonto)*. The healing method is touching and power *(dynamis)* that goes out from Jesus.

Conclusions

What may be gleaned from these two surveys? Various sufferings are mentioned, and different kinds of diseases or afflictions are lumped together. Within this variety there is a core of maladies, a certain stereotype so to say, namely, blindness, lameness, muteness, being deaf, and *lepra*.[1] Culture is at play in the way maladies are presented, and this is shown most clearly in the role occupied by demons and the "moon phases," as indicated by Greek *selēniazesthai*. Rudolf and Martin Hengel rightly note that Jesus' healings cannot be isolated from the worldview of his time. According to Luke 13:11, a woman had been crippled by a spirit *(pneuma astheneias)*. Jesus commands *(epetimēsen)* the fever to leave Peter's mother in law (Luke 4:38–39). Likewise, Jesus threatens *(epetimēsen)* "a spirit making a boy unable to speak"

---

1. Bernd Kollmann, "Krankheitsbilder und soziale Folgen: Blindheit, Lähmung, Aussatz, Taubheit oder Taubstummheit," in *Kompendium der frühchristlichen Wundererzählungen*, vol. 1, *Die Wunder Jesu*, ed. Ruben Zimmermann et al. (Gütersloh: Gütersloher Verlagshaus, 2013), pp. 87–93, also speaks of these as stereotypes in the tradition.

(Mark 9:25). The fact that fever and spirit or demon is addressed likewise demonstrates that Jesus was not exempt from culturally given assumptions, such as claiming that some suffering could be caused by demons.[2] However, it is important to notice that demons are neither the only, nor the major, cause of sickness in the New Testament. In most healing stories, demons are not mentioned, and naturalistic explanations appear more likely.[3] Religion is also at work here, most clearly in the cleansing of *leproi,* who were urged to see the priests.

The healing methods used include words or commands, touching, saliva, and power going out from Jesus. On several occasions, Jesus is portrayed as creating an intimate atmosphere by withdrawing the afflicted from the crowd. Furthermore, healing happens immediately; the sick in these stories do not enter a process through which healing will eventually happen. This is the picture New Testament scholarship has to make sense of, and this is also the picture against which current views held by New Testament scholars have to be tested.

2. Rudolf Hengel and Martin Hengel, "Die Heilung Jesu und medizinisches Denken," in *Der Wunderbegriff im Neuen Testament,* ed. Alfred Suhl (Darmstadt: Wissenschaftliche Buchgesellschaft, 1980), pp. 346-62.

3. Darrel W. Amundsen and Gary B. Ferngren, "The Perception of Disease and Disease Causality in the New Testament," in *ANRW* 37.3 (Berlin: De Gruyter, 1996), pp. 2934-56.

Jesus and Contemporary Healers

The New Testament evidence does not claim that Jesus was the only healer of his time. On the contrary, Jesus' response to the Pharisees undermines such a claim: "If I cast out demons by Beelzebul, by whom do your own exorcists [*hoi huioi hymōn*] cast them out?" (Matt. 12:27). In the Eschatological Sermon, Jesus says that many will be misled by false prophets performing miracles (Mark 13:22 par.). As a healer, Jesus belongs within a category of charismatic or shamanistic figures found in the ancient world. Simply put, he had "colleagues." The many Asclepius sanctuaries witnessed healings in which contemporary medicine and religion were intertwined.[1] More important are the individual miracle workers, such as Apollonius of Tyana (late first century CE), whose fourth-century biography by Philostratus shows many resemblances to Jesus.[2] Jewish traditions include miracle workers as well, such as Hanina ben Dosa.[3] Hence, Jesus was not unique, and he is therefore not to be separated from his "colleagues." But this does not rule out the distinctiveness of this aspect of his ministry.

1. Hans-Josef Klauck, *The Religious Context of Early Christianity: A Guide to Graeco-Roman Religions,* trans. Brian J. MacNeil (London: T&T Clark, 2003), pp. 153–77; Craig S. Keener, *Miracles: The Credibility of the New Testament Accounts,* 2 vols. (Grand Rapids: Baker Academic, 2011), pp. 36–40.

2. Keener, *Miracles,* pp. 53–56.

3. Keener, *Miracles,* pp. 58–61; John Dominic Crossan, *The Historical Jesus: The Life of a Mediterranean Jewish Peasant* (San Francisco: HarperSanFrancisco, 1991), pp. 148–58. Most contributions making up part 1 in Michael Labahn and Bert Jan Lietaert Peerbolte, eds., *Wonders Never Cease: The Purpose of Narrating Miracle Stories in the New Testament and Its Religious Environment* (London: T&T Clark, 2006), pp. 20–83, present these figures in detail. See also relevant articles in Graham H. Twelftree, ed., *The Cambridge Companion to Miracles* (Cambridge: Cambridge University Press, 2011), pp. 57–112.

The question of Jesus' distinctiveness as a healer has to be addressed against a wider background of healing and healers at the time. He was special with regard to the high number of healings posterity has ascribed to him. In other words, compared to contemporary healers, Jesus certainly healed more frequently — for obvious reasons such statements are based on the available sources. The prominence given to the practice of healing in the traditions about Jesus has no real analogy in comparable sources. The sheer number of healings attributed to him in the traditions about him therefore makes him almost unique. This fact reveals that there was something extraordinary about Jesus as a healer. With regard to the means or methods whereby he healed, Jesus equals his contemporaries to some extent, but only to some extent. Particularly his powerful words and his neglect of prayer when engaged in healing make him stand out among healers at the time. A comparison of the relevant sources, not to say the reputations involved, makes Jesus appear more efficacious and less ordinary in that he does not charge any fees.[4] Both points are illustrated by the story about the hemorrhaging woman, which states that she had suffered much from many physicians, and that she had spent all she had on their cures, which offered no help (Mark 5:26 par.).

The distinctiveness of Jesus is especially related to the parameters called on to make sense of his healings. The eschatological framework within which his healings were understood separates him from other healers.[5] His healings are construed as participating in a ministry in which the kingdom of God is at work. Ascribing such significance to the healings has no real equivalent. The healings of other healers were not conceptualized in ways comparable to what Jesus did.

Although Jesus had colleagues in the healing business, his followers came to see him as an unrivaled physician, indeed the supreme physician. Ignatius of Antioch gives witness to this (*Eph.* 7.2; 20.2), but these passages also demonstrate that this status owes much to the fact that Jesus is seen as treating the soul as well as the body. In healing both soul and body, Jesus became a unique healer with no one next to him. Furthermore, Ignatius

---

4. Hector Avalos, *Health Care and the Rise of Christianity* (Peabody, MA: Hendrickson, 1999) argues that the Jesus movement distinguished itself from contemporary healers in providing a health-care system that was cheaper and more accessible than what colleagues offered; for a list of costs involved, see p. 21.

5. According to Gerd Theissen and Annette Merz, *The Historical Jesus: A Comprehensive Guide,* trans. John Bowden (London: SCM, 1998), p. 309, this is really the distinctive character or the uniqueness of Jesus' miracles.

speaks of Jesus as the only physician in present tense, thus implying that the healing presence of Jesus is still at hand among the believers.

In the introductory chapter I mentioned the repute that spread in antiquity about Jesus as healer. It is clear that the above notices primarily affirm the repute, but they still give witness to the nature of the repute as well as to its extent, albeit legends of no specific historical value became part of this picture. Such a legend is rendered in detail by Eusebius's *Church History* 1.13 about Abgar of Edessa. Eusebius says the repute of Jesus as a unique healer made its way even beyond the Euphrates: "The divinity [*theiotēs*] of our Lord and Saviour Jesus Christ became famous among all men because of his wonder-working power, and led to him myriads even of those who in foreign lands were far remote from Judea, in the hope of healing from diseases and from all kinds of sufferings" (1.13.1).

King Abgar suffered badly from illness and wrote Jesus a letter asking him to come and heal him. According to Eusebius, this letter was still to be found in the archives of Edessa. In the letter, Abgar writes: "I have heard concerning you and your cures, how they are accomplished without drugs [*pharmakeia*] and herbs [*botana*]" (1.13.6, 18). Jesus responds in a letter that he is too busy, but "when I have been taken up, I will send to you one of my disciples to heal your suffering, and give life to you and those with you" (1.13.10). This is fulfilled in Thaddeus, one of the seventy from Luke 10, who comes and brings healing to the king through prayer and laying on of hands (1.13.18). He also preaches the gospel to the people.

The way this and other legends portray Jesus has bearings on the question of the extent to which he may be considered unique. He is presented as unique in healing with no media to help him. This was seen as indicative of his supernatural power; thus the healings were proofs of his divinity. Jesus' healing ministry is continued by his disciples; his power is at work in them. Finally, Jesus brings healing to body as well as to soul.

The present chapter has argued that Jesus was not unique in being the only healer. He belongs within a guild of healers in the ancient world, although this practice was not as widespread as is often assumed. It follows from this that the healings cannot prove the deity of Jesus, as has often been stated. However, the question of Jesus and contemporary healers is not sufficiently addressed in mentioning his colleagues; a closer look at the material makes Jesus appear as an extraordinary healer, albeit not unique. It is not justified to simply enroll Jesus among contemporary healers. Although Jesus was by no means the only healer, the general statement that "this was very common in those days" is misleading. It is worth quoting Annette Merz here:

We have to oppose the commonly held, but nonetheless false, opinion, that many wonder workers appear in the ancient contemporary literature, and that their miracles correspond to those of Jesus, and hence, are analogous. The opposite is, in fact, true. Apart from the Christian apostles — who for methodological reasons naturally are left out here — there is hardly any person in the ancient world to be compared to Jesus. This applies to the number of miracles, not only different in nature but also in detail, and with at least a claim to authenticity that can be meaningfully discussed.[6]

A consequence of this insight is that a religion-historical comparison, albeit necessary and helpful, is by no means sufficient in order to come to terms with Jesus the healer.

6. Annette Merz, "Der historische Jesus als Wundertäter im Spektrum antiker Wundertäter," in *Kompendium der frühchristlichen Wundererzählungen*, vol. 1, *Die Wunder Jesu*, ed. Ruben Zimmermann et al. (Gütersloh: Gütersloher Verlagshaus, 2013), p. 108 (my own translation).

Jesus as Healer in Current New Testament Scholarship

Contemporary friends and foes respectively gave various explanations of Jesus' ability to heal, but they were mostly unanimous that he did, in fact, perform strange and unexpected things on the verge of normality. Although these explanations are strongly contrastive, together they make a case for Jesus' reputation of being a healer. The preceding chapters have briefly touched on Jesus' foes; they saw him as practicing sorcery. We will later turn to the insider view found in the Jesus traditions as they were passed on.

Present-day scholars continue to wrestle with questions related to Jesus' ability to heal. Theirs is an etic perspective, a view of the academic "outside," trying to explain what *really* happened. The following will rehearse some influential ways of reasoning about this in recent New Testament scholarship.[1] This discussion has been limited to some works that have set an agenda by raising important methodological questions and also by addressing the need for making historically relevant definitions. I also find them especially helpful since engaging with them leads to a wide rehearsal of key points in the Gospel stories of healing. They have been chosen because they serve as foils for grasping what is narrated in these stories. These works have, albeit in different ways, marked the road for anyone interested in understanding Jesus' healing ministry today.

---

1. For a broader presentation, see, e.g., Bernd Kollmann, *Neutestamentliche Wundergeschichten: Biblisch-theologische Zugänge und Impulse für die Praxis* (Stuttgart: Kohlhammer, 2002), pp. 137–66.

A Healer Who Did Not Cure Diseases
(John J. Pilch and John Dominic Crossan)

Professor of biblical studies at Georgetown University for many years, John J. Pilch has published extensively on issues pertaining to interpreting New Testament texts in their contemporary culture and has become the doyen of cultural-anthropological studies among New Testament scholars. Some decades ago, following in the wake of a renewed interest in cultural anthropology for New Testament studies, Pilch introduced medical anthropology into the understanding of Jesus as a healer. This provided a new paradigm for studying the healing stories of the New Testament and paved the way for several important contributions. New Testament scholars started to draw on the work of scholars such as Arthur Kleinmann, *Patients and Healers in the Context of Culture: An Exploration of the Borderline between Anthropology, Medicine and Psychiatry* (1980), and George Peter Murdock, *Theories of Illness: A World Survey* (1980). Medical anthropology seeks to overcome ethnocentrism by proceeding from the fact that culture and subjectivity are components of any sickness. It studies cultural or indigenous representations of health, and aims to prevent imposing a biomedical framework onto the texts of other cultures. According to Kleinmann: "Disease refers to a malfunctioning of biological and/or psychological processes, while the term illness refers to the psychological experience and meaning of perceived disease. Illness includes secondary personal and social responses to a primary malfunctioning (disease) in the individual's physiological or psychological status."[2] In this definition, disease is about virus, bacteria, biology, or pathology — in short a universalized and objective phenomenon — while the patient's experience is a locally and culturally constructed phenomenon. Thus two interpretations address a single clinical reality. Questions of health are, to some extent, negotiable, due to culturally and subjectively dependent attitudes, on the part both of the person afflicted and of the society in question. Medical anthropology thus offers a taxonomy for understanding Jesus' healings historically in their proper context.

In *Healing in the New Testament: Insights from Medical and Mediterranean Anthropology* (2000), John J. Pilch's many previous contributions on this theme came together in a single volume. The book became very influen-

---

2. Arthur Kleinmann, *Patients and Healers in the Context of Culture: An Exploration of the Borderland between Anthropology, Medicine and Psychiatry* (Berkeley: University of California Press, 1980), p. 172.

tial. In fact, in an endorsement John Dominic Crossan writes: "Everything I know about healing in the New Testament I learned from John Pilch." Pilch's book represents a milestone, due to its new approach, its claim to represent the one and only way to an adequate understanding of healing in the New Testament, and because it challenges traditional views that Jesus in a miraculous way cured people suffering from sickness. In short, it has had an immense influence on the scholarly debate.

Pilch picks up on the fundamental distinction between disease and illness in medical anthropology. From this distinction follows another, namely, the distinction between curing and healing. Diseases are known by observable signs, and may be cured, while illnesses are known by the symptoms experienced by the patient, and may be healed. Hence, disease and illness are terms derived from different perspectives on the same phenomenon, namely, sickness. These distinctions have far-reaching implications for how we are to understand Jesus as a healer, and also for defining what Jesus actually did to those who were sick. It is important, says Pilch, to distinguish between etic and emic perspectives on how Jesus' healings are viewed. An etic perspective describes the outsider viewpoint, while an emic view is that of the native or insider.[3] The following table gives an overview of the distinctions urged by Pilch.

Biomedical framework	*Medical anthropology*
Cure	Healing
Disease	Illness
Biology and pathology	Symptoms and cultural construct
Activity	State (being or becoming)
Individualism	Relational or collectively oriented

The idea of health in the biomedical framework focuses on doing or activity, while medical anthropology implies states, that is, being and/or becoming. Within this pattern, health in the second perspective is primarily a relational status: "What a Western reader might interpret as a loss of function, namely lameness, an ancient reader would see as disvalued state of being."[4] It was

3. For the definitions argued and applied, see John J. Pilch, *Healing in the New Testament: Insights from Medical and Mediterranean Anthropology* (Minneapolis: Fortress, 2000), pp. 13–14, 19–25, 59, 73, 99, and his glossary. An etic analysis as given here by Pilch avoids the criticism that his definitions are not drawn from the New Testament itself since this takes an outsider's view. At the end of the day, however, even this heuristic perspective must face the question of whether it makes sense of the phenomenon of healing as it appears in the New Testament.

4. Pilch, *Healing in the New Testament,* p. 13.

this disvalued state of being that Jesus improved or changed when he healed. In all healings reported, Jesus "restored meaning to life and the sufferer is returned to purposeful living."[5] Healing was viewed as restoration to wholeness and integrity, whereas bodily functions were subordinated.

> Persons who have a blemish, who are blind or lame, who have a mutilated face or a limb too long, an injured foot or hand, a hunchback, a sight defect, an itching disease or scabs, or crushed testicles, all of these are certainly capable of doing. But their specific condition describes a state of unwholeness and thus they are permitted to join in the social behavior or group worship of God. Again, the issue is one of a state of unworthiness, not the loss of bodily activities. A Western observer whose culture favors doing over being would tend to interpret some of these handicaps as functional deficiencies.[6]

By mediating culture and community, Jesus restored meaning of life to suffering people. The key word in his healing was "interpretation." As with other folk healers, Jesus provided an interpretation that restored life within the community. Meaning mends, or metaphors heal, according to Pilch: "Healing boils down to meaning and transformation of experience. . . . What has changed? The life problems may or may not still be present, but their perception is no longer the same."[7]

Two types of healings stand out in Pilch's presentation, that of biblical leprosy and blindness in Luke's Gospel. As for biblical leprosy, it does not, according to Pilch, correspond to Hansen's disease, as modern medicine now knows it. It is about a reality constructed by the patient and the community; hence it is about pollution, not contagion. There is nothing biological involved in Leviticus 13–14 nor in Jesus' healing of those who were *leproi* according to New Testament texts. Jesus' actions toward these people provided them with a new, meaningful life, making them acceptable and welcome into the community. He made them clean. Hence, the way Jesus healed *leproi* can be compared to his associating with tax collectors and prostitutes.[8]

In Luke-Acts, blindness and seeing takes on metaphorical meaning; it refers to the heart zone, and therefore involves understanding and meaning.

---

5. Pilch, *Healing in the New Testament*, p. 14.
6. Pilch, *Healing in the New Testament*, p. 113.
7. Pilch, *Healing in the New Testament*, p. 35.
8. Pilch, *Healing in the New Testament*, p. 51.

Pilch argues this on the basis of Luke 4:18 and Acts 28:23–28. The opening and closing of Luke's double volume provide a framework within which all references to blindness and regaining sight, such as Luke 7:21–22, may be understood. Pilch writes that Luke 7:21 ("Jesus had just then cured many people of diseases, plagues, and evil spirits, and had given sight to many who were blind"), which sets the scene for Jesus' response to John the Baptist, refers to illnesses not diseases, and hence to blindness in this extended meaning.

From a historical and scientific point of view, Pilch tends to answer no to the question of whether Jesus ever cured anyone.[9] Jesus did *heal* illness though. Somewhat surprisingly, Pilch claims that the kinds of healing Jesus provided "take place always, infallibly, since everyone ultimately finds some meaning to given life situations: accidents, fate, will of God, providence etc."[10] At the end of day, this is what Jesus performed as a healer, namely, what most likely would happen anyway, with or without his assistance.

John Dominic Crossan, famous Jesus scholar and retired professor at De-Paul University, stands on the shoulders of Pilch in his view of Jesus as a healer. In his influential work *The Historical Jesus* (1991), Crossan refers to the distinctions urged by Pilch and considers them as key axioms in medical anthropology, providing him with a tool to explain what Jesus was doing as a healer. He offered healing for illnesses, not cure for diseases. In short, he offered "therapeutic comfort." Crossan says that he understands "the success both of Jesus and his missionaries against the background of what Arthur Kleinmann and Lilias Sung call 'the cross-cultural investigation of indigenous healing' in medical anthropology."[11] As a consequence, Crossan states in a rather dichotomous statement that "for disease you are better off with the doctor and the dispensary, but for illness you are better off with the shaman and the shrine."[12]

Since illness is culture-borne it is usually not treated by physicians but by popular or folk remedies provided by family, religion, or practitioners of healing. Jesus' healing miracles are to be seen within such a perspective. Crossan's contribution in *The Historical Jesus: Five Views*, reiterates this position, but now he asserts that healing is a sociosomatic complex.[13] As an

9. Pilch, *Healing in the New Testament*, p. 142.

10. Pilch, *Healing in the New Testament*, p. 60; see also p. 141.

11. John Dominic Crossan, *The Historical Jesus: The Life of a Mediterranean Jewish Peasant* (San Francisco: HarperSanFrancisco, 1991), pp. 336-37 (quotation p. 336).

12. Crossan, *Historical Jesus*, p. 336.

13. John Dominic Crossan, "Jesus and the Challenge of Collaborative Eschatology," in *The Historical Jesus: Five Views*, ed. James K. Beilby and Paul Rhodes Eddy (Downers Grove, IL: IVP Academic, 2009), pp. 127-29.

example, he mentions the movie *Philadelphia* from 1993, in which the lawyer Andrew Beckett, played by Tom Hanks, is fired by his firm since he has contracted AIDS due to homosexual practice. Andrew Beckett could not be cured, but he found healing in the support of his partner, his family, and his lawyer's successful suit against his firm for illegal discrimination: "*Curing* was not available, but *healing* was still possible. Not everything to be sure, but not nothing either."[14] Thus Crossan subscribes to the distinctions presented above as interpretive tools for understanding the healing acts of Jesus. Jesus of Nazareth did not cure diseases, he healed illnesses.

Assessing the Pilch-Crossan Model

Pilch has depicted Jesus' healings from an outsider (etic) perspective, not the "native viewpoint," which he labels the emic.[15] An etic perspective has its own right vis-à-vis an emic presentation, and is not to be judged by the latter. However, the etic perspective cannot dismiss the native viewpoint entirely, since an etic presentation constantly draws on information gained from sources that are genuinely emic. Thus the two are at points intertwined, and it is justified to ask if and how far the etic presentation in question accounts for what is claimed to be relevant in the healing stories. Does Pilch and Crossan's interpretation make sense of the New Testament material they set out to interpret?

Both Pilch and Crossan are unwilling to really engage with the emic claims made in the healing stories. I fully concur with Justin Meggitt's evaluation: "Jesus was not thought by his contemporaries solely to provide resolutions to the social and personal problems of meaning created by illness (the social experience of a sickness). He was also thought to cure disease (the physical experience of a sickness). Pilch is quite wrong to ignore this. He appears to do so because of his belief that someone can only think in terms of disease if they think in terms of contemporary biomedical models, which obviously first-century people did not. Hence his rather odd assertion that 'in the Bible there is no interest at all in disease.'"[16]

According to Pieter F. Craffert, the disease-illness distinction serves a theological or ideological agenda. The authenticity of Jesus' healing miracles

14. Crossan, "Jesus and the Challenge of Collaborative Eschatology," p. 128.

15. Pilch, *Healing in the New Testament*, p. 59.

16. Justin Meggitt, "The Historical Jesus and Healing: Jesus' Miracles in Psychosocial Context," in *Spiritual Healing: Scientific and Religious Perspectives*, ed. Fraser Watts (Cambridge: Cambridge University Press, 2011), p. 23.

is insisted on, but they are not really miraculous, only what any folk healer could easily have performed.[17] We may also add, what will happen anyway as time goes by.

When the stories about Jesus' healings are transferred and applied to present-day believers, they certainly create both hope and frustration. The view held by Pilch and Crossan may lighten the burden by telling those disappointed in failing to find a cure that Jesus himself never offered any cure for diseases either. Present-day sufferers should hope for a restored meaning in life, just like Jesus offered his contemporaries. The anthropological approach deserves to be seriously engaged, and any present claim on Jesus as healer demands that this challenge be taken seriously.[18] However, most readers who turn to the New Testament texts themselves will find that Pilch and Crossan do not come to terms with how the phenomenon of healing is addressed there. Having meaning restored to life certainly catches some aspects, but does not justify the often dramatic and sudden changes implied for the healee in the healing stories.

I grew up on the African savannah in Cameroon, the son of a medical doctor who was in charge of a hospital there. Almost daily I witnessed from the side the hopes nurtured in the hospital and its vicinity, the failures and the challenges of a culture where sickness and suffering were understood from a more group-oriented perspective. Looking back at my childhood, I realize now that I also witnessed that Pilch and Crossan were simultaneously right and wrong. Their observations on health and a collectivistic culture are basically relevant, but they oversimplify complex and complicated matters. I remember how those who were sick were surrounded by their families when hospitalized, how they cooked for the patient and cared for him or her during the time of treatment. I recall my father insisting that the bed provided by the hospital be reserved for the patient, though; it was not for grandma, auntie, or other family members. But I do not remember that this collectivistic setting with its emphasis on family and tribe made bodily functions and activity irrelevant, as Pilch in particular claims. These memories from childhood are, of course, not in themselves arguments, but they make me suspicious. Is it really likely that people who fell sick in Jesus' world

17. Pieter F. Craffert, "Medical Anthropology as an Antidote for Ethnocentrism in Jesus Research? Putting the Illness-Disease Distinction into Perspective," *Harvard Theological Studies* 67, no. 1 (2011): 12–13.

18. Twelftree, *Jesus the Miracle Worker* ignores this, although the influence of this approach was known in the nineties. Craig S. Keener, *Miracles: The Credibility of the New Testament Accounts*, 2 vols. (Grand Rapids: Baker Academic, 2011), addresses Pilch only in footnotes.

cared so little about their bodily malfunctions? Is Pilch's table (see above), of healing as opposed to curing, really the whole picture? I don't think so.

Pilch seems to tacitly proceed from the assumption that disease can only occur when our biomedical models are present, as though these models are the means whereby the realization of sickness appears. I think many suffering people in the ancient world and in the majority world would beg to differ. It is, however, against this backdrop that he asserts that "in the Bible there is no interest at all in disease, since this concept requires awareness of such things as microscopic viruses and bacteria."[19] Although the distinction between illness and disease serves to bring out the wider implications of what Jesus did, namely, that his healings were more than one thing only, Pilch's assertion in this citation is at best odd.[20]

In his article "Medical Anthropology as an Antidote for Ethnocentrism in Jesus Research? Putting the Illness-Disease Distinction into Perspective," Pieter F. Craffert questions what he considers to be New Testament scholars' uncritical use of the disease-illness distinction to understand Jesus as a healer.[21] He argues that it is impossible to keep these phenomena entirely apart. Pilch and Crossan make a dichotomy that cannot be upheld. Even within the world of biomedicine few would think of disease as purely organic or biological. Medical anthropology seems to accept more overlap than what these New Testament scholars have taken into account in their use of this model.

What in Kleinmann's definitions above are two interpretations of a single clinical reality becomes with some New Testament scholars separate entities, so that Jesus can be said to be involved in the one and not in the other. When Crossan and Pilch claim that Jesus did not cure, but healed, they subscribe primarily to the latter application of this methodology. Medical systems, however, are more "mixed' and multifaceted than Pilch and Crossan seem to envisage. There is every good reason to assume that illness may come as a secondary, culture-bound, reaction to a primary reason (disease), but the two are not necessarily separate realities. Furthermore, Craffert argues that Crossan and Pilch pick selectively from a variety of medical-anthropological sources in a proof-texting way, and hence make them appear more doctrinaire than the theory warrants.[22]

---

19. Pilch, *Healing in the New Testament,* p. 76.

20. The oddness of this is also pointed out by Meggitt, "The Historical Jesus and Healing," p. 23.

21. Craffert, "Medical Anthropology," p. 14. I concur with many of his critical points, and some of my points are drawn from there.

22. Craffert, "Medical Anthropology," p. 10.

The way Pilch and Crossan draw on medical anthropology neglects the fact that both disease and illness are *partial* ways of perceiving health and health systems. Neither of the terms captures sickness in its totality. Health is multifaceted. By equating the local experience with the totality of the situation of those who are sick, Crossan and Pilch are able to separate illness from disease, but illness is not necessarily only a cultural phenomenon: "Even if a sickness is experienced as an illness, this does not mean that someone is not suffering from an identifiable disease."[23] I think it would be helpful to distinguish between how the experience of illness is affected by culture on the one hand and illness per se as a purely cultural phenomenon on the other. Pilch and Crossan do not make this distinction, which enables them to keep disease and illness entirely separate. It is, however, fully possible, not to say likely, that at times disease and illness describe the same sickness phenomenon, but from different perspectives and by means of different explanatory models. Craffert takes as an example the many people in southern Africa who have been infected with HIV. Many of those affected will claim that they have been bewitched or that the devil has cast this on them. This experience is in accordance with the theory of illness given above. However, this does not of course mean that these people are not HIV positive. Alternative explanatory models are not necessarily indications that a known disease is not present. Craffert is, in my view, correct in pointing out that what comes out of the distinction urged by the Pilch-Crossan tradition is not the cross-cultural interpretation they claim it is: "Medical anthropology exists by virtue of the biomedical paradigm, and is not a way of bypassing it."[24] He demonstrates in detail the proximity of this discipline to Western medicine.

Diagnostics Based on Ancient Texts

Pilch and Crossan are entirely correct that the New Testament texts hardly provide any basis for making safe biomedical diagnoses. Not only are the texts vague in this regard, but they are also from a different and distant culture. If descriptions of sickness found in these texts comply with modern medicine, this may be due either to accident or to the general nature of the description. Pilch and Crossan, however, reduce the sickness descriptions throughout to support their claim for meaning and purposeful living of-

23. Craffert, "Medical Anthropology," p. 6.
24. Craffert, "Medical Anthropology," p. 3.

fered to people with disvalued states. Be it blindness, lameness, muteness, biblical leprosy, spirit possession, or death, they are all only different ways of describing one single sickness, the concern for restoring meaning in life. According to Pilch, there is an "almost total disregard of symptoms (something essential to disease). Instead there is constant need for meaning."[25] He writes the following: "By declaring lepers clean, by raising the dead, by healing a woman's hemorrhages (Mark 5:21-43), Jesus reduces and removes the experiential oppressiveness associated with such afflictions. In all instances of healing, meaning is restored to life and the sufferer is returned to purposeful living."[26] Here bodily dysfunctions, very different in nature, are lumped together under the umbrella of being in need of having meaning restored to one's life.[27] As Meggitt points out, the information that can be gleaned from the New Testament is so limited that it must force some restraint on scholars.[28] However, that is a point made according to how precise, not to say inaccurate, the sources are in addressing the matter. Pilch even ignores those distinctions that are explicit in the texts.

It is impossible to describe in modern pathological terms the complex experiences of ancient people who lived very long ago and under very different circumstances. We cannot accurately reconstruct or describe illnesses in the ancient world by our contemporary medical terms. This is the problem of doing diagnostics across both centuries as well as cultures, based only on texts *about* the phenomena. However, Klaus Berger has made an important point: "We must instead content ourselves with asking how the healthy made sense of the sick among them. Only the notions and reactions of the former have been preserved."[29] Berger brings the presence of an *audience or bystanders* into the picture here. Their presence is pointed out by New Testament texts themselves, and they seem to occupy a role of their own in these stories. Our analytical tools should take them and their role into account. Pilch and Crossan do not account for the role of the bystanders, who are those who witnessed the incident, in the healings stories.

In making the healings into matters of interpretation, Pilch overlooks

---

25. Pilch, *Healing in the New Testament*, p. 71.

26. Pilch, *Healing in the New Testament*, p. 14; cf. p. 81.

27. This critique also targets the psychosomatic attempts at coming to terms with Jesus' healing; see Donald Capps, *Jesus the Village Psychiatrist* (Louisville: Westminster John Knox, 2008).

28. Meggitt, "The Historical Jesus and Healing," pp. 29-31.

29. Klaus Berger, *Identity and Experience in the New Testament* (Minneapolis: Fortress, 2003), pp. 47-48.

the fact that many healings were accompanied by an audience, who sometimes played an active role as well. When Pilch describes healing of illnesses as a process of "restoring meaning to life,"[30] we have to ask if the role of the spectators in the texts is sufficiently accounted for. They are often said to *watch* the change. The reaction of the bystanders is a recurrent motif in these stories, even to the extent that it has been seen as typical to the form of healing stories. Already the classical works on form criticism by Martin Dibelius and Rudolf Bultmann pointed out that the reactions of the audience belonged to the basic format of miracle stories, be they about Christ or some other miracle worker.[31] The reaction of the bystanders implies that something was experienced on the spot. How this is accounted for when Jesus' healings are exclusively seen as restoring meaning to life is hard to understand. What spectators observed according to the healing stories Pilch moves to the interior of the patient. What happened to what the spectators observed on the spot? Restoring life to the community usually does not take place instantly, as it is recorded in the stories about Jesus. Furthermore, the reaction of the bystanders does not focus on the social aspect of the healing.

The amazement of the audience occurs in most healing stories. This element also has a bearing on the question of diagnosis, at least as a textual phenomenon. The spectators were witnessing something extraordinary, and are hence taken by surprise: "They were overcome with amazement [*ekstasis megalē*]" (Mark 5:42 par.).[32] Some of the stories enhance the wondrous and unexpected by giving details on how many years the patient had suffered from the illness, that the sickness had been there from birth, that physicians had been unable to deal with the matter, and that a dead body had already begun decomposing. Such details work together with the role of the spectators to emphasize an event that transcends normality,[33] but it also pertains to the question of diagnosis. Both observations in these stories imply that Jesus brought about a change observed then and there. To be sure, long-term effects are also part of the picture (see below), but the role of the spectators does not account for these.

---

30. John J. Pilch, *Visions and Healing in the Acts of the Apostles: How the Early Believers Experienced God* (Collegeville, MN: Liturgical Press, 2004), pp. 42–43.

31. See Keener, *Miracles*, pp. 27–28.

32. See the comments on *ta paradoxa* in the introductory remarks to part 1.

33. Ruben Zimmermann, "Grundfragen zu den frühchristlichen Wundererzählungen," in *Kompendium der frühchristlichen Wundererzählungen*, vol. 1, *Die Wunder Jesu*, ed. Ruben Zimmermann et al. (Gütersloh: Gütersloher Verlagshaus, 2013), pp. 14–15.

Inspecting "Meaning Restored to Life"

Pilch is certainly right in saying that Jesus "reintegrated" those suffering from biblical leprosy into society, but he does not account for the inspection they were directed to submit themselves to. My point can be illustrated by the texts where Jesus heals people suffering from some kind of a skin disease (Mark 1:40–44//Matt. 8:2–4//Luke 5:12–16 and Luke 17:12–19). The person suffering from this sickness is in Greek described as *lepros*, suffering from *lepra*. Pilch is right that this is hardly what we today call Hansen's disease (leprosy). Suggestions have been made for psoriasis, favus, leukoderma, or vitiligo. The Old Testament regulations involved here (see below) make all these suggestions unlikely, due to the fact that disappearance and visible change are supposed to occur within weeks.[34] Jacob Milgrom calls it "scale diseases," implying visible peeling off of the skin.

Jesus urges the person healed to show himself to the priest, in accordance with law requirements. Hence, the texts apply the set of rules laid down in Leviticus 13–14. This finds corroboration in the fact that all relevant texts speak of healing in terms of being "cleansed." Furthermore, the terminology of the Gospel stories, such as showing *(deiknymi/epideiknymi)* oneself to the priest, offering the prescribed sacrifices *(prospherō)*, and being healed *(iathē)*, all echo the language of Leviticus 13–14 in the Septuagint.

Pilch's urging of the disease-illness distinction on the material makes him emphasize purity, the disvalued state, and reintegration of the patients. These stories, however, are not merely about removal of "experiential oppressiveness,"[35] but also about a bodily change subjected to inspection. How are the healed supposed to show the priest that meaning has been restored to their life? What kind of inspection would that be? Leviticus 13–14 speaks throughout of examination by the priest, and this inspection is based on *observable* outward signs. In the Septuagint, forms of the verb *horaō* (to see, or to be shown) are used repeatedly. The priest is supposed to observe potential changes and to let these changes or lack thereof be decisive for the question of purity. Looking for spots, blemishes, changes — all outward signs — are what this inspection is really about. Against this background, being healed involves restoration of cleanliness and thus being included into the fellow-

---

34. See Jacob Milgrom, *Leviticus: A Book of Rituals and Ethics* (Minneapolis: Fortress, 2004), pp. 127–29; David P. Wright and Richard N. Jones, "Leprosy," in *The Anchor Bible Dictionary*, ed. David Noel Freedman (New York: Doubleday, 1992), 4:277–82.

35. Pilch, *Healing in the New Testament*, p. 14.

ship. Here Pilch is truly right! But this is preceded by visible changes on the surface of the body, such as the disappearance of blemish spots, the abating of itches, and so on.[36]

According to Luke 17:15, the Samaritan "saw that he was healed." This makes sense only if the healing brought on the lepers by Jesus served to prepare for the inspection by the priest in such a way that they were announced clean, since no bodily blemish was visible any longer. The manner in which we envisage the healing that came on this person must take into account the priestly examination; these are not only scenes about individuals finding meaning restored to their lives. Certainly this aspect is included, but only after and dependent on the bodily changes observed by the priest. The matter of purity — certainly the primary one here — can only be justified if bodily changes were brought about by Jesus' healing.

Frederick J. Gaiser accepts the distinction between healing and cure as helpful but nonetheless makes a pertinent observation: "The distinction makes more sense in the language of the observer than in the language of the participant."[37] Certainly those who were ill would hope for bodily cure, not just meaning restored to their life. As Gaiser points out, in the moment of pain most sufferers would opt for cure rather than healing, if those were the alternatives. Hence I find Pilch's assertion that "it is not the physical problem that concerns this society, but the state of pollution or impurity which makes one incapable of approaching God in worship or even living in the holy community"[38] to be misleading, if applied generally, as Pilch seems to do. I think people suffering from physical problems would disagree with Pilch. In her book *The Christ of the Miracle Stories,* Wendy J. Cotter argues convincingly that these stories are to be understood as encounters. This means that they not only convey something about Jesus but also about the petitioners, those seeking Jesus' help: "More than the miraculous act itself holds center stage. The petitioners remain spunky, noisy, pushy, and outrageous. Jesus meets them on their ground and moves to their side, recognizing their need, their confidence, and the rightness of radical resolution when salvation from dis-

36. This is also pointed out by Annette Weissenrieder, "Stories Just under the Skin: *Lepra* in the Gospel of Luke," in *Miracles Revisited: New Testament Miracle Stories and Their Concepts of Reality,* ed. Stefan Alkier and Annette Weissenrieder (Berlin: De Gruyter, 2013), pp. 82–85.

37. Frederick J. Gaiser, *Healing in the Bible: Theological Insight for Christian Ministry* (Grand Rapids: Baker Academic, 2010), p. 180.

38. John J. Pilch, "Jesus' Healing Activity: Political Acts?" in *Understanding the Social World of the New Testament,* ed. Dietmar Neufeld and Richard E. DeMaris (London: Routledge, 2010), p. 150.

ease, demons, death, or danger is within reach."[39] Pilch ignores the physical needs of these petitioners who remain so vocal in these stories.

A similar disregard for bodily changes claimed in the healing stories applies to how Pilch views Jesus' healing of lameness or paralysis. According to the healing of a lame man in Mark 2 and parallels, Jesus says to him: "I say to you, stand up, take your mat and go to your home" (v. 11). The amazement of the bystanders is caused by the lame man walking away. Furthermore, verse 11 comes as a continuation of what Jesus says in verse 9: "Which is easier, to say to the paralytic, 'Your sins are forgiven,' or to say, 'Stand up and take your mat and walk'?" The activity of walking serves as a demonstration here. This demonstration does not work if it simply means being restored to a purposeful life. The "restoring to life" interpretation leaves the demonstration void, almost invisible, and spectators with no role to play. This happens because of the definitions Pilch and Crossan impose on the New Testament texts. There are similar instances which emphasize that Jesus' healings restore the body to function properly as well (e.g., Mark 5:41-42). Jesus' dictum to the lame at Bethesda (John 5:8) echoes his words in Mark: "Stand up, take your mat and walk." That this is to be interpreted as a bodily change is evident from the reaction that follows. It was a Sabbath, and the lame man healed was therefore accused of breaking Sabbath rules by carrying his mat (vv. 10-12). The Sabbath rules targeted precisely actions or activities in defining what to do and what not to do. How a healed mind affects the Sabbath rules is not obvious. In Pilch and Crossan's interpretations there is, simply put, not much body left to be healed, nor is there much left to be seen by bystanders either.

Allegories and Parables?

When Pilch lumps different kinds of healing together under the heading of removing "experiential oppressiveness," and when the healing is a kind of restoration that must have taken time, sometimes even considerable time, one senses that Pilch tacitly reads the Gospel healing stories as parables or allegories. Regrettably, he does not state this explicitly, but it is nevertheless conveyed through the way he conceives of illness and healing in the Gospels. To take one example, Pilch mentions lepers, tax collectors, and prostitutes

---

39. Wendy J. Cotter, *The Christ of the Miracle Stories: Portrait through Encounter* (Grand Rapids: Baker Academic, 2010), p. 256.

together as beneficiaries of Jesus' therapeutic fellowship.[40] It is nowhere said that Jesus healed tax collectors and prostitutes, but it is said about lepers. Pilch does not touch on this difference in his presentation. A text like Luke 5:27–32, built on the proverbial saying in verse 31 ("Those who are well have no need of a physician, but those who are sick"), may be supportive of Pilch's viewpoint here. Nonetheless, this proverbial saying does not, in my opinion, justify making metaphors of Jesus' healings in general. It is a stock saying about teachers and philosophers in antiquity who were often described as soul physicians.

Spiritualizing interpretations of Jesus' healing certainly exist in the Gospel traditions (e.g., Mark 8:18–26; see below). Most scholars recognize this in John 9. Pilch has rightly pointed out that blindness and gaining sight in some Gospel texts as well as in Acts has a metaphorical meaning.[41] The problem is that the disease-illness distinction by its nature seems to remove physical problems from the scene, at least from having any significance. Hence, these scholars end up with very modest claims about what Jesus did when he healed. There is no doubt that the Gospels tell about Jesus successfully healing people from their sufferings, whatever they are labeled. The significance of this in the Gospels is expressed in a theological and christological framework, to which we will return later.[42] If these healings were primarily ways of restoring meaning, and if such healing "always takes place," as Pilch repeatedly states, a wide gap opens between what the bystanders are said to have observed and the interpretative framework in which the performances of healing are placed in the Gospels. Pilch illustrates his point with the example of his late wife, who suffered from cancer. She was not cured, but she was 100 percent healed because healing, the restoration of meaning to life, "occurs always."[43] According to Pilch, such a healing process might take a long time. This illustrates what Jesus could not do, and also what he could, and did, as a healer. Jesus offered healing but not cure. When Jesus' healings are trivialized in this way, it becomes hard to understand why his healings play such a prominent role in the way he was remembered.

It seems to me that at the end of the day these scholars have found their own interpretations of Jesus' healing performances insufficient or not fully convincing. Hence, they interpret the healings both politically and allegorically.[44] The physical body is a microcosm of the social body so that there is a

---

40. Pilch, *Healing in the New Testament*, p. 51.

41. Pilch, *Healing in the New Testament*, pp. 113–16.

42. See pp. 70–80 below.

43. Pilch, *Healing in the New Testament*, p. 141.

44. Pilch, "Jesus's Healing Activity." Somewhat similarly, Gerd Theissen sees the ailments

dialectic between the personal and the social, the individual and the corpo-
rate. According to Crossan, the Gospels were hardly meant to be taken literally. In his book *The Historical Jesus: The Life of a Mediterranean Jewish Peasant,* "healing" becomes a term referring to Jesus' "religious and economic
egalitarianism that negated alike and at once the hierarchical and patronal
normalcies of Jewish religion and Roman power."[45] That these elements are
present in Jesus' ministry is not contested here, but I do indeed question the
way the healings of Jesus are construed as internal to the patient only, referring to social integration or to political actions while ignoring physical sickness. According to Craffert, Pilch and Crossan's picture of Jesus' miraculous
deeds is so unimpressive that they feel the need for additional explanations:
"This is where modern political ideology comes into the picture: in the healings Jesus actually performed deeds of political resistance if not treason."[46]

What started out as a question of the relevance of medical anthropology
for Jesus research seems to have become a discourse on whether the Gospels
are meant to be taken literally as stories or if they conceal another political
and allegorical agenda. The step from the first to the second is not sufficiently
addressed by Pilch and Crossan, if at all. It is assumed to follow from the
models and definitions applied.

A First-Century Psychiatrist? (Don Capps)

In his book *Jesus the Village Psychiatrist* (2008), Donald Capps, professor
of pastoral theology at Princeton Theological Seminary, takes a different
approach. He presents himself as an opponent of "the miracle theory" claiming that Jesus in his healings contradicted known scientific laws: "In fact,
it was Jesus' deeper knowledge of these laws, especially as they concerned
the interaction of the mind and the body, that enabled him to be a more effective healer than the physicians of his day."[47] The laws Capps has in mind

---

as a consequence of broader economic and social contexts; *Miracle Stories of the Early Christian
Tradition,* trans. Francis McDonagh (Edinburgh: T&T Clark, 1983; German version, 1974),
pp. 249–51.

45. Crossan, *Historical Jesus,* p. 422. Similarly in his *Jesus: A Revolutionary Biography*
(San Francisco: HarperSanFrancisco, 1994), pp. 76–82, where Crossan says that Jesus did not
cure disease through an intervention in the physical world, but through an intervention in the
social and political world.

46. Craffert, "Medical Anthropology," p. 12.

47. Capps, *Jesus the Village Psychiatrist,* p. xiv.

here are those governing the relationship between mind or brain functions and the rest of the body. Furthermore, Capps also opposes Pilch's much-referred-to "social illness theory." Both Pilch and Crossan tend to overlook the fact that some diseases may result from psychological disorders. Capps says: "In my view, the distinction between curing a disease and healing an illness breaks down where psychosomatic disorders are concerned. They are diseases because they have physical — organic — symptoms, but they are illnesses because the primary causes of the diseases are psychosocial."[48] Jesus understood this to be the case, and he used healing methods accounting for it. He "anticipated the truly innovative Sigmund Freud himself."[49] While some have presented Jesus himself as a case in need of psychological treatment, Capps views him instead as a forerunner of the psychiatrist league "concerned with prevention of disorders of the mind, including neuroses, emotional maladjustments etc."[50]

Capps believes that most of the people Jesus healed suffered from mental or emotional disorders, and he claims that the Gospel writers themselves acknowledged this. In other words, the suffering of those mentioned in the Gospels was psychosomatic. Their suffering was not faked or less real for that matter; it was altogether real, but it was caused by mental and psychological problems that turned into and surfaced as physical disabilities. Hence, Capps strongly claims that Jesus did cure, but not due to divine intervention. Jesus brought healing and cure that amazed and impressed the community, says Capps. In this way he accounts for the reaction of the bystanders in a way the Pilch tradition does not.

Capps does not consider psychological problems to be individual problems only. Although they emerge as the problems of individuals, they are part of a larger historical and cultural picture. He portrays the life of village dwellers in Galilee as strongly disturbed by the Hellenistic political structures and life in Tiberias and Sepphoris. They were heavily taxed and received little in return. Life in these Hellenistic cities thus posed a threat to the lives of those who lived in the surrounding villages, and was a major factor in disturbing their mental harmony. It is disputed whether the Hellenistic influence that guides Capps's theory was really this dominant

---

48. Capps, *Jesus the Village Psychiatrist,* p. xviii. New Testament scholar Stevan Davies suggested in 1995 that those healed by Jesus suffered from somatization of psychological problems; see Stevan L. Davies, *Jesus the Healer: Possession, Trance and the Origins of Christianity* (London: SCM, 1995).

49. Capps, *Jesus the Village Psychiatrist,* p. xxii.

50. Capps, *Jesus the Village Psychiatrist,* p. xxii.

this early.[51] And despite making cursory references to this larger picture of politics and culture in Galilee, Capps is nevertheless unable to bring his presentation of Jesus as a healer into contact with it. Throughout, the psychological diagnostics presented remain individually based, as the following will make clear. This bigger picture is thus a dead end in the book itself. Capps does not make any effort to prove that this cultural climate really affected the individual diagnoses he provides.

Sigmund Freud's Fräulein Elisabeth von R. and the Paralytics of the Gospels

In order to add some flesh to the bones of his diagnostic descriptions of the biblical stories, Capps turns to *The Diagnostic and Statistical Manual of Mental Disorders* (DSM-IV) of the American Psychiatric Association (1994). On that basis Capps works out both the illnesses involved and a diagnostic scheme to be applied to the textual descriptions of the Gospels. He distinguishes (though not sharply) between conversion disorder and undifferentiated somatoform disorders. I will briefly present the latter before proceeding to conversion disorder, which is more helpful for making relevant observations pertaining to what the texts describe.

Undifferentiated somatoform disorders are characterized by physical complaints that persist for six months or more and that cannot be explained by any known medical condition, drugs, or the like. The symptoms relate to organs and processes within the body. According to Capps, the textbook examples of this are the woman who had been hemorrhaging for more than twelve years (Mark 5:25–34) and the daughter of Jairus (Mark 5:21–24, 35–43 par.). He supports his psychiatric diagnosis with references to ancient ideas about women suffering from hysteria, which includes the notion that women were especially susceptible to out-of-control behavior.[52] Capps suggests that the cases referred to in Mark are excessive, and that they are probably paralleled because the women both suffered from sex-related anxieties. Their bodily disorders served to reduce the anxiety and offered camouflage for the real psychological conflict, namely, the woman's unfulfilled sexual desires

---

51. Jonathan L. Reed, *Archaeology and the Galilean Jesus: A Re-examination of the Evidence* (Harrisburg, PA: Trinity Press International, 2000).

52. Margaret Y. MacDonald, *Early Christian Women and Pagan Opinion: The Power of the Hysterical Woman* (Cambridge: Cambridge University Press, 1996).

and fantasies. For Jairus's daughter, the underlying problem was anxiety for assuming all the responsibilities of womanhood.

Conversion disorders represent psychological sufferings (primary problem) converted into physical pains or sickness (secondary problem), which cause deficits that affect voluntary motor or sensory function and suggest a neurological or other general medical condition. The symptoms carry a primary gain, which is to transform the conflict into a bodily symptom, thereby reducing anxiety and keeping it out of awareness. A secondary gain may also be implied, namely, possible benefits such as the evasion of unpleasant duties or responsibilities.

An example Capps gives of such a conversion disorder is Sigmund Freud's patient Elisabeth von R. The patient had developed severe leg pains that made it virtually impossible for her to walk. There was no sign of any physical reason for this disorder. However, as Freud used his "free association method," Elisabeth von R. revealed a hidden, deep sense of guilt, owing to the fact that she had nurtured a hope of marrying the husband of her late sister. The memory of the guilt for seeking to profit from her sister's death was long gone, but her leg pains remained. To Freud there was an apparent connection between the repressed desire and her paralysis. Against this background, Capps turns to the stories about the paralytics in Mark 2 and John 5. He claims that there is "indirect evidence" of psychological conflict à la Elisabeth von R. when these texts are read in light of the diagnostic scheme of DSM-IV. The fact that they were able to walk when Jesus told them to do so proves beyond any doubt that there were no physical obstacles holding them back. Based on the fact that Jesus tells the lame man (Mark 2) to go home (v. 11), Capps suggests that the home was the origin of the conflict: "The man must have felt threatened by the abusive treatment, aggressive or sexual or both, to which he was subjected."[53]

The role of Jesus in these healings resembles the role of Freud vis-à-vis Elisabeth von R. He helped her regain her health, and his charismatic personality was certainly also involved in making this possible. Similarly, "there was something about Jesus — his bearing, his voice, his eyes — that inspired in the two men the necessary confidence that they could, in fact, be cured. In effect, their *faith* made a huge difference in the outcome."[54] Thus

53. Capps, *Jesus the Village Psychiatrist*, pp. 48-49. This is a good example of how little Capps's sociocultural climate really brings to his analysis.

54. Capps, *Jesus the Village Psychiatrist*, p. 50.

the story of Fräulein Elisabeth von R. becomes an important tool for Capps's interpretation of the texts about the paralytics in the Gospels.

Ralph Waldo Emerson and Two Blind Men of the Gospels

Like the paralytics, Capps sees the men whom Jesus healed from blindness also to be afflicted with conversion disorder. Just as the psychological problems of the paralytics were converted into lameness, the problems of the blind likewise attacked their sensory function, making them unable to see. Again Capps bases his analysis on two factors, the criteria for conversion disorder in DSM-IV and on a nineteenth-century case, that of the American poet Ralph Waldo Emerson (1803–1892).

During a period when Emerson struggled with fundamental doubt, he was temporarily struck by blindness. His eyes failed him in the middle of finishing an essay on a controversial topic, the unity of God. He also had psychological conflicts related to forbidden erotic desires, as he found himself deeply disturbed by his fascination with a man. He probably suffered from "bisexual confusion."[55] Emerson's temporary blindness appeared after his fascination with Mr. Martin Gay, but "the symptoms of conversion disorder may begin months, even years after the original stressful experience,"[56] in analogy with Freud's analysis of the case of Fräulein Elisabeth von R.

As for the blind man at Bethsaida (Mark 8:22–26), Jesus urges him to go home, and not to return to the village. Capps takes this to indicate that he may have had "eyes for a woman in the village who belonged to another man or was otherwise inaccessible to him because they belonged to different social classes."[57] While Capps admits that this is pure speculation, it is nevertheless more or less a given with the approach he chooses and the sources he draws on. The act of leading the man out of the village was, according to Capps, the initial process of healing. Capps claims that blindness is a traditional "punishment" for sexual licenses; hence he assumes that Jesus "recognized that sexual anxieties had caused the man to be blind in the first place, and that sexual anxieties might be reawakened as a consequence of his being cured. . . . This may explain why he advised the man not to return to the village where his eyes had begun to fail."[58]

55. Capps, *Jesus the Village Psychiatrist*, pp. 63–68.
56. Capps, *Jesus the Village Psychiatrist*, p. 68.
57. Capps, *Jesus the Village Psychiatrist*, p. 69.
58. Capps, *Jesus the Village Psychiatrist*, pp. 76–77.

The story about Bartimaeus (Mark 10:46–52 par.) demonstrates that Jesus' curative method was to focus on the primary gain of the problem, not the secondary, which in this case was that Bartimaeus was allowed to beg for his living. Based on the fact that Bartimaeus is named after his father (Son of Timaeus), Capps suggests that there is a father issue at play, a deep resentment that this blind man felt for his father. His cry for help to Jesus, which does not name him by his father's name (Joseph), but instead "Son of David," further strengthens the observation that a father issue is involved.

Assessing Capps's Model

Compared to the Pilch-Crossan approach, Capps rehabilitates Jesus as a healer with a concern for bodily disorders. Body and bodily functions matter here. Jesus really did cure; he was, in fact, unique in this. This was not so because he was divinely inspired, but because he understood the unconscious conflicts underlying the illnesses he confronted. His therapeutic skills and curing methods simply surpassed those of his contemporary healers; he was more skilled and knowledgeable.[59] In Capps's presentation Jesus comes out rather unique. If Jesus' uniqueness consisted in his skills and know-how, one has to ask what it entails for his ministry that he instructed his disciples to continue his healing activities (see below). Were they equally skilled; did they have a "deeper knowledge" of how mind and body interacted? This question is, of course, not answered by Capps, since he limits himself to the Jesus traditions.

In a review of Capps's book, Craffert says that it is important to distinguish between what is possible and what is likely.[60] This targets precisely the duality of Capps's approach. He has explored some new paths, and it cannot be denied that it is possible that Jesus was equipped with a unique intuition regarding the origins in the mind of severe bodily disorders. The question is whether this makes sense based on the information given in the New Testament healing accounts.

Although Capps bases his diagnostic analysis on several observations and methods, the foundations are indeed fragile. The sociocultural climate

59. Capps does not mention that Jesus as a prophet is perceived to have special insight into the secrets of the human heart (Luke 7:39; 19:5; John 4:18–19).

60. Pieter F. Craffert, review of *Jesus the Village Psychiatrist,* by Donald Capps, *Review of Biblical Literature* 10 (2008): http://www.bookreviews.org/bookdetail.asp?TitleId=6392.

of villagers in Galilee is not developed in his book, and when it comes to the precise diagnosis he works out, Capps notes hardly any specific links between the political climate of Galilee and the disorders from which Jesus' patients suffered. Parental and sexual conflicts do not call for a specific cultural or political explanatory model, and Capps, aside from the few references mentioned above, for the most part leaves any such analysis out of his book.

In one of his observations, Capps points to ancient hysteria concerning the evil eye. This is the most promising diagnostic background he provides. In antiquity, it was believed that some people, through the power of their eyes, had the ability to cause malignant effects on other people.[61] Here Capps draws on substantial historical evidence, which he assumes Jesus may have been familiar with. Ancient hysteria provides a historically relevant starting point, for instance, for the analysis of the demon-possessed boy (Mark 9:14–19 par.). Capps claims that hysteria is here disguised as epilepsy (primary gain), which was believed to be caused by a demon. Since hysteria as described in ancient literature is especially connected to women and female issues, Capps goes on to suggest that the suffering of this boy was probably caused by base and evil wishes against his parents. These wishes, in turn, were caused by his mother's beating him from childhood. Because of the beating, the boy had internalized his rage against his mother, and, moreover, he "may have had sexual responses, possibly evoked by the sexual stimulation of the physical beating he received from her."[62] At some point in this argument one comes to think that, although the point of departure is relevant, speculation prevails.

At one point I find a tension in Capps's presentation, which goes to its very heart. The idea behind his explanatory model is that Jesus has a unique understanding of how the mind affected the body, and that this made him stand out from most, not to say all, of his contemporary healers. However, when it comes to the demon-possessed boy, Capps says that "Mark and all the other actors in the story, including Jesus, would have assumed that the boy was suffering from epilepsy."[63] What has happened here to Jesus' insight that bodily disorders were caused by mental problems? This special insight, which is the crucial point in Capps's thesis, is here simply lacking.

61. John H. Elliott, "Paul, Galatians, and the Evil Eye," in *The Social World of the New Testament: Insights and Models,* ed. Jerome H. Neyrey and Eric C. Stewart (Peabody, MA: Hendrickson, 2008).

62. Capps, *Jesus the Village Psychiatrist,* p. 97.

63. Capps, *Jesus the Village Psychiatrist,* p. 91.

Drawing on the DSM-IV, Capps uses criteria originally established based on clinical situations where the patients were observed and questioned over some time. The criteria themselves, however, are rather flimsy, and they do not provide much help in extracting diagnoses from the ancient texts that Capps investigates. Most of the diagnoses Capps deduces through his reading are, in fact, more an intrusion on than a deduction from the texts themselves. This is not at all surprising since the details in the texts are sketchy at best in their descriptions of the maladies of those healed (see above). Capps himself is aware of this and even admits that the stories do not say anything about these disorders being preceded by conflicts or stressors.[64] It follows from this that Capps's reading stretches the evidence here and that the diagnoses conferred on the sick really come from outside the texts, from *Capps's* set of criteria.

This weakness might have been remedied by claiming that Jesus had shown himself to be unique in knowing unconscious conflicts of the mind; this need not be spelled out in every text. But Capps assumes that the Gospel writers also shared the insight that Jesus healed those suffering from mental disorder.[65] This gives them a share in the uniqueness of Jesus. However, if they knew about this, why is it never indicated in the texts? It would not be far-fetched to assume that this kind of knowledge would have been brought to expression, but this does not happen. The near silence of the texts on the matter is difficult to explore.

Throughout Capps's presentation, Jesus appears in his healings as devoted to the real issue, which is the unconscious conflict; it is psychological in nature. According to Capps, these conflicts are often derived from parents, home, or village. But this picture of Jesus as generally calming people's unrest stands in stark contrast to the way he was remembered. If Capps's picture is not entirely wrong, it certainly does not explain the whole picture. An important piece of the picture is that this "psychiatrist" was also an apocalyptic, prophet-like figure who stirred conflicts and problems, and this affected precisely the contexts of family, home, and village. It is germane to cite here Luke 12:51–53: "Do you think that I have come to bring peace to the earth? No, I tell you, but rather division! From now on five in one household will be divided, three against two and two against three; they will be divided; father against son and son against father, mother against daughter and daughter against mother, mother-in-law against her daughter-in-law and

64. Capps, *Jesus the Village Psychiatrist*, pp. 61, 95, 117–18.
65. Capps, *Jesus the Village Psychiatrist*, p. xii.

daughter-in-law against mother-in-law." Jesus not only dissolved problems but also created some of them for his disciples, who did not, by the way, fall sick from them! Any model of Jesus as psychiatrist has to deal with this aspect of the tradition as well.[66] An apocalyptic prophet like Jesus does not easily fit the counseling type reconstructed by Capps.

Capps's examples of Elisabeth von R. and Ralph Waldo Emerson in his diagnostic analysis of the biblical texts certainly serve his purpose by making it evident that bodily illnesses may be caused by mental problems. But these cases do not just set a stage for biblical interpretation; they also lead Capps to deduce information from the texts that in fact is gained from nineteenth-century psychiatry rather than from the texts themselves.

There is, in my view, a troubling discrepancy between Capps's examples and the biblical material they are supposed to serve. This has to do with the aspect of time. Freud's treatment of Fraulein Elisabeth von R. lasted for a year at least.[67] And although Ralph Waldo Emerson did not undergo any professional treatment, his eyes recovered over time, primarily due to the time he spent together with laborers in his uncle's field, among whom a man named Tarbox played a significant role. He reminded Emerson that prayers were granted, and the poet started to pray for the recovery of his sight, which gradually returned after about a year.

At this point these cases fail to meet the New Testament passages they are supposed to serve. In the case of the two paralytics, Capps writes the following: "In both cases Jesus enjoins the men to stand up, take their mats, and begin walking. In both cases, their ability to do so is immediate. In a moment, the flicker of an eye, two men who had been lying prone were able to stand and, as they stood, were able to walk."[68] The cure was instantaneous. This aspect finds no real analogy in either Elisabeth von R. or Ralph Waldo Emerson. Capps would have done well to address this difference directly since it pertains to the helpfulness of his models. Instead, he confuses his own statement given above by saying concerning the demon-possessed boy, "I doubt that the effectiveness of the cure was due to a single physical or verbal act on Jesus' part. Instead, the cure was effected by many individual acts that were beautifully orchestrated into a composite whole. There was the

66. Rightly pointed out by Gerd Theissen, "Jesus and His Followers as Healers: Symbolic Healing in Early Christianity," in *The Problem of Ritual Efficacy*, ed. William Sax et al. (Oxford: Oxford University Press, 2010), pp. 57–59.

67. The treatment is said to have started in the autumn 1892, and the therapy was finished as the summer was approaching; which summer is not said.

68. Capps, *Jesus the Village Psychiatrist*, p. 43.

convenient fact that his disciples had tried to cure the boy but had failed."[69] However, there is no less "a flicker of an eye" in this passage than in those about the blind men, and Capps does not address this difference. His dictum about the demon-possessed boy has been adjusted to fit his model in a way that stretches the texts.

Capps's nineteenth-century cases interestingly demonstrate the significance of key persons in effecting healing. Jesus attributes the healing to the faith of those healed, demonstrating the mutuality involved, that those who are suffering are responding to Jesus' voice and touch. In the words of Justin Meggitt, "It takes two to make a 'miracle.'"[70] This parallels Freud's charismatic personality and also the impression Tarbox made on Emerson. According to Capps, the relationship between the sick and Jesus developed because of Jesus' voice, eyes, and touching. These are relevant analogies for explaining the healing method of Jesus.

As we will soon see with Gerd Theissen, Jesus took those who were sick away from the crowd, away from the village, in order to build the intimacy on which their relationship was based. However, Capps's perspective on these observations instead mirrors the difficulties involved, pointing to the background that caused the problems. According to Capps, Jesus withdrew his patients from the contexts that helped create their bodily disorders.

The Power of Faith — Placebo? (Gerd Theissen)

The Heidelberg New Testament Professor Gerd Theissen has written extensively on Jesus and his miracles.[71] In the edited volume *The Problem of Ritual Efficacy* (2010), Theissen has recently written an essay titled "Jesus and His Followers as Healers: Symbolic Healing in Early Christianity." He considers the historicity of Jesus' healing ministry to be based on multiple attestations in independent traditions: "As a whole, they are no invention."[72] Theissen understands Jesus' healings as charismatic, symbolic, and social. They are charismatic in creating a personal and intimate relationship between the healer and the client (see above). In the Gospel tradition, this intimacy is labeled "faith." Jesus' healings are symbolic since they are understood within

---

69. Capps, *Jesus the Village Psychiatrist*, p. 101.
70. Meggitt, "The Historical Jesus and Healing," p. 43.
71. Theissen, *Miracle Stories of the Early Christian Tradition.*
72. Theissen, "Jesus and His Followers as Healers," p. 50.

a cognitive imagination surrounding their significance and meaning. In the tradition, this comes to expression as the antagonistic struggle of freeing the sick from the power of evil, or the healing is an indication of an eschatological transformation of the world (see pp. 118–21 below). Jesus' healings are ritual due to his use of external aspects, such as the laying on of hands, touching, and the use of saliva (Mark 7:33; 8:23; John 9:6). Theissen points out, however, that ritual elements play a smaller role in the Gospel stories when compared to other relevant elements. Prayer, for instance, strikingly plays no role in the tradition of Jesus as healer: "He never prays in order to heal a person."[73] Finally, Jesus' healings are social, as they reintegrate the client into fellowship. The stories usually end with Jesus sending the sick back to the household or the family, although the healings at times also provoke protest from and conflict with the community.

Fundamental to the efficacy of Jesus' healings is that he "discovered the power of faith."[74] The role attributed to faith permeates the stories of Jesus and the sick, abbreviated in the repeated formula: "Your faith has healed/saved you."[75] According to Mark 2 and parallels, Jesus *saw* the faith of those who brought him the lame man. Was what Jesus observed the fact that they carried the man to him? Faith is confidence leading to either an initiative or a responsive act. This confidence in the healer is preceded by a rumor about Jesus as a powerful healer worthy of believing and putting one's trust and hope in. Thus faith reacts to rumors of healings, but also produces them. The Jesus tradition's motif of faith has no real analogy in antiquity. It does not grow naturally from Christian tradition either, since "faith" very early became faith in doctrines about Jesus, and it definitely works differently in the miracle stories. According to Theissen, faith is the power of healing attributed to Jesus, who himself reattributes this power to the faith of the sick. Contrariwise, lack of faith also explains failure of healings according to the Jesus tradition, as when he visited his hometown (Mark 6:5–6; Luke 4:23–30). Jesus' healings were thus products of both healer and the expectations of the sick or those bringing the sick to him.

Jesus' discovery of the power of faith dovetails with modern research on the so-called placebo effect.[76] The expectations of the patient activate

73. Theissen, "Jesus and His Followers as Healers," p. 49.

74. Theissen, "Jesus and His Followers as Healers," p. 53. On p. 54, he writes that Jesus intuitively discovered the healing effect of faith.

75. For the Greek *sōzein*, see BDAG, s.v. The clear meaning in the context is healing. The soteriological meaning becomes dominant in Pauline tradition, and partly in Acts.

76. Meggitt, "The Historical Jesus and Healing," pp. 32–42, argues similarly on the basis

the body's own therapeutic powers and work like "a wonderful drugstore" inside the client herself. This power, not manufactured by medicine, is strengthened in Jesus' healings when he takes the sick aside, thus creating an intimate atmosphere in which he touched the sick or whispered words of healing. These rituals were expressions of personalized actions that heightened the intimacy between Jesus and the sick person. As noted above, Theissen points out that there is a poverty of ritual gestures in the stories about Jesus' healings. However, he considers this poverty increases the significance of those rituals that are there, that is, words, touching,[77] and even kissing. The repertoire of ritual gestures is small but all the more significant in that they all enhance "the proximity to the sick person."[78] These hallmarks create the exact context modern research holds to be critical to placebo healing. This placebo effect is, according to Theissen, not able to cure diseases, but to "improve the general conditions of health and thereby make it easier to live with an illness."[79] He thus combines medical-anthropological theory and placebo theory to explain Jesus' healings: "Jesus and his followers treat illness, they transform the social role, the self-estimation, and the confidence of the sick person, independent of organic disease."[80] According to Theissen, this does not imply that Jesus "generally reduced social conflicts and stress"; sometimes he even enhanced stress and social conflicts (see above).

Assessment of Theissen's Model

The combination of faith and ritual elements does create intimacy and personal relationship worth considering as analogous to what present-day scholars may label placebo. This claim is, of course, of much relevance for New Testament studies. Theissen's argument needs to be assessed from two angles, that is, the placebo theory he applies, and the ability of this theory to make sense of the relevant New Testament passages.

---

of medical anthropologist Daniel Moerman, *Meaning, Medicine and the "Placebo Effect"* (Cambridge: Cambridge University Press, 2002).

77. Zimmermann, "Grundfragen," pp. 15–18, emphasizes the touching method as a reminder of the physical aspect of Jesus' healings.

78. Theissen, "Jesus and His Followers as Healers," p. 61.

79. Theissen, "Jesus and His Followers as Healers," p. 55; cf. p. 57.

80. Theissen, "Jesus and His Followers as Healers," p. 57. Theissen thus adheres to the Pilch tradition, albeit in a way not sufficiently explained or accounted for in his article.

Placebo Theory

Although the Jesus tradition by and large lacks ritual elements, Theissen still holds that Jesus healed by using rituals in a way that makes it relevant to consider placebo the closest explanatory model, particularly since the ritual gestures that are there increase the proximity to the patient, which is crucial for placebo in bringing about healing. Placebo here refers to the positive expectations and visions of hope that can stimulate natural processes of healing in a patient. Placebo thus refers to how self-healing may be stimulated and strengthened.

According to Howard Brody, "Theissen's analysis matches very closely the meaning model I [i.e., Brody] have presented."[81] The meaning model — namely, "when the meaning of the illness experience for the patient is altered in a positive direction" — rests on two fundamental conditions: expectancy and conditioning. While expectancy is forward-looking, awaiting healing to take place, conditioning is backward-looking; "it *requires* a previous, repeated exposure to a particular stimulus."[82] Rituals are by definition repetitive bodily actions. As pointed out, to some extent Jesus' healings follow this pattern. The meaning model and Theissen's analysis share the following characteristics:

- The patient experiences intimacy with the healer (importance of community or therapist)[83]
- The patient is given an explanation for the illness which coheres with her general worldview
- The patient feels taken care of
- The patient experiences mastering of or control over the illness

One significant difference, in my opinion, is not accounted for in Brody's statement that Theissen's analysis perfectly fits this placebo model.[84] I am

81. Howard Brody, "Ritual, Medicine, and the Placebo Response," in *The Problem of Ritual Efficacy*, ed. William Sax et al. (Oxford: Oxford University Press, 2010), p. 163.

82. Brody, "Ritual, Medicine, and the Placebo Response," p. 157 (emphasis original).

83. In the classic study, Jerome Frank, *Persuasion and Healing: A Comparative Study of Psychotherapy* (Baltimore: Johns Hopkins University Press, 1974), the role of the healer himself is emphasized; in entering into an intense relationship with the patient, the healer comes to play a crucial role.

84. Meggitt, "The Historical Jesus and Healing," draws on the following characteristics: knowledge about medicine or healing presented to the sick; the therapist or therapeutic agent; the form of the therapeutic intervention; and the expectations of the patient.

referring to the repeated actions and the conditioning that, according to Brody, are crucial for the theory. The theory primarily addresses healing that takes place within a continuous relationship where the healer repeatedly does the same thing, and where the patient is exposed to the same actions over some time. However, it is also necessary to address how this can be transferred to healings that take place, apparently accidentally, through a short encounter with a patient. This is precisely how the tradition depicts Jesus' healings. He is not a "doctor" caring for his patient over time; that is, his patients are not "hospitalized." The patients are generally brought to him or they appear to him then and there, and are then sent home. As Capps puts it, in the flicker of an eye their situation is changed. Thus elements essential to the placebo definition seem not to apply to the textual material Theissen addresses.

To my critique it may be objected that the ritual elements and the repeated stimuli, although not necessarily present in the situation, were carried by spreading rumors. Hence, a rumor might have created both the expectancy and conditioning required, and therefore a positive placebo response might follow. This possibility cannot be ruled out, but here I find that both Theissen and Brody stretch the biblical material to fit their theory. The question to be asked is the following: Is it likely that repeated actions and stimuli experienced by different patients at different places and passed around by rumor could create the necessary expectancy and conditioning required by the theory in ever new patients? As for expectancy, I am inclined to agree that rumors might accomplish precisely that. With regard to conditioning, I am more reluctant. Although some recurrent patterns are observable, Jesus' healings were not always performed in the same way.

Variety in the Rituals and Placebo

Gerd Theissen points out that although Jesus' healings were not rich in rituals, he did perform some gestures of importance, namely, Jesus' withdrawal of the patient from the crowd, his words or commands, touching, use of saliva, and healing at a distance. Prayer is not included in these rituals, although Jesus at times looks up and sighs (Mark 7:34; Matt. 14:19), and medicine is nowhere mentioned.[85] These do not form one fixed set of rituals. Sometime they occur together, but not always. There are instances where only one of them appears, and there are instances where Jesus heals at a dis-

---

85. Hendrik van der Loos, *The Miracles of Jesus* (Leiden: Brill, 1965), pp. 305–36.

tance without even having seen the sick (Mark 7:25–30; Matt. 8:5–13//Luke 7:1–10; John 4:46–54).[86] This lack of consistency is important to notice since regularity, as both Brody and Theissen point out, is usually a prerequisite for placebo to work.[87] Theissen addresses this objection, referencing a documented story that a healer in Munich in the 1950s was able to heal patients in Hamburg. Without their knowledge about the healer, nor his about the patients, no improvement was registered. However, after they were told about a man in Munich with extraordinary power to heal, were given books to read about him, and were told that the healing would take place at an appointed time (fictive though, since the healer was not informed), healing actually took place. According to Theissen, "In order to explain the distant healings of Jesus we must presuppose only that the Syrophoenician woman told her little daughter that she was looking for help from a famous Galilean healer, and the servant of the centurion of Capernaum had knowledge of his master's attempt to meet this healer in order to ask him for help. This may even explain why the daughter and the servant felt better."[88] Again we are touching on an observation that seems to apply to most present-day models aimed at explaining Jesus' healings. Most of them assume relationships and situations developing over some time, and thus they fail to meet the short perspective implied in the New Testament passages. Reading books about the Munich healer provides time for placebo to work, a span of time that in the New Testament stories is shorter, if present at all.

In the story of the blind Bartimaeus (Mark 10:46–52) regaining his sight, the only ritual present is the words of Jesus: "Go, your faith has made you well." This does not necessarily mean that placebo is out of the question here, but Theissen's argument for a setting that enhances a potential placebo effect appears more questionable. The only thing to suggest this is the words by which the healing is performed. The placebo explanation may go a long way toward providing an answer to what Jesus did when he healed, but it is not a sufficient explanation. This becomes acute when we approach the stories claiming that Jesus restored life to people already dead, like Lazarus, who already smelled (John 11:39) (see below). If this and similar stories refer to

---

86. This variety is pointed out by Zimmermann, "Grundfragen," p. 15, as well.

87. This is not sufficiently accounted for by Meggitt, "The Historical Jesus and Healing." Meggitt rightly points out that Jesus at times used techniques associated with folk practices at the time, but this is not the general impression. On the contrary, "the historical Jesus appears to have been set apart from many of his contemporaries" (p. 41) in this regard. Unforeseen methods are hardly conducive of placebo.

88. Theissen, "Jesus and His Followers as Healers," p. 56.

physical death, and are not only metaphors, placebo would not work at all. Placebo effects are, of course, entirely dependent on factors that stimulate and affect the brain, mind, emotions, and body of the person fallen sick. The whole idea is that placebo is a responsive reaction to received stimuli. Hence, the patient must be alive. Gerd Theissen constructs, on the basis of New Testament evidence, an environment for this to work within Jesus' healing ministry, but this construction proceeds from a situation of mutuality, contact, and communication between Jesus and the afflicted. Death brings an end to all mutuality, responsive acts, information, and communication. Death is not a modern experience only; people at Jesus' time of course experienced the reality of death as well (more on this below).

The Absence of Prayer in Jesus' Healings?

We have seen that Theissen makes the important observation that prayer was not among the rituals[89] Jesus turned to in his healing practice.[90] (An exception to this is John 11:41-42, where Jesus offers a prayer before commanding Lazarus to come out of the tomb. This prayer, however, is explicitly said to be offered for the sake of the crowd, and it is thus not really a ritual part of the healing performance.) Theissen's observation deserves some elaboration, and the significance of the absence of prayer will be considered. Its significance appears if we see Jesus' healing power against the backdrop of a failure of his disciples to heal, which occurs in the story about the moonstruck[91] boy in Mark 9:14-29//Matthew 17:14-20//Luke 9:37-43.

This story throws some interesting light on the manner in which Jesus was thought to be able to heal people. All versions say that the disciples were unable to heal the boy: *ouk ischysan* (Mark 9:18); *ouk ēdynēthēmen* (Mark 9:28); *ouk ēdynēthēsan* (Matt. 17:16, 19; Luke 9:40). This is a rather strong expression of their failure. In Mark and Matthew, the disciples approach Jesus privately about their incompetence: "Why could we not cast out or

---

89. "Ritual" here refers to any act, gesture, or word accompanying the healings of Jesus.

90. Jesus here differs from most contemporary figures relevant to compare him with; see above.

91. NRSV has "epileptic," which is most likely a precise rendering of the Greek here and which also makes sense of the symptoms described. However, "moonstruck" is the explanatory model, shared by the authors and most likely by Jesus as well, that this sickness was connected with the phases of the moon; see Ulrich Luz, *Matthew 21-28,* trans James E. Crouch, Hermeneia (Minneapolis: Fortress, 2005), p. 407; and BDAG, s.v.

heal the boy?" According to Mark, Jesus says: "This kind can come out only through prayer" (v. 29). This reading finds limited support in the textual witnesses, but the support it does find is all the more significant.[92] A number of witnesses[93] add "and through fasting."

Matthew elaborates on this scene, turning it into a didactic text, that is, on how the disciples may perform healing. Matthew in particular reveals that Christians from early on grappled with the question of how miracles were possible, and 17:14-20 gives kind of a manual for Christian healers, though not for Jesus. Matthew 17:20 makes the disciples' failure a matter of faith — "your little faith" — and Jesus adds to this the dictum that faith is able to move mountains.[94] This theme may also be found in other places in Matthew's Gospel (6:30; 8:26; 14:31; 16:8).[95] Faith in these passages denotes trusting God, nurturing no doubt in God's power, and is something achieved through prayer (and fasting).

Present-day commentaries mostly devote themselves to treating what is considered the "original text"; hence Mark 9:29b "and fasting" is often left unaddressed. "This kind does not come out (or is not being cast out) without prayer (and fasting)," found also in Matthew 17:21, is certainly an insertion, but is nonetheless important in grasping how these texts were read. By focusing on the alleged "original," commentaries in this way cut themselves loose from some of the earliest witnesses to how a given text was transmitted and interpreted. It is precisely the appearance of praying and fasting together that guides us to see how a text about Jesus becomes didactic, on how the disciples are to heal, and hence prayer also comes into the picture.

In this perspective, Matthew 17:21, albeit most probably a later insertion, is highly relevant. However, the textual support of Mark 9:29b and Matthew 17:21 is, if not in the oldest manuscripts, still immense, and demonstrates that this was a widely read text. Against this background, Matthew 17:21 pertains to the question of how *disciples* could perform healings. The phrase "without prayer and fasting" makes this not a matter of technique, but of a regimen of preparing oneself before embarking on healing. The idea is that through

92. This includes Sinaiticus prima manus, Vaticanus, one other majuscule (0274, fifth century), and one Old Latin version (k, fourth/fifth century).

93. E.g. P45, Sinaiticus corrector 2, a number of majuscules with A and D as the most prominent, many minuscules, the Majority Text, Latin, Syrian, and Coptic versions.

94. This dictum also appears in slightly different versions in Matt 21:21; Mark 11:22-23; Luke 17:6; 1 Cor. 13:2.

95. Cf. the Synoptic scenes where Jesus pays a visit to his hometown Nazareth, where he "could not" perform miracles (Mark 6:5; Matt 13:58; Luke 4:16-30).

this preparation the necessary power becomes available. Praying and fasting, particularly as a tandem, hold pride of place in early Christian ideas of preparing oneself for ministry, baptism, or moments of divine presence. This is also evident in Acts 4:30, where the believers engage in a prayer, saying: "while you stretch out your hand to heal, and signs and wonders are performed through the name of your holy servant Jesus" (cf. Acts 9:40).

The temptation scenes are relevant here, as preparation scenes for Jesus' ministry. Other relevant examples include Acts 9:11, together with 9:19; 13:2; 14:23;[96] 1 Corinthians 7:5; *Didache* 7; and Tertullian, *On Baptism* 20. These texts are, in spite of their differences, united in making prayer and fasting the crucial preparation for God's powerful work, be it in mission, in times of devotion, or in baptism. According to the text-critically doubtful reading of Mark 9:29b and Matthew 17:21, healing is possible, depending on the required preparation. According to the temptation traditions rendered in Matthew 4, Jesus did likewise before embarking on his ministry. But this is not described as a ritual Jesus repeated whenever he was confronted with sickness. When this didactic text on healings brings together faith and preparatory rituals, such as prayer (and fasting), it is implied that faith applies to the healer as well. It does not make sense to reserve faith for the sick in these passages. Against this backdrop, the absence of prayer when Jesus heals becomes important.

In the healings of Jesus, "healing words are at the center."[97] This is certainly not to say that Jesus was not a man of prayer — he certainly was, as emerges from the Lord's Prayer as well as Matthew 11:25-26 — but prayer definitely appears in the background when he heals. Compared to the significance of prayer in the didactic passage on healing, Jesus therefore appears unique in not using these preparatory rituals.[98] Jesus' person, identity, and proximity to God appear as the very reasons why he was perceived as able to heal people who were suffering from sickness. The miracles in themselves do not prove Jesus' uniqueness since they are not without analogies. What is unique is that these performances are seen within a wider horizon where Jesus' identity, his access to divine power, is also involved. Hence, it follows

96. Acts 10:30 is another example where alternate readings show that praying and fasting were seen in tandem as means of preparing for God to act.

97. Theissen, "Jesus and His Followers as Healers," p. 61.

98. Annette Merz, "Der historische Jesus als Wundertäter im Spektrum antiker Wundertäter," in Zimmerman, *Die Wunder Jesu,* pp. 119-20, makes the same observation, namely, that Jesus, who himself hardly prays when involved in healing, instructs his disciples to do precisely that.

naturally that Jesus in his response to John the Baptist, after summarizing his healings (Q 7:23), says, "And blessed is anyone who takes no offense in me." The reaction of the bystanders (Mark 2:12; Luke 5:26; Matt. 9:7), though put in somewhat different forms, paves the way for the question of who Jesus really is.

A Cultural Phenomenon (Pieter F. Craffert)

Craffert, a South African scholar who has published widely on the historical Jesus, claims that "anthropological historiography" is the appropriate method for the study of the historical Jesus.[99] This method is grounded in ontological pluralism, which recognizes that reality and events are grounded in multiple worldviews, and are thus socially and culturally constituted and construed. The texts about Jesus, he goes on to argue, have to be read in a way sensitive to the cultural system in which they came into being. In order to make sense of the "events" claimed in these texts, we must therefore offer a culture-plausible interpretation. Craffert claims that this will overcome ethnocentrism and arrogance vis-à-vis cultures foreign to modern scholars,[100] which of course includes the world of the Gospels. Jesus was a figure in a different world; his audience made sense of his life and ministry within parameters set by their culture. It is therefore crucial for studies on the historical Jesus to find appropriate categories with which to think and reason: "a description that can account for Jesus' social type, profile and biography that is well established historically and cross-culturally, fits the first-century Mediterranean Galilean setting, and can account for the underlying traits, stories and deeds ascribed to him in his lifetime and continued to make sense in the life of the followers after his death."[101]

The figure Craffert finds most appropriate for understanding Jesus is the shaman. He worked within a culture where such figures operated, and he met with such expectations. Specific for shamans, wherever they appear, are altered states of consciousness (ASC), which manifest themselves in vision-

99. See Pieter F. Craffert, "Crossan's Historical Jesus as Healer, Exorcist and Miracle Worker," *Religion & Theology* 10 (2003): 243–66; and his main contribution Craffert, *The Life of a Galilean Shaman: Jesus of Nazareth in Anthropological Perspective* (Eugene, OR: Cascade, 2008), especially pp. 245–99.

100. In his article, Craffert targets Crossan in particular for claiming that Jesus was a healer who did not heal. The healings of Jesus made sense precisely as healings to his audience.

101. Craffert, "Crossan's Historical Jesus," p. 250.

ary experiences of all sorts, among which healing, divination, and exorcism are the most typical. A shamanic worldview is populated with spirits and powers of various kinds. Many aspects of Jesus' life and ministry fall into this category, among which healing and exorcism hold pride of place.

Craffert pleads for a "biopsychosocial approach," which means that sickness and healing are culturally conditioned. This approach goes beyond the biomedical paradigm assuming that illness (or sickness) and the healing thereof are universal and similar phenomena: "The healing accounts can be seen as normal and typical activities of someone controlling and manipulating the symbols of meaning in his cultural world, and in that way affecting sick people — this is precisely what shamanic figures do all the time."[102] Healing and illness are thus real, but simultaneously culturally dependent. In effect, Jesus as a healer remains within his culture and the expectations at work there. The healings are cultural events, as are the texts telling about them.[103] And it is equally true that they fall outside *our* view of reality.

What did Jesus do when he healed? According to Craffert, we should distinguish among autonomous responses (the body's power to heal and placebo), specific responses (herbs, saliva, etc.), and meaning responses (mediating forgiveness, faith). These means were conveyed to the sick via touching, a belief relationship, and rumor of the power of the healer.

Assessing Craffert's Model

Craffert's contribution raises many important issues; my assessment here is limited to the implications for healing. Fundamental to Craffert's argument is that the shaman was a familiar social type in the world of Jesus as well as of those who passed on the stories about his healings. The social figure of the shaman embodies culture-specific traits, but is simultaneously a cross-cultural type. Although Craffert provides a helpful heuristic model for understanding the indigenous and culturally dependent nature of Jesus' healing, he leaves crucial details of his study somewhat vague and abstract. He claims that the sicknesses Jesus faced were "Galilean conditions,"[104] or Galilean in nature. What this entails Craffert substantiates in principle only, not in detail, nor with historical sources. This is in my opinion not a minor

102. Craffert, *Life of a Galilean Shaman*, pp. 298–99.
103. Craffert, *Life of a Galilean Shaman*, p. 261.
104. Craffert, *Life of a Galilean Shaman*, pp. 277, 287.

matter, since Craffert's claim regarding "Galilean conditions" comes as a result of his emphasizing the culture-driven aspect of sickness. His argument boils down to this claim, which he leaves unwarranted. In a study so bent on contingency, this is surprising.

Craffert is right in claiming both that sickness is ingrained in culture and that the New Testament accounts do not provide sufficient basis for precise diagnosis. But this observation also makes the most evident aspects of some texts rather ambiguous. According to Craffert, "a remarkable feature of the healing episodes is that none of the healings ascribed to Jesus contains a reference to an injury or serious bodily wound (with the exception of the episode where Jesus replaced a soldier's removed ear)."[105] But there are several episodes where Jesus heals the blind, the lame, and the deaf, so that they recover sight, walk, and hear. Furthermore, these events are witnessed by audiences. In what way these stories count as Galilean conditions per se is not easily seen.

Craffert is right in pointing out that realities (note the plural) can be distinct due to cultural aspects. This is not to be underestimated. In the present study, we have seen that cultural parameters were at work to explain sickness, such as possession and the phases of the moon.[106] Nonetheless, sickness does not disappear with a culture-specific explanation.

ASC Experiences

As ASC experiences, Jesus' healings were "cultural versions of cultural events," "most of which could not have been tape-recorded or video-recorded."[107] This illustration in effect withdraws the events from observation. While such healings according to Craffert have "a serious and profound effect on the life of an individual or a community,"[108] they are about "people in an alternate state of consciousness."[109]

At this point, Craffert's argument becomes muddled. He makes no distinction between the state of consciousness that caused the healing and its effect. What started out as the driving force that turned Jesus into a healer now applies also to those healed. The two are not necessarily the same. By

---

105. Craffert, *Life of a Galilean Shaman*, p. 277.
106. See pp. 19–20 above.
107. Craffert, "Crossan's Historical Jesus," p. 261.
108. Craffert, "Crossan's Historical Jesus," p. 261.
109. Craffert, "Crossan's Historical Jesus," p. 261.

turning the healing into events of consciousness only, the role of the spectators in the New Testament stories becomes hard to understand. To this Craffert may object that the bystanders also shared the cultural system that brought about the healing. The problem is then that the shamanic theory and ASC in Craffert's theory are applied to Jesus as healer, to the sick as healee, and to the bystander who watched the incidents. I do not think the healings Jesus performed were so one-sidedly culture-specific as Craffert claims. This applies particularly to the view chosen in the present study, namely, how Jesus was remembered. The way his healings were remembered brought with it a perspective *beyond* Galilee and beyond contingency. The healings become stories of relevance for posterity.

A Summary of the Works Presented

According to Gerd Theissen and Annette Merz, the miracles of Jesus have become a problem, and modern theologians tend to "excuse" them.[110] The models applied by the scholars discussed above do provide important partial perspectives, but they do not fully come to terms with what the texts actually say and imply in terms of how Jesus' healing practice was remembered. This is not to assert that things happened according to the texts, but explanatory models are expected to account for the texts before proceeding to reconstruct what is behind them.

I have focused on four explanatory models for Jesus' healing activity and have assessed them according to their ability to explain Jesus' reputation as an effective healer. I have come to view these models as providing no more than partial help for understanding this aspect of Jesus' ministry. John J. Pilch inaugurated a new paradigm in New Testament scholarship on this topic. His use of medical-anthropological models and definitions is a reminder that sickness is not always a given, independent of culture. He also reminds us that healing is a matter more complex than curing. However, Pilch uses his models in a rather doctrinaire way, which at times overrules the texts themselves. An indication that the Pilch-Crossan tradition falls

110. Gerd Theissen and Annette Merz, *The Historical Jesus: A Comprehensive Guide,* trans. John Bowden (London: SCM, 1998), p. 285. Theissen's own rationalism is expressed clearly in his *The Shadow of the Galilean: The Quest for the Historical Jesus in Narrative Form,* trans. John Bowden (London: SCM, 1987), p. 120. Theissen argues that Jesus made people "feel that there was always food there" (p. 115), and "once the people believe that there's enough food for everyone they lose their fear of hunger."

short of explaining the healings of Jesus as a phenomenon is their need to make metaphors out of the texts. At times this appears justified, but it becomes a problem with texts that address bodily sicknesses, and particularly so since this interpretation owes more to Pilch's model than to the texts themselves. Pilch's interpretation of this aspect of Jesus' ministry therefore implies a certain reductionism. Bodily healing becomes irrelevant and is of little importance in the Pilch-Crossan view. Sharon V. Betcher has therefore recently accused Crossan and others of turning disabled bodies into "stage props" for other concerns.[111]

Don Capps emphasizes the charismatic personality, be it Sigmund Freud, Tarbox, or Jesus, to make sense of the biblical material. This perspective is developed in Gerd Theissen's emphasis on the proximity between healer and patient, which in Jesus' case enhanced faith and enabled them to respond to and to produce healing. However, Theissen's claim that healing is equivalent to placebo leaves certain aspects of the texts unaddressed. A common problem with both Capps's and Theissen's models is that they assume a certain lapse of time, which does not correspond to how the Gospels depict Jesus at work; on the contrary, this time lapse speaks against the textual evidence. In principle, it is of course fully possible that Jesus' healings manifested themselves over some time, and that this has been suppressed into moments in the texts. But the texts do not say so.

As Theissen points out, relating the healing stories, making them relevant for posterity by telling about them, is a "*symbolic* act of opposing real problems."[112] The act of telling transcends the events told and makes them relevant for subsequent audiences. Thus the telling and the didactic perspective that emerge represent the same idea, namely, that there is no cessation in Jesus' healings. This is a fundamental insight, which forms a bridge to the second part of the present volume, about the present-day relevance of the healing tradition about Jesus (more on this later).

Craffert reminds us that sickness always comes in cultural garb. But in my view, he overstates his case, which can be seen in the fact that he fails to substantiate the specific cultural dependence of the sicknesses healed by Jesus.

The four influential theories presented above are united in explaining

---

111. Sharon V. Betcher, "Disability and Terror of the Miracle Tradition," in *Miracles Revisited: New Testament Miracle Stories and Their Concepts of Reality*, ed. Stefan Alkier and Annette Weissenrieder (Berlin: De Gruyter, 2013), pp. 169–70.

112. Theissen, "Jesus and His Followers as Healers," p. 46 (emphasis original).

Jesus' healings as caused by natural reasons. Indeed, they present alternative explanations, but they are all, albeit in different ways, attempts to explain away the wondrous in these stories, that which is said to have caused the amazement of the spectators. Jesus' reputation as a healer probably did include cures stemming from natural reasons. Healing today may at times be due to natural reasons, and there is no reason to assume that the healings of Jesus were entirely cut off from some such reason.[113] But the approaches presented in this chapter more or less exclusively claim natural reasons behind Jesus' healings. Hence, they depend heavily on analogies. As a consequence, Jesus becomes one among other contemporary healers. But while Jesus certainly was not alone in being remembered as a healer, the nature of his reputation and the extent of this aspect of his ministry also made him extraordinary when compared to others.[114] The theories presented above hardly come to terms with this reputation. Furthermore, the contributions presented here unanimously, albeit in very different ways, aim at explaining Jesus as a healer by isolating certain aspects of the healing, be it the difference between disease and illness, psychological diagnostics, or placebo. A common weakness is therefore that they fail to account for the effects of the numerous factors involved. Attempts to identify and separate singular aspects do not come to terms with what is most likely a plurality of reasons behind Jesus' healings, including biological effects.

113. Keener, *Miracles*, pp. 620–30.
114. See pp. 21–24 above.

Raising the Dead — Implications for Jesus as Healer?

Definitions and limitations matter; they do make a difference. The previous chapters have presented some influential explanatory models for what Jesus actually did when he healed. Rarely does the claim that Jesus even raised people from the dead come into play in these models. If, however, this tradition is included among the healings, then that would open grounds the above models do not sufficiently touch on. As Graham H. Twelftree points out, "The stories of the raising of the dead stretch the credulity of Western post-Enlightenment readers to the limit, if not beyond."[1]

From the Gospels themselves, it seems right to consider the raising of the dead as closely related to the healings of Jesus, as extreme cases, so to say. This becomes apparent not only from Jesus' response to John the Baptist (see below), but also from the raising of Jairus's daughter (Mark 5:22–43//Matt. 9:18–26//Luke 8:40–56). The way this story is sandwiched around a healing story in all three Gospels has attracted attention. What starts out as a request for healing turns out to be the raising of a girl who has passed away. Within this story, all three versions interpolate the healing of the woman with hemorrhages. From this it becomes clear that the raising of the dead is to be considered the ultimate healing.

Above I pointed out that it seems to make little if any difference for John J. Pilch whether Jesus declared a leper clean, raised someone from the dead, or healed hemorrhages. Either way, it is about removing experiential oppressiveness.[2] Raising someone who is dead makes sense only if it is

---

1. Graham H. Twelftree, *Jesus the Miracle Worker: A Historical and Theological Study* (Downers Grove, IL: InterVarsity Press, 1999), p. 304.

2. John J. Pilch, *Healing in the New Testament: Insights from Medical and Mediterranean Anthropology* (Minneapolis: Fortress, 2000), p. 14.

seen from the perspective of the family afflicted, namely, Jairus himself, the widow in Nain, and Mary and Martha, the sisters of the deceased Lazarus. However, Pilch goes on to say that "Jesus restored meaning to life and the sufferer is returned to purposeful living."[3] If I read Pilch correctly here, he is not referring to the family members left behind, but to the dead person. Does the restoration of meaning to life make sense when it comes to someone already dead? Their death can hardly be described as "experiential oppressiveness," unless death is to be understood purely allegorically. Although this seems to be a likely interpretation in the Pilch-Crossan tradition, Pilch never says so explicitly.

The sheer number of Jesus' healings sets him apart from what we know about contemporary healers. Summaries found in the Gospels give the impression that Jesus' ministry in Galilee was constantly accompanied by healing the sick. By comparison, Jesus' resurrections of the dead are strikingly rare, making up only three stories: the raising of the daughter of Jairus found in all Synoptic Gospels (Mark 5:21–43 par.), the raising of the son of the widow in Nain, found only in Luke 7:11–17, and the raising of Lazarus, found in John 11 alone.[4] This is a rather tenuous set of attestations compared to other healings. Only one of the incidents is witnessed in three different accounts, although all Gospels include the raising of the dead as an aspect of Jesus' ministry.

The tradition has clearly not multiplied itself here, a fact that adds weight to the few instances included. The fact that the raising of Lazarus is left unmentioned in the Synoptic Gospels raises a lot of questions. It is, however, not evident what consequences may be inferred from this, as the same applies to a number of other stories as well.[5] Whatever the case, different sources witness that Jesus on occasion, though not often, restored the dead to life. Furthermore, in his response to John the Baptist, Jesus includes the raising of the dead in his healing ministry (Matt. 11:1–6//Luke 7:18–23; i.e., in Q).

The following observations deserve some space in a study on Jesus as healer. First, two out of three beneficiaries of this act are named. Jairus, the father of the daughter, is mentioned in Mark and Luke. John 11 gives the name Lazarus, and also includes the names of his sisters. The only other instance where the healed person is named is in the case of blind Bartimaeus.[6] The

---

3. Pilch, *Healing in the New Testament,* p. 14.

4. The book of Acts mentions two instances where Peter (9:40–41) and Paul (20:9–12) raise people from the dead.

5. See Twelftree, *Jesus the Miracle Worker,* pp. 214–15.

6. Twelftree, *Jesus the Miracle Worker,* p. 309, makes the point that names are attached to two of what were presumably the most difficult kinds of healing in which Jesus was involved.

names add individuality to the stories. Furthermore, both Nain and Bethany are specified as the places where these wonders happened. This gives local color to the texts as well. The Jesus tradition abounds with fictitious stories: the parables. In none of these narratives are names found, however; they are generalized stories. Only one such story gives a local name, the parable of the good Samaritan, where the road between Jericho and Jerusalem provides a setting for what is told. However, this stretch of road is a stereotype for a deserted road that exposes a lonely traveler to all kinds of dangers. Naturally, such observations do not by themselves exclude the possibility that the stories of Jesus raising others from the dead are fictitious, but they might represent obstacles for that view (see below).

Second, although medical diagnosis at Jesus' time was less precise than it is today to say the least, people would normally understand when a person had passed from death to life. This is also evident in the stories in question. In the case of Jairus's daughter, the house is already filled with professional mourners. The son of the widow is being carried to his resting place, and Lazarus has been in the tomb for four days and already smells (John 11:17, 39). If the details of four days and the fact that Lazarus's body is decomposing already are read in light of John 20, it appears that the raising of Lazarus is not meant to be a metaphor only (see below), but the story of a real event. Notwithstanding all the questions involved, this seems to be the authorial intent behind the story.

The details in John 11 find correspondence in the shaping of Jesus' resurrection in John 20. The latter chapter is aimed at refuting polemics against Jesus' bodily resurrection.[7] Two observations favor this view. First, the text shifts the perspective from the fact that Mary from Magdala was the first to find the tomb empty to assign a key role to two male disciples. Furthermore, Mary is completely unprepared for encountering her deceased Lord, and says three times that someone must have removed the body (John 20:2, 13, 15). Mary's skepticism serves to point out that Christians are not credulous people. Verses 6–8 are strangely detailed in telling how neatly the linen clothing had been left and placed at two different places, implying that this is not the way grave robbers would leave a tomb. Hence Jesus' body was not stolen. The mention of Thomas touching the wounds of Jesus three times

---

7. Most likely arguments against the belief in the resurrection are mirrored in the resurrection story in John: grave robbery (refutation: The head cloth was neatly rolled up), the body was relocated (refutation: so thought Mary Magdalene until she met Jesus), a rumor (refutation: many witnesses, males in particular, even the doubting Thomas), a spirit (refutation: touching and eating).

(20:20, 25, 27) also implies that the believers are not credulous people.[8] These stories, already in John's Gospel, are shaped to justify Christian belief in the bodily resurrection. That Jesus called to life a body that for four days had been disintegrating and was stinking fits into a picture where claims of a bodily resurrection are being made.

Third, both Matthew and Luke (Q) render Jesus' response to John the Baptist (Matt. 11:1–6//Luke 7:18–23) within a context where he is at work as a healer. The different aspects of Jesus' answer reiterate the preceding stories. This link becomes most obvious in Luke 7:11–17, where the resurrection of the widow's son at Nain is an immediate manifestation of this part of the response: "the dead are raised."[9] As a consequence, the answer to the Baptist refers to physical acts of restoration.

However, there is some duality in Jesus' response to the Baptist. On the one hand, Jesus' answer is preceded by healing activities and thus clearly has this as its primary reference. On the other hand, the scriptural basis this passage leans on (Isa. 26:19; 29:18; 35:5–6; 42:7, 18) includes renewal in a wider sense.[10] The Septuagint inserts *hōs* ("like" or "as") before "lame" in Isaiah 35:6, thus indicating a tradition where healings were also seen as metaphors for a total renewal of the people.[11] With John 11, this surplus of the text becomes obvious. The story is the last and ultimate "sign" performed by Jesus. His raising Lazarus from death gives the Jewish authorities the opportunity to destroy him. A paradox appears: Jesus' death is thus implicitly caused by his raising Lazarus to life. This final sign mirrors the belief that Jesus' death and resurrection brings about eternal life. The presence of this life is emphasized in 11:25–26, in accordance with John 5:24, and culminates in Jesus saying, "I am the resurrection." In the words of Graham H. Twelftree, the miracle is turned "into a parable of the eternal life."[12]

---

8. Quadratus's fragment (second century), preserved by Eusebius in his *Hist. eccl.* 4.3.1–2, clearly understands these stories as physical restorations, and mentions witnesses.

9. This is pointed out very clearly by François Bovon, *Luke 1: A Commentary,* trans. Christine M. Thomas, Hermeneia (Minneapolis: Fortress, 2002), pp. 266–67.

10. See Pilch, *Healing in the New Testament,* pp. 114–16; Hans Kvalbein, "The Wonders of the End-Time: Metaphoric Language in 4Q 521 and the Interpretation of Matthew 11.5 Par.," *Journal for the Study of the Pseudepigrapha* 18 (1998): 87–110.

11. *Targum Isaiah* of the relevant texts proves the existence of such a tradition; see Brice D. Chilton, *The Isaiah Targum: Translation, Apparatus and Notes* (Edinburgh: T&T Clark, 1987).

12. Twelftree, *Jesus the Miracle Worker,* p. 216. A metaphorical usage of Jesus' healings is observable already in Mark's Gospel where understanding and lack thereof is addressed in terms of eyes seeing or failing to see, or ears hearing or not hearing (Mark 4:12; 8:17–18), thus paving the way for John 9 on the man born blind, and the sign character of the miracles in the Fourth Gospel.

Fourth, for some scholars such observations pave the way for considering these stories fictitious. Furthermore, the raising of the widow's son in Nain is clearly modeled on the story of Elijah raising someone dead. This Elijah story is mentioned in the so-called Praise of the Fathers in Sirach: "You raised a corpse from death and from Hades, by the word of the Most High" (Sir. 48:5), indicating its role in the memories about Elijah. The biblical background for this summary is found in 1 Kings 17:8–24. Elijah is here told to go to a town and to meet a widow at its gates. Her son passes away, and Elijah restores him to life and gives him to his mother. Luke 7:11–17 echoes this story; elements resound there, and verse 15 is a verbatim citation of 1 Kings 17:23. Furthermore, verse 16, "a great prophet risen among us," alerts the reader to such context. Some scholars therefore consider Luke's story to be a Christian appropriation of this text, not due to historical events but to the imitation of this biblical story.[13] We should not jump to conclusions here. A number of differences between the stories are also apparent, though some of these may be accounted for as emulations of Elijah, the pattern story.

According to theories and practice on ancient mimesis, or imitation of literary patterns, comparisons were generally also expected to include transcending aspects. This is particularly relevant in texts claiming to represent fulfillments of previous patterns or texts.[14] However, some of the narrative differences in Luke 7 are so striking and numerous that they hardly find satisfactory explanation within a mimesis approach. Be that as it may, the practice of mimesis does not in itself lay the foundation for historical judgments, although this kind of imitation certainly disturbs historical particularity. Imitations of classical texts in New Testament narratives has received much attention in recent decades, whether they be imitations of the Old Testament or Homer.[15] For obvious reasons, the frequent use of the Old Testament particularly lends itself to such studies.

It was a narrative ideal to imitate and emulate ancient classical texts. We should not be surprised to see this happening in the Gospels' use of the Old Testament. By itself imitation is no evidence of an event's fictitious nature, but of a narrative rhetorical style that shapes stories considerably.

---

13. Thomas L. Brodie, "Towards Unraveling Luke's Use of the Old Testament: Luke 7:11–17 as an Imitatio of 1 Kings 17:17–24," *New Testament Studies* 32 (1986): 247–67.

14. Here recent rhetorical investigations into the role of mimesis link up with the insight conveyed long ago by Leonhard Goppelt, *Typos: Die typologische Deutung des Alten Testaments im Neuen* (Gütersloh: Gerd Mohn, 1939).

15. For references, see Karl Olav Sandnes, "*Imitatio Homeri?* An Appraisal of Dennis R. MacDonald's 'Mimesis Criticism,'" *Journal of Biblical Literature* 124 (2005): 715–32.

Imitation of given patterns facilitates remembrance and recollection. For obvious reasons, imitation and emulation have repercussions on historical studies, but primarily because of their rhetorical nature. Proving mimesis does not necessarily imply that a text has no historical bedrock.[16] Any assumption that remembrance, to be reliable, must find idiosyncratic form, is to be questioned.

The view held by scholars on Jesus' own resurrection will often mirror the view they take on the wonder stories in the Jesus tradition. As for John Dominic Crossan, it is no surprise that he ends up making metaphors or allegories out of the resurrection stories.[17] Historical judgments are indeed difficult to pass on these matters. The main question is therefore, which interpretation makes sense of the New Testament material itself; that is, how do these stories fit into an emic New Testament perspective? In this perspective, a mythic, fictitious, or parabolic interpretation is unable to account for these texts. However, the history behind the stories may nevertheless be a more complex issue.

---

16. This is also pointed out by Ruben Zimmermann in "Grundfragen zu den frühchristlichen Wundererzählungen," in *Kompendium der frühchristlichen Wundererzählungen*, vol. 1, *Die Wunder Jesu*, ed. Ruben Zimmermann et al. (Gütersloh: Gütersloher Verlagshaus, 2013), p. 41. Brodie, "Towards Unraveling Luke's Use," may of course be right, but hardly for the reasons he advances.

17. In John Dominic Crossan, *Jesus: A Revolutionary Biography* (San Francisco: Harper-SanFrancisco, 1994), p. 159, Crossan introduces the chapter on the Easter traditions under the headline "How Many Years Was Easter Sunday?"

Jesus as Healer in the Gospels

The present chapter will look at how Jesus' healings are perceived from an emic perspective. How are they interpreted, and what parameters are used to make sense of them? The focus will be on the Synoptic Gospels. Two chapters previous, we examined four scholarly contributions as a foil to engage the healing stories of the New Testament, occasioning several observations pertaining to the emic perspective. We now turn to this more in detail.

Acts of Mercy and Compassion: "I Want!"

Already in the earliest remembrances of Jesus, his healing activities provided material for theological considerations of far-reaching implications, such as Christology, soteriology, and cosmology. Present-day theologians tend to jump immediately to these -logies, and this has some significant repercussions on our topic. In his significant and influential book *Jesus Remembered,* James D. G. Dunn addresses Jesus' miracles and healings under the heading "Who Did They Think He Was?"[1] This is certainly an important question. Nevertheless, as pointed out in the chapter on Jesus' healings and current New Testament scholarship, it is pertinent to see Jesus' acts of healing first and foremost from the perspective of his beneficiaries, those who were sick. Jesus was remembered as having healed people out of compassion for their needs. Inherent in the significance accorded to the perspective of those who benefited from Jesus' healings is also a reminder not to cut Jesus loose from his contemporary context. The many -logies involved will often label Jesus as unique from the very outset of the presentation.

---

1. James D. G. Dunn, *Jesus Remembered* (Grand Rapids: Eerdmans, 2003), pp. 615, 667.

To avoid this we will start from the fact that Jesus wills to help to those in need. In doing so, Jesus was no different from other miracle workers (pp. 21–24 above).

In one of his first healings according to Mark's Gospel, namely, the cleansing of the leper (Mark 1:40–42), the person afflicted approaches Jesus, begging on his knees: "If you will, you can make me clean." Jesus responds: "I want." The Greek *thelō* may also be rendered "I choose" (as in the NRSV), but "I want" more appropriately brings out the purpose of Jesus. There is a will to help, and this intention motivates the healing. While this is also relevant for theological reasons, in itself it hardly sets Jesus apart from other miracle workers of his time.

The passage in Mark 10:46–52 tells about the blind Bartimaeus, son of Timaeus, begging by the road when Jesus passes by. Mark alone names him, and Matthew mentions two blind men here. The situation assumed is a typical one. Bartimaeus's blindness leaves begging as the only way for him to make a living, and people around him are bothered by the man's shouting for help. A physical (primary) as well as social (secondary) problem is thereby visualized. This is vividly expressed in the attempts at silencing his cries of "Have mercy on me" *(eleēson me)*. His cry for help is mentioned twice. Such cries for help are a recurrent motif in the healing stories where those in need raise their voices, often emotionally. They are about need, mercy, and help.

There is in this story an afflicted person, in Mark's Gospel even a named individual, not only repressive structures and powers. Bartimaeus's situation for obvious reasons cannot be cut loose from the religious, social, and political perspectives it is embedded in.[2] Jesus mentions the vulnerability of the sick in Matthew 25:36 ("I was sick and you took care of me"). Limited access to worship in the temple, loss of work and income, and social stigmatization — all are involved. Bartimaeus's begging clearly proves that he is caught in the middle of these consequences. Jesus' healing of this blind man started out as a benevolent act of compassion demonstrated to a suffering individual, but it is implied here that healing is more than the offer of a cure. Here Pilch's conception of healing as "restoring meaning to life" and "liberation from oppressive structures" may come into play, thus reminding us that the

---

2. Bernd Kollmann, "Krankheitsbilder und soziale Folgen: Blindheit, Lähmung, Aussatz, Taubheit oder Taubstummheit," in *Kompendium der frühchristlichen Wundererzählungen*, vol. 1, *Die Wunder Jesu*, ed. Ruben Zimmermann et al. (Gütersloh: Gütersloher Verlagshaus, 2013), pp. 90–92.

healing stories are comprehensive in their view on human beings. The cure appears instantaneously, in the flicker of an eye, while the full healing, as indicated above, is a process toward change.

At times the reports about Jesus' healings include the names of those afflicted, thus reminding us that there are individuals behind these stories, and probably also that Jesus' response resonated in the recollections of those who remembered the accounts: "What do you want me to do for you?" (Mark 10:51//Matt. 20:32//Luke 18:41). Hence the cry of those tormented as it is found in these passages very early found its way into Christian worship: *Kyrie eleison* (Lord have mercy). Here the healing stories have taken on another and more general function; they are universalized. We may surmise that a first step in this process is seen in the fact that only Mark names Bartimaeus. For the other Gospels his name is of no importance, and Matthew even says there were two blind men. This may be a first step toward universalizing, and thereby also toward inspiring a hope for others out of what was originally an individual healing.

Jesus' compassion for those healed is in some texts expressed through the Greek verb *splanchnizesthai*. The verb is found in the Synoptic Gospels only, and most occurrences pertain directly to our topic.[3] The background of this term is the insides or intestines of sacrificial animals.[4] Gradually the term came to refer to the seat of feelings and emotions. In the Testament of the Twelve Patriarchs, the term "expresses the guiding inner disposition which leads to mercy," applied also to God's mercy.[5] The term and its cognates may be used of parental love and care. The motherly love of the martyrs' mother in 4 Maccabees (14:13, 20; 15:23, 28–29) exemplifies this, and particularly so since she is said to imitate Abraham's love for his son (Gen. 22). His love for Isaac is mentioned in such terms in Wisdom of Solomon 10:5.

In the Synoptic Gospels, the verb is used exclusively about Jesus. Some parables are exceptions, but the figures described there are characterized according to an attitude that elsewhere characterizes Jesus solely. The king who out of compassion forgives the servant his debt of ten thousand talents (Matt. 18:27) echoes forgiveness in the Lord's Prayer (Matt. 6:12). The parable of the loving father who pities his prodigal son and embraces him (Luke 15:11–32) serves as an illustration of Jesus' association with tax collectors and

---

3. The texts are the following: Mark 1:41; 6:34; 8:2; 9:22; Matt. 9:36; 14:14; 15:32; 20:34; Luke 7:13. All these instances are found in contexts of healing activities. Furthermore, the verb also appears in three parables (Matt. 18:27; Luke 10:33; 15:20).

4. This applies particularly to the noun *splanchna* (plural); see LSJ, s.v.

5. Helmut Köster, "Σπλάγχνον, κτλ," *TDNT* 7:551-52.

sinners (Luke 15:1–2). The parable on the good Samaritan (Luke 10:25–37) is, of course, more questionable, since it obviously sets an example to be followed by Jesus' disciples. Regardless, it is worth considering what the occurrence of the term "compassion," which is elsewhere exclusively connected to Jesus' ministry, does to this parable. Augustine's allegory of this parable as encapsulating the Jesus story from beginning to end is famous, but certainly far off. Nonetheless, he proceeds from what appears to be a polyvalent potential in the text.[6] I disagree with Helmut Köster, who sees the verb as a "Messianic characterization." The term as such is not so, but the way it is narratively unfolded and exclusively related to Jesus makes it a term that expresses not only his emotions but also identifies him with the presence of divine mercy among those in need.

Bible translations render this Greek verb somewhat differently, but most have either "moved by compassion," "filled by compassion," or something similar. Examples to be mentioned in particular include the way Jesus' reaction to the widow in Nain (Luke 7:13) is translated in NIV ("his heart went out to her") and in NLT ("his heart overflowed with compassion").[7] These translations attempt to portray Jesus as responding with compassion so strong that it finds *bodily* expression in him. The verb in question often appears as a result of Jesus' "seeing" people in need.

Matthew 9:36 deserves particular mention: "When he saw the crowds, he had compassion for them, because they were harassed and helpless, like sheep without a shepherd" (cf. Mark 6:34). This dictum follows a summary of Jesus' activities that also mentions his healings (Matt. 9:35). Hence, his compassion for those in need is the motivating factor behind his healing ministry. Furthermore, this compassion is also the guiding motivation for extending his mission to the disciples (10:1).

Jesus' compassion is motivated by a situation that is paralleled in other scriptural passages, Ezekiel 34 being the most important. This chapter describes the people of Israel as sheep without shepherds, that is, scattered, each going their own way, bound to be lost, without someone to feed them, prey to wild animals. According to Ezekiel 34:4, 16, the weak have not been strengthened, the sick not healed, the injured not bound up, the strayed not brought back, and the lost not sought; these are precisely the things God will do for his people. Jesus' ministry in Matthew 8–9 is to be understood

---

6. See Augustine, *Quaestiones evangeliorum* 2.19.

7. These translations bring to mind Hos. 11:8, although our term is not used there in the Greek version.

against this biblical backdrop. His compassion is the divine presence among the sick among the people.

We have seen that Jesus' compassion at times takes on a wider meaning, making it relevant to the readers as well. In this process toward a general application, Jesus' compassion finds new ways to manifest itself to new audiences. When the healing ministry of Jesus is made relevant to posterity, the fact that Jesus healed out of compassion for the sick is a constant reminder to look at his healings from the perspective of the healee.

The Time Has Come: The Kingdom of God and Jesus' Healings

Jesus' healings are fundamentally attached to the fact that he inaugurated the time of salvation announced in the Old Testament. Mark 1:15 sets the stage for the whole ministry of Jesus: "The time is fulfilled, and the kingdom of God has come near." The story then immediately turns to Jesus casting out demons in Capernaum (Mark 1:23-28) and healing Peter's mother-in-law (1:29-31). The arrival of the kingdom also brings with it a struggle with the devil and the evil powers (see below). Matthew's Gospel also speaks about the dawning of the time appointed by God in which Jesus was to address and to act on behalf of his people: "From that time Jesus began to proclaim, 'Repent, for the kingdom of heaven has come near'" (Matt. 4:17). When Matthew summarizes Jesus' ministry, his healings are included and mentioned alongside his teaching (Matt. 4:23; 9:35), but they appear subordinated to the proclamation of his message.[8]

In Luke's Gospel, the inauguration of the promised time is found in the story of Jesus in his hometown (4:16-30), which encapsulates key themes resonating throughout both Luke and Acts: "Today this scripture has been fulfilled in your hearing" (Luke 4:21). The time for opening the eyes of the blind is at hand, that is, the eschatological fulfillment of the Year of Jubilee (Exod. 23:10-11; Lev. 25; Deut. 15). The pastiche of biblical texts that forms the point of departure for Jesus' announcement that the time has arrived (Isa. 29:18-19; 35:5-6; 58:6-7; 61:1) is taken from passages that prophesy complete renewal, physical and spiritual. Jesus' ministry is here portrayed as the fulfillment of the prophetic visions announcing the promised future. This is also the implication of Luke 10:23-24: "Blessed are the eyes that see

---

8. Thus also Joachim Gnilka, *Jesus of Nazareth: Message and History* (Peabody, MA: Hendrickson, 1997), pp. 112-13.

what you see! For I tell you that many prophets and kings desired to see what you see, but did not see it, and to hear what you hear, but did not hear it." The immediate context of Matthew's version (Matt. 13:16–17) of this Q dictum makes it evident that regaining sight and hearing are metaphors for understanding and grasping.

John the Baptist's question to Jesus ("Are you the one who is to come, or are we to wait for another?"; Luke 7:19; Matt. 11:3) links up with the idea of the ripening of time and its fulfillment. The reference to "what you see and hear" found in both Luke 7 and Matthew 11, makes Jesus' answer a comment on his healings, which are being performed simultaneously, as Luke spells out most explicitly: "Jesus had just then cured many people of diseases, plagues, and evil spirits, and had given sight to many who were blind" (Luke 7:21).

Gerd Theissen points out that there were expectations that God in the last days would perform miracles, as stated in Isaiah 29:18–19; 35:5; 42:18; 61:1; 4Q 251.[9] Such eschatological expectations form the background of the Baptist's question, and also for Jesus' response. The breaking in of the kingdom of God is already making its presence felt in the healings wrought by Jesus and in his freeing the people from the power of evil. The arrival of God's kingdom brings a salvific power extending to both troubled minds and bodies. Naturally, Jesus' healings gain their fundamental significance from the fact that they bear witness to the dawning of the kingdom, as they themselves are the results of its arrival. This intimate connection between Jesus as healer and the arrival of the kingdom of God marks the distinctiveness of Jesus and serves to separate him from contemporary miracle workers.

Healing and Proclamation

With the coming of Jesus, a time has drawn near in which renewal is envisaged along the lines of key passages in the book of Isaiah.

> Then the eyes of the blind shall be opened,
> and the ears of the deaf unstopped;
> then the lame shall leap like a deer,

9. See also Hans Kvalbein, "The Wonders of the End-Time: Metaphoric Language in 4Q 521 and the Interpretation of Matthew 11.5 Par.," *Journal for the Study of the Pseudepigrapha* 18 (1998): 87–110.

and the tongue of the speechless sing for joy.
For waters shall break forth in the wilderness,
and streams in the desert.

(Isa. 35:5–6; see also 29:18–19; 58:6–7; 61:1–2)[10]

Parabolic and poetic dimensions emerge from this passage. It is not surprising that Jesus' healing activities carry similar notions, as they are often explained by the help of precisely these visions.

In Mark's Gospel, the healings are an aspect of Jesus' ministry alongside his proclamation. They serve to substantiate or confirm his words. Thus, in the healing of the lame man in Mark 2, Jesus first announces the forgiveness of the man's sins and then restores power to him, thus enabling him to walk. In Matthew's Gospel the healings are intimately associated with Jesus' teaching. In Matthew 4:23 (= 9:35), the triad of teaching, preaching, and healing summarizes the ministry of Jesus in a more conscious way than do the other Gospels; this triad to some extent structures the presentation of Jesus' activity.

Matthew's focus on the spoken word subordinates the healings to the proclamation, but also implies that the healings are rightly assessed only within the context of Jesus' proclamation. This particular insight is true also of the other Gospels and finds a special expression in the signs of the Fourth Gospel. In Luke's Gospel, a duality between physical and spiritual restoration is present already in Jesus' inaugural speech (see above). In the pastiche of biblical texts drawn on in Luke 4:18, *aphesis* is a key word. In Luke's writings, this term is ambiguous. It refers to setting someone free from evil powers and sickness, as the stories immediately following this text make clear (4:33–41). But elsewhere *aphesis* mostly appears in combination with the genitive *hamartiōn*, that is, forgiveness of sins, thus echoing the way *11Q Melchizedek* interprets the eschatological Year of Jubilee in a spiritual way.[11]

Jesus' healings thus become powerful illustrations of what Jesus' proclamation accomplished. They become parables. This brings us back to John Dominic Crossan's understanding of these texts. Crossan has grasped an important aspect of the healings, but the physical restoration is, according to Crossan, primarily parabolic. I disagree, as pointed out above, but it is still

10. For the role of such passages in Jesus' proclamation, see Werner Grimm, *Die Verkündigung Jesu und Deuterojesaja* (Frankfurt am Main: Peter Lang, 1981).

11. Robert Bryan Sloan, *The Favorable Year of the Lord: A Study of Jubilary Theology in the Gospel of Luke* (Austin, TX: Scholars Press, 1977).

important to see the metaphorical dimension as an extension of the physical or bodily reference included in the texts.

Fighting Evil Powers and Restoring Life Intended

Jesus' ministry was remembered as challenging Satan and evil powers. Before embarking on his ministry, Jesus was tempted by the devil (Mark 1:12–13; Matt. 4:1–11; Luke 4:1–13).[12] At the end of his story, Luke makes the comment that the devil departed "until an opportune time," thus implying that this battle will last throughout Jesus' ministry. This comment, albeit Luke's only, is relevant also for understanding Jesus' ministry in the other Gospels. Jesus' calming of the storm is in all these Gospels shaped in such a way that it symbolically encapsulates Jesus' ministry in its entirety, as opposing evil powers in order to defeat them.[13] His healing ministry belongs firmly within this interpretational pattern.[14] Jesus is seen fighting all evil, remedying sickness, and thereby also restoring life to how it was intended to be.

In Mark 3:22–27 and parallels (Matt. 12:24–29; Luke 11:15–22; see also Matt. 9:34), a dispute arises over the power that enables Jesus' healing activities: "He has Beelzebul, and by the ruler of the demons he cast out demons." Only in Matthew does this dictum immediately follow a demoniac who was blind and mute. In all versions, Jesus argues that it does not make sense to imagine that the ruler of demons is enabling Jesus to cast out his own allies. Such an argument would bring with it an intolerable tension, since it implies that Satan's dominion is being divided, and therefore torn apart. Hence, the argument of Jesus' opponents falls short of validity. On the contrary, Jesus says that he is plundering the house of the evil one by casting out demons. Before he can do that, Jesus has the devil bound. According to Matthew, this

---

12. In John's Gospel this tension equals the contrast between "from above" and "from below"; see Karl Olav Sandnes, "Whence and Whither: A Narrative Perspective on Birth *Anōthen* (John 3,3–8)," *Biblica* 86 (2005): 153–73. In John's Gospel the casting out of demons is caught up in the interpretation of Jesus' death (John 12:31). It is hardly adequate to say that John left out this aspect of Jesus' ministry; on the contrary he construed it differently, and addressed it more theologically instead of telling about incidents.

13. Karl Olav Sandnes, "Markus — en allegorisk biografi?" *Dansk Teologisk Tidsskrift* 69 (2006): 285–95.

14. It is worth noticing that Jesus according to Matthew and some mss to Luke's version taught his disciples to pray: "rescue us from the evil," be that a masculine (the evil one) or neuter (evil things).

means that it is by the power of God that Jesus is performing the healings: "But if it is by the Spirit of God that I cast out demons, then the kingdom of God has come to you" (Matt. 12:28). In the words of James D. G. Dunn, "Jesus was remembered as claiming to be especially (eschatologically) empowered by God, and his consequent success as an exorcist was attributed to that fact."[15]

According to Gerd Theissen, "Neither the healing energy nor the demons are physical realities; instead, they are powerful symbols working within the brains of the sick person and the healer."[16] I find this logic to be a short-circuit. It is equivalent to saying that since Jesus and his contemporaries considered a man to be "moonstruck," that is, his sickness was due to the phases of the moon, there was no physical reality there. Explanatory models and the reality they make sense of are to be kept apart. There may well be a physical reality in these texts; after all Jesus is said to bring about healing. To say so is not the same as subscribing to demons as the plausible reason behind the situation remedied by Jesus. The explanation for the origin of the sickness may well be culturally dependent without this affecting the events that took place. A phenomenon like healing will very often receive different interpretations or explanations, but the phenomenon as such is not questioned by its explanatory models, be they convincing or not.

In Jewish biblical traditions, overthrowing Satan and his allies paves the way for life as it was meant to be. Jesus' concern for bringing things back to the will of creation is explicitly stated in his dispute over marriage and divorce (Mark 10:2–8), a concern that also applies to health and sickness. The book of Jubilees envisages a renewed creation preceded by the removal of Satan and his powers (Jub. 1:29; 23:29). In the Testament of the Twelve Patriarchs, it is said that Levi and Judah will wage war against Beliar, defeat him, and then the people will rejoice in the garden of Eden. In the New Testament, the book of Revelation witnesses to this idea in its final visions. The vision of the new heaven and new earth recapitulates the creation stories of the Old Testament, and is preceded by the binding of Satan (Rev. 20:2–3)[17] and followed by physical restorations (21:3–4), bringing back the scene of Genesis 1.

15. Dunn, *Jesus Remembered*, p. 400.

16. Gerd Theissen, "Jesus and His Followers as Healers: Symbolic Healing in Early Christianity," in *The Problem of Ritual Efficacy*, ed. William Sax et al. (Oxford: Oxford University Press, 2010), p. 51.

17. See Udo Schnelle, *Theology of the New Testament*, trans. M. Eugene Boring (Grand Rapids: Baker Academic, 2007), pp. 122–24, for more references.

The perspective of restoring life to how it was intended to be is implicit in the texts where Jesus engages the devil by healing those who are suffering. This is brought to the surface in Mark 7:31–37, where Jesus heals a deaf man. Jesus' powerful words, the means by which he heals, have been preserved in Aramaic in the Greek text, a fact in itself worth pondering. Jesus healed by his powerful words, and these precise words have been preserved in what was perceived to be the master's voice. This brings to mind God's powerful word by which the world was created according to Genesis 1: "God said . . . and it was so." This world is celebrated in Psalm 33, which says that God created heaven and earth by his word.

> For he spoke, and it came to be;
> he commanded, and it stood firm. (v. 9)

Furthermore, the comment of the bystanders is worth observing: "He has done everything well" *(kalōs panta pepoiēken)* (Mark 7:37), echoing the formula repeated in Genesis 1 (LXX): "God saw that it was good" (vv. 12, 18, 21, 25, 31). Particularly the last occurrence, Genesis 1:31, demonstrates significant overlapping with the vocabulary of Mark 7:37: "God saw everything that he had made, and indeed, it was very good" *(ta panta hosa epoiēsen kai kala lian).*[18]

Summarizing the Emic Perspective

The emic perspective on the significance of Jesus' healings worked out above cannot be taken as a witness to what really happened when Jesus was healing. This perspective is not synonymous to what bystanders saw and witnessed, but is the inside or native view interpreting these acts. This interpretation is by its very nature prone to enhance the healing ministry of Jesus. The eschatological and cosmological perspectives make cognitive sense of the miracles. For posterity these perspectives have certainly left the impression that Jesus' healings were unique, special, and miraculous in every aspect, a picture that owes much to the symbolic emic point of view presented in this chapter. On the other hand, it is difficult to understand how this theological worldview was integrated into the remembrance about

18. Thus also Robert A. Guelich, *Mark 1–8:26,* Word Biblical Commentary 34A (Nashville: Thomas Nelson, 1989), pp. 397–98.

Jesus, if his healings were simply "not everything to be sure, but not nothing either," as Crossan puts it,[19] or that "healing occurs always," or anyway, as Pilch says and implies.[20] The discrepancy between their views and the emic perspective worked out here is indeed fundamental.

Ruben Zimmermann makes the pertinent point that the texts as stories should be at the center of studies on Jesus as a healer.[21] Rather than doing so, however, New Testament research has often concentrated on the history, analogies, or meaning of these narratives. This has led many scholars to neglect that they are really stories about individuals in need, and their experiences of having their bodies restored. Thus this chapter may be summarized in the following way: New Testament texts about healing refer to acts or events that were perceptible to the senses, often observed by bystanders, and reported as something concrete; these acts or events transcended normality and thus challenged the expectations of those to whom these stories were passed on.[22] It follows from this that the healing stories claim to be about experiences that were also observable to outsiders. These experiences are not sufficiently accounted for when they are said to refer to the mind or level of meaning only. While they do refer to the human body as such, they also include other aspects of human life. These experiences move beyond normal expectations, and hence cause amazement. They transcend normality as they are perceived as signs of the kingdom of God at work.

19. John Dominic Crossan, "Jesus and the Challenge of Collaborative Eschatology," in *The Historical Jesus: Five Views,* ed. James K. Beilby and Paul Rhodes Eddy (Downers Grove, IL: IVP Academic, 2009), p. 128.

20. John J. Pilch, *Healing in the New Testament: Insights from Medical and Mediterranean Anthropology* (Minneapolis: Fortress, 2000), p. 141.

21. Ruben Zimmermann, "Grundfragen zu den frühchristlichen Wundererzählungen," in Zimmermann, *Die Wunder Jesu,* pp. 12, 22, 34.

22. This definition is inspired by Zimmermann, "Grundfragen," p. 13.

Jesus Still a Healer through His Disciples

According to the New Testament, Jesus' healing activities continued *beyond* his own ministry. This and the following two chapters in this book will therefore present healing in the early church as a continuation of Jesus at work. The didactic aspects included in the healing stories make them more than stories of the past; they are told with a view to carrying on the healing ministry of Jesus among the believers. This will be the perspective of the following; hence, the presentation is limited to working out precisely how the healing ministry of Jesus was seen to continue through the disciples. The exemplary nature of Jesus' healing ministry is affirmed in different New Testament genres: commission texts, be they pre- or postresurrectional, epistles, and narratively in the book of Acts. We will start with the oldest written evidence, the epistles of Paul.

Paul — A Healer Suffering from Sickness?

The Pauline letter tradition is not vocal on the question of healing. Based on this fact, New Testament research has turned Paul into a thinker or theologian, and the miraculous has been sidetracked. According to Graham H. Twelftree in his recent book *Paul and the Miraculous: A Historical Reconstruction* (2013), the historical Paul should be portrayed more as complex. If Paul's experiences[1] are taken into account, new light is shed on Paul's ministry, and the scattered references to healings in his letters become inte-

---

1. Graham H. Twelftree, *Paul and the Miraculous: A Historical Reconstruction* (Grand Rapids: Baker Academic, 2013), pp. 153–78.

grated into his ministry. Acknowledgment of the role of the Spirit in Paul's theology works in the same way.[2]

The gift of healing appears in the lists of spiritual gifts (Rom. 12:3-8; 1 Cor. 12:9-10; Eph. 4:11-13), but more relevant here are the places where Paul intimates that his apostolic ministry was accompanied by wondrous events. In what is possibly the first extant Christian writing, Paul reminds the Thessalonians that the gospel came to them through him, accompanied by "power and in the Holy Spirit, and with full conviction" (1 Thess. 1:5). The contrast between "not in words only" but "in power and the Holy Spirit" is indicative of some kind of charismatic manifestation, although it remains open what precisely is in view here.[3] The contrast to "words only" implies more than a reference to the potency of the word but makes clear that Paul's gospel was not given through his preaching alone. Accompanying phenomena served to authenticate Paul and his ministry.[4]

An analogous passage is found in 1 Corinthians 2:3-4. Again Paul contrasts his own weak *(en astheneia)*[5] appearance with the "demonstration of the Spirit and power." The Greek noun used here *(apodeixis)* is taken from rhetoric, and denotes a compelling argument or demonstration.[6] These passages are incorporated into heavily rhetorical contexts, but it is nonetheless justified to deduce that Paul's gospel manifested itself in ways deemed to be powerful, most likely in miracles of some kind. Objections that Paul says Christ crucified is the exclusive power of his gospel probably owes more to our ideas of *theologia crucis* than to a historical interpretation of Paul.[7] Furthermore, the contrast between his weakness and the power of his gospel is a rhetorical way of emphasizing its divine legitimacy. What kind of events these were, and whether healing is included among them, Paul does not state, although it appears likely that some kind of acts beyond normality are involved.

---

2. See Hermann Gunkel, *The Influence of the Holy Spirit: The Popular View of the Apostolic Age and the Teaching of the Apostle Paul,* trans. Roy A. Harrisville and Philip A. Quanbeck II (Philadelphia: Fortress, 1979).

3. Thus also Gordon D. Fee, *God's Empowering Presence: The Holy Spirit in the Letters of Paul* (Peabody, MA: Hendrickson, 1994), p. 45.

4. Twelftree, *Paul and the Miraculous,* pp. 183-87.

5. Although *astheneia* in this epistle hardly means sickness, as is the case in Galatians (see below), it certainly implies a contrast between Paul the preacher and the power that surrounded and accompanied his appearance.

6. BDAG, s.v.

7. See Twelftree, *Paul and the Miraculous,* pp. 196-201.

In Romans 15:19, Paul summarizes his ministry in "word and deed" in the following way: "by the power of signs and wonders [*en dynamei sēmeiōn kai teratōn*], by the power of the Spirit of God." This text proves helpful for understanding the group of texts relevant for Paul on this issue. The phrase "signs and wonders" brings to mind God's presence through miraculous events in the history of Israel as well as that of the early church.[8] Paul's apostolic ministry is thus enrolled in this history of God making his presence known through various kinds of miracles. Furthermore, this sentence is found in the context of Paul summarizing his ministry from Jerusalem to Illyricum. It follows from this that miracles were a regular part of the apostle's ministry, not a random phenomenon.[9]

Paul's epistle to the Galatians witnesses to this aspect of his ministry. According to Galatians 3:5, the Spirit had from the inception of the Galatian churches manifested itself by "working miracles [*dynameis*]"[10] among them. By implication, the miraculous was a continuous characteristic among these Christians. Now Paul appeals to such experiences as evidence of divine approval for his gospel. Simultaneously, this letter says that Paul came to preach the gospel to them "because of physical infirmity" *(di' astheneian tēs sarkos),* which probably refers to some kind of "ophthalmic complaint" (Gal. 4:12–15; cf. 6:11).[11] This is a reasonable guess. In any case, the double message of Galatians pertains to our topic: Paul, suffering from some illness, proclaims the gospel in words and deed. This concurrency probably caused Paul's concern that he might not be welcomed. His physical condition could have been taken to undermine his trustworthiness in proclaiming a powerful gospel. This was a test *(peirasmos)* to them, "but[12] [they] welcomed me as an angel[13] of God, as Christ Jesus" (v. 14), which echoes the tradition of Jesus commissioning disciples (see below).[14] Paul includes himself among the emissaries of God, representing Christ in his ministry.

This picture emerging from Galatians 4 finds an analogy in 2 Corinthians

---

8. Arland J. Hultgren, *Paul's Letter to the Romans: A Commentary* (Grand Rapids: Eerdmans, 2011), pp. 543–44.

9. Twelftree, *Paul and the Miraculous,* pp. 218–23.

10. If the reference of the singular *dynamis* in 1 Thess. 1:5 may be uncertain, the plural *dynameis* used here is synonymous with miracles; see Twelftree, *Paul and the Miraculous,* p. 184.

11. Twelftree, *Paul and the Miraculous,* pp. 156–57.

12. This is to be taken as a contrastive *alla.*

13. May also be rendered "emissary."

14. Nestle-Aland 28th ed. *(Novum Testamentum Graece)* makes a reference to this particular tradition in Matt. 20:14 in the margin here.

12:11–12. Paul here says that he performed "the signs of an apostle . . . signs and wonders and mighty works" (v. 12), and simultaneously suffered from "a thorn in the flesh" (vv. 7–9).[15] Jacob Jervell has labeled this paradox of Paul's appearance "the sick charismatic."[16] If Paul appeared so enigmatic, this certainly called for a proper theological rationale, one option being the background of Paul's concern expressed in Galatians 4:13–15, while Paul himself worked out what he in the Corinthian correspondence labels "boasting in weakness." The apostle's weakness served precisely to convey that any miracle he performed is truly nothing but a gift of God, not from an especially gifted person.

Although the instances of healing in Paul's letters are indeed few,[17] they are not at all isolated texts. References to miracles and healings emerge from a theology that fostered such activities; namely, they are intimately connected to the role of the Spirit in the apostle's theology. In the words of Gordon D. Fee, miracles are "something Christ does by his Spirit."[18] Dynamic experiences are not random events in Paul's ministry; instead, they follow naturally from the role he assigns to the Spirit as evidencing divine presence and power. Paul's gospel "was always word and deed."[19] James Carleton Paget accurately formulates the picture given by Paul's letters: "Behind Paul's sober tones, there may lie a richer and more vivid theology of miracles, and a more important role in his ministry, which letters written to believers, only hint at."[20]

Twelftree raises the question of why Paul still does not come out as a miracle worker, neither in his letters nor in the way he was viewed in his churches nor in rhetorical situations where such a portrayal might have settled some of the disputes about his authority. The picture of a physically poor preacher remains. Twelftree summarizes the ambivalence of the material in this way: "Although miracles took place in association with his ministry, Paul neither set out to perform them nor orchestrated those that took place. Rather, as he preached, the Spirit's powerful presence was spontaneously

---

15. Twelftree, *Paul and the Miraculous,* pp. 142–46, 158–62.

16. Jacob Jervell, "Der schwache Charismatiker," in *Rechtfertigung: Festschrift für Ernst Käsemann zum 70. Geburtstag,* ed. Johannes Friedrich, Wolfgang Pöhlmann, and Peter Stuhlmacher (Tübingen: Mohr Siebeck, 1976), pp. 185–98.

17. The letter genre may not invite much about healing, simply because the epistles are occasional writings addressing things on the agenda among the addressees.

18. Fee, *God's Empowering Spirit,* p. 631.

19. Twelftree, *Paul and the Miraculous,* p. 225.

20. James Carleton Paget, "Miracles in Early Christianity," in *The Cambridge Companion to Miracles,* ed. Graham H. Twelftree (Cambridge: Cambridge University Press, 2011), p. 142.

manifested in the miracles. This was God's doing, not Paul's. In the simplest terms, if pressed, Paul might say that the gospel was proclaimed when he did the preaching and Christ, through the Spirit, performed the miracles."[21]

This has some interesting repercussions for the question of whether Jesus was an exemplary healer. The idea that Paul continues the healing ministry of Jesus is only vaguely present in Galatians 4, where a commission tradition is likely present (see above and below). Furthermore, the contrast Paul urges between his own weakness and God's power to work wonders in effect makes Jesus' miracles more unique than we would expect. Although miracles and healing accompanied Paul's mission, the apostle somehow distances himself from them; he is not a powerful miracle worker or healer alongside Jesus. It is now apt to turn to the book of Acts, and to see how the miracle and healing tradition is reworked there.

"Jesus Christ Heals You" — The Book of Acts

The claim that Christ is present among his disciples through their preaching and healing is substantiated particularly in the book of Acts. The story told is an unfolding of the prophetic words of Joel 2, cited in Acts 2:19: "And I will show . . . signs [*sēmeia*] on the earth." This statement finds two immediate follow-ups in chapter 2, the first in 2:22: "a man attested to you by God with deeds of power [*dynameis*], wonders [*terata*], and signs [*sēmeia*] that God did through him among you." God's presence in the midst of the people through the wonderful things done by Jesus paves the way for a similar pattern with regard to the apostles: Christ is present through their healing performances. Second, the miracles and healings performed by Jesus attest to him as chosen by God. Thus, in the midst of a narrative that emphasizes the exemplary nature of Jesus, one is reminded of his *special* status; what he did proved him chosen. Third, the prepositional phrase "to you" assumes witnesses; in other words, what Jesus did was visible to bystanders. It is thus assumed that the healings of Jesus manifested themselves among others and were acts to be watched.

The statement in Acts 2:19 finds its second follow-up in 2:43, which states that many signs and wonders were done "through the apostles," and thus includes their healings as part of the fulfillment of the Joel prophecy. The following passages in Acts mention healing done by the apostles:

---

21. Twelftree, *Paul and the Miraculous,* p. 225.

3:1–8: The healing of a lame man at the Beautiful Gate

5:12, 16; 6:8; 8:6–7; 14:3; 15:12: Summary statements

5:15: The healing shadow of Peter

9:17–18: Restoration of sight

9:32–35: The healing of the paralytic Aeneas

9:36–42: The raising of the dead Tabitha

14:8–10: Healing of a crippled man

16:16–18: Casting out demons

19:11–12: Healing handkerchiefs and aprons

20:7–12: The raising of the dead Eutychus

28:3–6: Paul is himself miraculously rescued from a snake bite

28:7–9: The healing of Publius's father

Most of the healings are carried out by Peter and Paul, the main human protagonists in the story. This list is telling in the way it recalls the kinds of healing performed by Jesus in the Gospel tradition. A certain model of parallelism between the apostles and their master is at work here. Narrative forms of healings tend to coalesce in whatever context they are found; hence, the parallelism is in itself not striking, but the similarities go beyond that. The apostles perform the miracles in other ways that bring Jesus to mind. They lay their hand on the sick, they touch them, and they command the sickness to leave. They see faith pave the way so that healing may take place. The power of their presence, manifested in their passing shadow (Acts 5:15)[22] or in pieces of cloth worn by the apostles (Acts 19:12), bears a semblance to the healing power of Jesus as mentioned in Mark 6:56 and the story about the woman with hemorrhages in Matthew 9:20–22. Twelftree has worked out in detail how the healing stories in Acts are modeled on what Jesus did.[23]

The Relationship between Jesus' Healings and the Apostles' Healings

Some differences between Jesus and the apostles are worth noticing, however. On three occasions, the apostles pray before healing. Twice the healing is done "in the name of Jesus." In their healing activity, the apostles call on

22. See Pieter W. van der Horst, "Peter's Shadow: The Religio-Historical Background of Acts v.15," *New Testament Studies* 23, no. 2 (1977): 204–12. Later mss of this verse have enhanced the healing effect of Peter's shadow.

23. Twelftree, *Paul and the Miraculous*, pp. 229–71.

the name of Jesus (Acts 3:6; 16:18). Acts 4:29–30 renders a prayer: "Grant to your servants to speak your word with all boldness, while you stretch out your hand to heal, and signs and wonders are performed through the name of your holy servant Jesus." This prayer assumes an understanding in which healings involve God, Christ, and the apostles. God stretches out his hand to the apostles to perform healings and signs in the name of Christ. The notion of God stretching out his hand to perform miracles is taken from the Old Testament (see Exod. 3:20; 7:5; Deut. 4:34; 5:15; 6:21–22). That Jesus' name is mentioned on such occasions certainly bears some resemblances to magic. Acts 19:13, which is about some itinerant Jewish exorcists trying to use the name of Jesus, implies that this is precisely how outsiders might have understood the name of Jesus (see Acts 8:9–11, 17–19).[24] According to Acts, it is more appropriate to say that the name of Jesus refers to the power and authority by which the healings are done, not to a spell or incantation. Three times healings are wrought "through the hands of the apostles," an expression that makes them instruments of divine help or healing (see Acts 9:17–18). All these characteristics set the apostles apart from Jesus' way of healing simply because they have no analogies in the miracle stories about him. The apostles are subordinated to Jesus; they are his instruments and act on his authority.

Three observations are of special importance for understanding the role of healing in this literature. In the first place, the apostles are agents of God's healing power, and Christ is at work through the miracles they do. The strongest possible expression of this is found in Acts 9:34: Peter says, "Aeneas, Jesus Christ heals you; get up and make your bed!" This is also implied in the texts that state, "God did extraordinary miracles [*dynameis*] through the hands of the apostles." The apostles mediate God and Christ's acts in the world, thus bringing to mind the commission texts from the ministry of Jesus about the apostles as Christ's representatives, who preach and act on his behalf but who are also his subordinates (see below).

In the second place, the consequences of the salvation brought by Jesus are holistic; they embrace the spiritual as well as the physical dimension. Jesus restores "perfect health" *(holoklēria)*[25] to the crippled man in Acts 3:16. He is physically restored: "stand up and walk" (Acts 3:6; cf. vv. 12, 16). While being interrogated about this incident by the priest, Peter says that the lame man has been *sesōtai (sōzein),* which is to be rendered "has been healed."

---

24. *The Greek Magical Papyri* (PGM) provides examples.
25. For this term, see BDAG and LSJ s.v.

This physical meaning is retained throughout the story, as can be seen in Acts 4:14, which states that the lame man was now seen by all to have been cured *(tetherapeumenon)*. However, Acts 4:12 gives a twist to the meaning of "salvation" here; hence hardly any Bible translator (to my knowledge) renders this as "healing" *(sōteria)* in no one else; that is, it does not read, "for there is no other name under heaven given among mortals by which we must be *healed*." Lexically and contextually such a rendering is possible, but rarely made — for good reason. Jacob Jervell, to take a prominent counter-example, overlooks the twist taken here when he says that "here salvation is the healing of a crippled man."[26] The author of Acts uses the healing story as a point of departure for saying something fundamentally theological about the role of Jesus' name.[27] Likewise, the blindness of Paul in the stories about his calling (Acts 9 and 22)[28] also becomes a narrative vehicle for depicting his radical turn in terms of insight. This comes to expression in Acts 26:18, where Paul's commission is precisely to "open the eyes of the blind."

Third, although salvation in Acts is holistic, and includes both mundane and spiritual aspects, the healing and miracles generally serve a primary purpose, the preaching of God's message. The prayer given above in Acts 4 might be understood in this way. None of the three versions of Paul's commission (Acts 9; 22; 26) mention healing or signs. Acts 14:3 pertains to this: "speaking boldly for the Lord who testified to the word of his grace by granting signs and wonders to be done through them." The miracles give testimony to the gospel proclamation; they serve a subordinate role. I agree with Ben Witherington III, who points out that while a mundane sense of salvation seems to dominate in the Gospel of Luke, we find a "more specifically Christian use of the salvation language more often in Acts than in the Gospel."[29] This concurs with Jervell, who says that "the primacy of the word is evident."[30] As for Paul's miracles in Acts, Jervell asserts that they "comprise a secondary part of his preaching and teaching, and so the proclamation is legitimized as the word of God." From a hermeneutical perspective this primacy is of much im-

---

26. Jacob Jervell, *The Theology of the Acts of the Apostles* (Cambridge: Cambridge University Press, 1996), p. 95.

27. Karl Olav Sandnes, "Beyond 'Love Language': A Critical Examination of Krister Stendahl's Exegesis of Acts 4:12," *Studia Theologica* 52 (1998): 43–56.

28. The blindness is not pointed out in chap. 26.

29. Ben Witherington III, "Salvation and Health in Christian Antiquity: The Soteriology of Luke-Acts in its First Century Setting," in *Witness to the Gospel: The Theology of Acts*, ed. I. Howard Marshall and David Peterson (Grand Rapids: Eerdmans, 1998), p. 165.

30. Jervell, *The Theology of the Acts*, p. 93.

portance, though it does not deny the importance of Jesus' continuous presence through the healings performed by his apostles. Within this continuity there is, however, also a discontinuity. Jesus is exemplary and simultaneously in some respects still unique compared to the healings of the disciples.

Jervell has consistently argued that the healing narratives of Acts fill in the gaps left open by the Pauline remarks addressed above, thus adding to the picture and making it complete.[31] I essentially agree, but this view misses out on the fact that the question of Jesus' uniqueness is being negotiated within the New Testament.[32] As pointed out above, Paul, without in any way rejecting the occurrences of miracles, tends to emphasize that Jesus is unique. This question also comes to the surface in Acts, but it is addressed in a different way. Here, there is a balance between Jesus being exemplary and his being unique, but the balance certainly tips in favor of the first. As Twelftree points out, Luke creates a catena of stories aimed at depicting Paul as a successor of both the apostles and Jesus himself. Due to this aim, Paul comes out as a powerful healer and miracle worker. Paul's being a successor of Jesus implies that Jesus is exemplary. "Paul did not see himself as a miracle worker, let alone a great one, even though from time to time he is likely to have conducted miracles."[33] In Acts, Paul appears as a man of power, which is not easily reconciled with his own emphasis on his weakness. In the words of Harold Remus, "Paul, the wounded healer of his letters, appears in the Acts of the Apostles as an invulnerable healer."[34] This hardly implies that Luke and Paul are in disagreement when it comes to whether Paul wrought healings and miracles, but it does imply two almost contradictory ways of reasoning about Paul's miracles. Two somewhat different concepts are also implied with regard to how the role of the healer is construed.

The Healing Stories in the Book of Acts and History

The question of the historical veracity of the evidence in Acts needs to be briefly addressed. This issue should not be turned into a simple question of

31. This is one of the main points in the essays collected in Jacob Jervell's *The Unknown Paul: Essays on Luke-Acts and Early Christian History* (Minneapolis: Augsburg, 1984).

32. Although Twelftree, *Paul and the Miraculous,* does not frame his presentation this way, it is a consequence of his presentation of Paul and Luke.

33. Twelftree, *Paul and the Miraculous,* p. 325.

34. Harold Remus, *Jesus as Healer,* Understanding Jesus Today (Cambridge: Cambridge University Press, 1997), p. 99.

whether miracles and healings are possible at all.[35] It has to be addressed as a proper source-critical question, and is also not to be subsumed under the discussion of the reliability of Acts in general. It is worth noticing that some of the healing stories are attached to named persons (Tabitha, Aeneas, Eutychus). This adds specificity to the stories. Of special interest here is Paul's healing of Publius's father (Acts 28:7-10). He was a well-known figure of the island, called *ho protos tēs nēsou,* which refers either to his official position or to his being a wealthy man. Be this as it may, he was a prominent and leading figure on the island. Accordingly, the father is not named but simply mentioned as the father of Publius. This adds not only specificity but even a historical dimension to the text. Nonetheless, there are no external sources nor multiple attestations for the healings told of in Acts. In this way the healing stories of the apostles are poorly based compared to the Jesus tradition. Viewing Acts as narratives that fill in the gaps left open in the Pauline epistles serves to ameliorate this source-critical situation, but only to some extent.

The healing stories in Acts are inscribed into theological patterns of significance for grasping the whole story, such as God's salvation history, an analogy with the ministry of Jesus and also a parallel between the two main human protagonists, Peter and Paul.[36] In itself, this is not enough to dismiss these stories in a historical inquiry. Healing stories will often be incorporated into stories that also offer an interpretation. The obvious parallels between Peter and Paul as healers should be seen as a common example of the rhetorical exercise *synkrisis* (comparison), which also forms the backbone of Plutarch's *Parallel Lives.* The fact that a story is structured with parallel lives or ministries does not rob it of any historical value, but such comparisons and doublets do shape the stories in ways that affect strict historical access to the events narrated.

According to Acts 5:15-16, even the shadow of Peter falling on the sick caused healing, and 19:11-12 says that just touching the handkerchiefs or

---

35. Critics as well as advocates sometimes simplify in this way. As for critics, see Gerd Lüdemann, *Early Christianity according to the Tradition in Acts: A Commentary,* trans. John Bowden (Minneapolis: Fortress, 1989), pp. 54, 145. As for advocates, see Ben Witherington III, *The Acts of the Apostles: A Socio-Rhetorical Commentary* (Grand Rapids: Eerdmans, 1998), pp. 223-24; Charles H. Talbert, *Reading Acts: A Literal and Theological Commentary,* rev. ed. (Macon, GA: Smyth & Helwys, 2005), pp. 248-50.

36. See Andrew C. Clarke, *Parallel Lives: The Relation of Paul to the Apostles in the Lucan Perspective* (Milton Keynes, UK: Paternoster, 2001); as for the miracles in particular see pp. 209-29.

aprons[37] of Paul caused diseases to depart. These stories share similarities with the one about the hemorrhaging woman in the Gospels, but they also point forward to legends about the apostles (see below). The remarkable stories of healings in the apocryphal literature are influenced by the New Testament, not the other way around. Nonetheless, these summary statements from Acts find analogies in the apocryphal traditions. These apocryphal pieces of information lack the fundamental encounter or intimacy of the miracle stories of the Gospels, the hemorrhaging woman being an exception due to the lack of intimacy. There is in Acts 5 and 19 no real contact between the sick and the healer; this sets these incidents apart from most, if not all, biblical miracle stories. Hence, they raise suspicion with regard to their historicity.

Furthermore, Acts also includes punitive miracles among the performances of the apostles (Acts 5:1–11; 12:20–23; 13:11). These kinds of miracles are not a part of the Gospel traditions, though the cursing of the fig tree is an exception (Mark 11:12–14, 20–21). These punitive miracles contrast with the image of Jesus' healings in Acts 10:38–39, where these are seen as having been done out of compassion, as acts of benefaction *(euergetōn)*. Punitive miracles like "healings reversed," where sickness is imposed on people, abound in apocryphal traditions. Taken together these observations imply that the historical foundations of the healing stories in Acts are less certain than those told about Jesus. Analogies found in the apocryphal material (see later) are at least an indication that these stories in Acts were prone to spin off further legends about the apostles.

Finally, the attempt in Acts to fill the gaps in the Pauline letter tradition is a procedure we will (later) see developed and thrived in the apocryphal traditions. However, I am reluctant to see these as parallel phenomena. Apocryphal texts draw heavily on gaps in the narrative material in the New Testament, much less on letters. Moreover, in comparison with apocryphal traditions, the book of Acts is indeed moderate, even if some elements may betray initial steps into a wider legendary legacy. It is well known that the *Apocryphal Acts* have a marked biographical interest compared to the New Testament evidence. Generally speaking this is certainly true, but the way Peter and Paul appear in Acts as powerful miracle workers, able to heal even through the presence of their shadow or their belongings, is possibly an anticipation of what is widely attested to in the apocryphal traditions.

37. Rick Strelan, "Acts 19:12: Paul's Apron Again," *Journal of Theological Studies* 54 (2003): 154–57.

Jesus' Commission of His Disciples during His Ministry

The relevant texts in the Synoptic Gospels are the following: Mark 6:7–13; Matthew 10:1–42; Luke 9:1–6, 10–11; 10:1–23; 22:35–36. According to Mark, Jesus sent the twelve disciples out two by two. Their being sent as well as given authority imply a commission to act on his behalf.[38] The emissaries proclaimed repentance, cast out many demons, and anointed with oil and cured *(etherapeuon)* many sick people (Mark 6:12–13). No doubt, Jesus' ministry at large is echoed here. The last part of this sentence brings to mind the philanthropic attitude of the good Samaritan (Luke 10:34) toward an injured man, but church practice described in James 5:14 is also echoed here. Although anointing with oil was used for medical purposes,[39] we never hear that Jesus did so. There is a possibility that a church setting where this was common is mirrored here.[40]

It is clearly conveyed in these texts that healing among Jesus' followers is done through his authority and power. The disciples are his representatives, who make the blessings of his ministry present and available while he is absent. This finds corroboration and elaboration in Matthew 10. On Jesus' authority, the disciples embark on a ministry that models the performances of Jesus (vv. 1, 7–8): preaching, healing, raising the dead, and casting out demons. Jesus even states an explicit link between them as recipients of the benefits of his ministry and their own commission: "You received without payment; give without payment." Thus there is a fundamental similarity between the ministry of Jesus and his disciples. They represent Jesus among people, making him present to them: "Whoever welcomes you welcomes me" (v. 40; cf. vv. 24–25, 41–42); hence, their destiny is also an imitation of Jesus (v. 38).

According to Luke 9, the ministry of Jesus and his disciples are intertwined, so that their commission, to proclaim and to heal (vv. 1–2; cf. 10:9),

---

38. The implication of authority *(exousia)* may well be illustrated by reference to Acts 9:14, about Paul's coming to Damascus; that is, he was sent by the chief priests of Jerusalem to arrest Christ followers there. He acts on their behalf, under their authority; in short he is the presence of the Jerusalem priesthood when they themselves are absent.

39. H. Schlier, "Ἔλαιον," in *TDNT* 2:470–73.

40. In principle it may also be the other way around. But since this is an isolated instance of anointing in the Gospel stories, I tend to think that church practice is mirrored here. For a detailed and recent study on James 5, see Sigurd Kaiser, *Krankenheilung: Untersuchungen zu Form, Sprache, traditionsgeschichtlichem Hintergrund und Aussage zu Jak 5,13–18* (Neukirchen-Vluyn: Neukirchener Verlag, 2006).

is more or less a verbatim repetition of what Jesus does to the people who gather around him (v. 11). This is narratively visualized (vv. 12–17) when Jesus tells them that they are to feed those present: "You give them something to eat" (v. 13). Luke 10:16 puts this in a pointed saying: "Whoever listens to you listens to me, and whoever rejects me rejects the one who sent me." The healings to be performed by the disciples in all these texts are seen as acts of representing Jesus, imitating him, but also of acting on his authority. This implies that they continue his ministry, but theirs is subordinated to his; hence, both continuity and discontinuity mark their relationship to Jesus' healing ministry. In all these commission texts, healing stands out as an important aspect.

Mark's Two (Secondary) Endings

The two endings in Mark's Gospel, both certainly of later date,[41] address the issue discussed in this book. The secondary nature of these passages should not distract us from the fact that they, like all Gospel texts, bear witness to how Jesus was remembered in various ways. According to the shorter version (added after v. 8), Jesus sent his disciples to preach the message of "eternal salvation." Although *sōteria* and its cognates are in many places ambivalent terms, though nevertheless with a primary reference to healing, that is hardly the case here, simply due to the fact that the adjective "eternal" narrows the perspective to the spiritual. The longer version (vv. 9–20), however, gives a pivotal role to the miracles in the ministry of discipleship after the resurrection. Signs will accompany the believers; in Jesus' name they will cast out demons. They will lay hands on the sick and cure them, thus bringing to mind how Jesus performed miracles (Mark 5:20). The passage brings to mind Psalm 91:13 (cf. Luke 10:19), about God's protective presence, which in Mark is seen as available in Jesus Christ. It is on the basis of this notion of divine presence that the longer version addresses the question of wonders.

Mark 16:20, the final verse, is worth quoting: "And they went out and proclaimed the good news everywhere, while the Lord worked with them [*synergountos*] and confirmed [*bebaiountos*] the message by the signs that accompanied it." The Lord is here seen as continuously active in the mission of the church, working alongside the disciples and confirming the message

41. See Craig A. Evans, *Mark 8:27–16:20,* Word Biblical Commentary 34B (Nashville: Thomas Nelson, 2001), pp. 540–51, for a discussion of how these endings came into being.

with signs. The continuing presence of Jesus through miracles is thus empha-sized, but the signs are also subordinated to the oral message here, justifying the proclamation. Furthermore, the confirming role of Jesus vis-à-vis the mission of the disciples is indicative of his superior role. Hence, the signs performed by the apostles continue his work and are simultaneously subor-dinated to him. The passage in Mark 16:19–20 addresses the mission of the apostles accompanied by signs in a way remarkably similar to the story told in the book of Acts.

Matthew 28:19–20: The Commission Text Par Excellence

The didactic nature of Matthew's Gospel earned it pride of place in early Christianity, mirrored in its prominent place in the New Testament canon. Jesus' final instruction to his disciples, although its form is clearly later, fits this didactic nature nicely. His disciples are sent "to make disciples." The Greek verb *mathēteuein* holds the key to the rest of Jesus' command here. Both "baptizing" and "teaching" are subordinated; they are the means by which disciples come into being. Discipleship is therefore primarily an issue of obeying *(tērein)* the words of Jesus. What to obey is not clear, however. In Matthew 23:3 *tērein* is synonymous with "doing" *(poiein);* hence interpret-ers of Matthew often refer to Jesus' ethical instruction in Matthew 5–7. The concluding section of this sermon (7:21–27) even criticizes the performance of healing in the name of Jesus if it is not accompanied with obedience to Jesus' teaching, thus demonstrating that healings are here subordinated to proclamation. Ulrich Luz, rightly in my mind, argues that obedience should not be limited to the Sermon on the Mount as the ethical A-to-Z, but should include the entire teaching of Jesus, which of course would include Matthew 10 as well.[42]

Miracles or healings are seemingly absent from this commission text. Nonetheless, two caveats are worth considering. First, this is a text about making disciples, less about how disciples live. Second, it is worth consid-ering the implications of the last sentence: "And remember, I am with you always, to the end of the age" (v. 20). The continuous presence of Jesus is especially highlighted in his last dictum. This saying serves the purpose of giving comfort (cf. Matt. 1:23; 18:20). Readers who found comfort in this

---

42. Luz, *Matthew 21–28,* trans. James E. Crouch, Hermeneia (Minneapolis: Fortress, 2005), pp. 632–34.

statement are likely to have understood it on the basis of how Jesus made himself present among those in need in the story told. This would, of course, include his powerful actions, even though this is not spelled out here.

In commenting on Matt 28:20, Donald Hagner says: "Jesus, though not physically present among them, will not have abandoned them. He will be in their midst, though unseen, he will empower them to fulfill the commission he has given them."[43] The emphasis on Jesus' unseen and nonphysical presence may be taken to bring into the picture an elusiveness that I think owes more to present-day concerns than to biblical thoughts on Christ's presence among his followers. Empowerment in the New Testament is shown to *manifest* itself in ways seen, heard, or noticed. This charismatic aspect of early Christian beliefs needs to be restored in order to gain an adequate understanding of how early Christianity thought of and experienced Christ's presence among them. In this perspective it is hardly conceivable that Christ's presence among and empowerment of his disciples are not experienced dynamically.

Luke 24:47-49: Empowered by the Spirit

Luke's version resembles those addressed above, but is also distinct in some important ways. Of special significance is the disciples' empowerment by the Holy Spirit (cf. Acts 1:4-5, 8). The mission entrusted to them is inaugurated by the giving of the Spirit, as promised in the Old Testament (Joel 2; Ezek. 11; 36). This echoes the beginning of Jesus' ministry according to Luke 4:14: Jesus was "filled with the power [*dynamis*] of the Spirit" and "anointed with the Holy Spirit" (Luke 4:18). This anointment initiated a ministry of healing and preaching of the good news to the poor, proclaiming God's favorable year to them (Luke 4:18-19). Although Luke here includes biblical passages in which salvation is addressed as inclusive of both physical and spiritual restoration, a one-sided spiritual interpretation of the ministry described here does not account for how this passage in Luke 4 is echoed in Acts 10:38: "how God anointed Jesus of Nazareth with the Holy Spirit and with power [*dynamis*], how he went about doing good and healing all who were oppressed by the devil, for God was with him." This passage from Acts is helpful in order to grasp what Luke 24:47-49 envisages.

43. Donald Hagner, *Matthew 14-28*, Word Biblical Commentary 33B (Dallas: Word, 1995), pp. 888-89.

In Acts 10, Spirit and power work synonymously, as they do in Luke 24. Endowment of the Spirit manifests itself charismatically. The power of the Spirit is noticeable; it also manifests itself in healing, just as it did with Jesus: "and the power [*dynamis*] of the Lord was with him to heal" (Luke 5:17). The nature of *dynamis* as something observable is obvious. Christ pouring out the Spirit from his exalted position is both seen and heard according to Acts 2:33,[44] very much in line with what Paul says in Romans 15:18–19. From this we may conclude that the power of the Spirit often includes signs and wonders (see Luke 4:36). It is no wonder, therefore, that the plural *dynameis* becomes a technical term for miracles wrought either by Jesus or by his disciples. Finally, the phrase "God was with him" as the motivation for Jesus' healing activities in Acts 10 brings us back to Matthew 28:20, where I cautiously suggested that this implied miracles as well (see above). This now appears to find external substantiation here.[45]

The empowered witness about which Jesus speaks in Luke 24, and Peter in Acts 10, includes the power of healing in accordance with what Jesus himself did. According to Luke 24:19, Jesus was "mighty [*dynatos*] in word and deed," which is likewise stated about Moses in Acts 7:22. This duality of word, that is proclamation, and acts, mostly healing miracles, is also what Luke envisages in the commission of the risen Jesus to his disciples.

44. Similarly in, e.g., Acts 8:13, 18–19; 10:45–46.

45. It is worth noticing that the phrase "God with him" also in John 3:2 motivates the signs Jesus was doing.

New Testament Apocrypha

The healings of Jesus were remembered not only in the texts that came to be canonical. The New Testament apocrypha attest to a wider interest in this aspect of Jesus' ministry, and also depicts apostolic ministry in accordance with healing traditions. This chapter serves to exemplify the wider interest in Jesus as a healer, but also provides a backdrop against which the New Testament material may be seen.

The apocryphal *Infancy Gospel of Thomas (IGT)* and the apocryphal *Acts of the Apostles* are replete with miracles and healing stories about both Jesus and the apostles. Thus they affirm the significance of Jesus as a healer and miracle worker for those who remembered him. This literature also construes the miracles as signs of Jesus' continuous presence among the apostles. Hence, these sources are affirmative vis-à-vis our findings in the canonical sources, the book of Acts in particular. But there are indeed differences worth noticing. The stories found in the apocryphal traditions are lengthy stories, rich in detail and more sensational. The apocryphal Gospels and apocryphal acts are remarkably different from their canonical counterparts in their marked biographical interest, which also indicates their fictional status.[1] The diverse textual traditions and versions of these writings witness to their popularity and fluidity as well as to the thriving of this literature.

The narratives within which the healing stories are embedded are largely driven by miraculous events. Hence, healings may, for example, be intertwined with conversion stories or stories that affect whole cities visited by the apostles. The healing stories are embellished in ways that distance

---

1. See Richard Bauckham, "*The Acts of Paul* as a Sequel to Acts," in *The Book of Acts in Its First Century Setting*, vol. 1, *The Book of Acts in Its Ancient Literary Setting*, ed. Bruce W. Winter and Andrew D. Clarke (Grand Rapids: Eerdmans, 1993), pp. 105-52.

them from their counterparts in the New Testament. They become means of showing extraordinary power. The Gospels' perspective on healing as acts of mercy is often downplayed, although it is present at times in the *Apocryphal Acts.* The following will delve into how Jesus is presented in the *Infancy Gospel of Thomas,* and then provide a cursory reading of some stories in *Apocryphal Acts.*

The *Infancy Gospel of Thomas*

Apocryphal Gospels and acts fill in gaps in the biblical stories. The open spaces in the latter triggered the imagination and the development of many legends. The birth and infancy of Jesus provide natural grounds for such continuation and elaboration or embellishment. This can be seen most vividly in the so-called *Protevangelium of James,* where the author (or authors) delves into the birth and upbringing of Mary, Jesus' mother, before turning to the miraculous events accompanying the birth of Jesus.

The complicated and variegated history of the text of *IGT* reflects its popular use. Scholarly agreement places this text sometime in the second century, although it is a collection of tales. Both Irenaeus (*Haer.* 1.13.1) and *Epistula Apostolorum* make reference to a story that figures prominently in *IGT,* namely, Jesus' learning the alphabet at school. This is likely indicative of their familiarity with this particular story. Since it might have circulated independently, we cannot, however, assume that they are familiar with *IGT* as we now have it. Nonetheless, these sources attest to an early interest in stories of the kind found in *IGT.*[2]

IGT demonstrates that Jesus' infancy becomes a starting point for stories to develop, which seems natural since the New Testament is indeed meager in its attestation of this period in his biography. Not surprisingly, the story of Jesus' childhood closes (*IGT* 17.1–5) with the retelling of Luke's passage about Jesus in the temple at age twelve (Luke 2). Scribes and teachers are silenced, and they marvel at his wisdom. Elizabeth's dictum about Mary in Luke 1:42 is now echoed in the mouths of scribes and Pharisees. "Blessed

2. The Greek text and English translations are taken from Reidar Aasgaard, *The Childhood of Jesus: Decoding the Apocryphal Infancy Gospel of Thomas* (Eugene, OR: Cascade, 2009). Translations are also available at www.tonyburke.ca and in Wilhelm Schneemelcher and Robert McL. Wilson, eds., *New Testament Apocrypha,* 2 vols. (Louisville: Westminster John Knox, 1991–1992). Readers should be aware of the textual differences between the available translations.

are you, for the Lord God has blessed the fruit of your womb. For we have never known or heard such wisdom as his, nor such glory or virtue" (*IGT* 17.4). This knowledge of Jesus' superiority becomes the point of departure for depicting Jesus' infancy as equally marvelous.[3]

IGT is, in fact, one long continuous miracle story, consisting of different kinds of marvelous acts wrought by Jesus as a child. He gathers a rushing stream into pools and makes the water pure by his mere words. Then he forms twelve sparrows out of clay, and brings them to life. This play takes place on a Sabbath (*IGT* 2.2–5). The father of one of his playmates therefore destroys the pool. Jesus is enraged and causes his playmate to be withered (*IGT* 3.1–3). Such punitive miracles occur throughout the story. Jesus brings death upon another playmate because he bumps into Jesus' shoulder. He blinds the parents of this boy when they accuse him because of what he has done to their son (*IGT* 4.1–2).

At school, Jesus marvels his teachers, and at times he brings shame upon them. This makes up two sections in this story (*IGT* 6.1–10; 13.1–14.4). Here we also find an incident where a teacher is so annoyed by his pupil Jesus that he strikes him on the head. Jesus becomes angry and tells him that his teaching is nothing more than a "noisy gong or a clanging cymbal which can't provide the sound or glory or power of insight" (*IGT* 6.8; cf. 1 Cor. 13:1). In his anger toward the teacher who struck him (*IGT* 13.1–2), Jesus curses him so that he falls dead to the ground. It is not strange, therefore, that Joseph and Mary are afraid to let him out of the house, lest his anger should cause more deaths. Although Jesus restores all those cursed by him (*IGT* 8.1–2), no one dares to make him angry. The anger of the boy is an important motif in these stories of Jesus' punitive miracles. In Jesus' miracles and healings, it seems that the world and those who inhabit it are his playthings. This is also stated in *IGT* 6.7: "I was playing [*epaizon*] with you, for I know that you are easily impressed and small-minded."

However, Jesus also rescues his brother James from dying of a viper bite. Jesus only has to breathe on the bite, and James is instantly healed and the snake destroyed (15.1–2). According to 9.1–3, he raises his playmate Zeno from the dead. In other versions,[4] two other similar instances are told, thus

---

3. According to *IGT* 10.1–2, Jesus filled his cloak with water and brought it to his mother. *IGT* 10.12 also tells a story about Joseph, his carpenter-father, working with two pieces of wood not equally long. Jesus stretched the shorter so they became even. Jesus' superiority to his teachers (see later) also underlines Luke 2 as a source of inspiration. These stories owe much to Luke 1–2; see Aasgaard, *Childhood of Jesus*, pp. 111, 123.

4. See *IGT* 17.1; 18.1 in Schneemelcher and Wilson, *New Testament Apocrypha*. These two

demonstrating how these legends thrived and fluctuated. A creative and expansive power is certainly at work in this narrative tradition about Jesus. He is likewise said to heal a foot injured from an ax (*IGT* 16.1–3), and also heals one of his teachers who was struck *(ho plēgeis sōthesetai)*, though it is not clear precisely what kind of suffering this refers to (*IGT* 14.1–4).

IGT gives a picture of Jesus aimed at amusing its readers.[5] At times he appears naughty; this is not only a modern observation, but is clearly reflected in the response and reaction of the bystanders as well. Jesus represents a constant danger to his surroundings. People appear as playthings to him in a world he runs completely. Nonetheless, he also at times brings healing and curing, and on one occasion he sows seeds and gathers one hundred measures, which is then distributed to the poor and orphans (*IGT* 11.1–2). This is an example of acts done out of mercy, though the text itself does not point this out. The near absence of compassion and mercy in this literature is probably the reason why miracles other than healings hold pride of place.

Jesus' miracles and healings serve a larger purpose in the story, easily extracted from the reaction some of his marvels cause. This is clearly seen in what one of his teachers says about him: "The child is simply not of this earth — he is even able to tame fire. Perhaps this child existed before the creation of the world? What kind of womb bore him? What kind of mother raised him? I really don't know. Dear me brother, he outdoes me! My mind can't comprehend this" (*IGT* 7.2).[6] This reaction follows from a question resonating throughout the story, namely, where this boy is really from: "From where was this child born, since his word becomes deed?" (*IGT* 4.1). According to *IGT* 6.5, this christological mystery is formulated like this: "This child is only five years old, and oh, what words he utters. We have never known such words. No one, neither a teacher of the law nor a Pharisee, has spoken like this child." The teachers assigned to teach him find themselves put to shame and become mouthpieces for christological insight.

His wisdom, his miracles and healings, and his raising of the dead distance Jesus from ordinary men. He is truly unique, which his miracles serve to demonstrate. His poking fun at his surroundings works narratively to distance him from people. Jesus himself explicitly states the answer to the

---

stories are told in a way that brings to mind Mark 5 and Luke 7. Aasgaard, *Childhood of Jesus,* renders these texts on pp. 241–42.

5. Aasgaard, *Childhood of Jesus,* p. 215.

6. Aasgaard, *Childhood of Jesus,* pp. 152–62, points out that the main point of *IGT* is to demonstrate the superiority and power of Jesus already as a child. Hence the miracles engage in christological discourse.

question of his true origins in *IGT* 6.4–6: "For I am from outside of you" and "When you were born, I existed."[7]

In this literature, Jesus' healings and miracles are not exemplary, but rather absolutely unique. They have become proofs of his divinity, a kind of divinity shaped by the entertaining nature of this literature. From the perspective of *IGT* it is hard to imagine that others, even the apostles, could be seen to perpetuate the healings performed by Jesus. However, we should not jump to conclusions here. After all, *IGT* is a piece of amusement literature, and even though it certainly includes theological aspects, this is not a genre that recommends itself to far-reaching conclusions. Finally, *IGT* demonstrates that some traditions indulged in the miracles of Jesus, and that these thrived in storytelling about him. In this way *IGT* confirms the importance of this aspect of Jesus' ministry in the remembrances about him, and simultaneously *IGT* shows how fundamentally different the Gospel stories are.

Jesus at Work in the Healing Stories of the *Apocryphal Acts*

Just a glance at the *Apocryphal Acts* is sufficient to tell how important the miracles and healings are in their portrayal of the apostles' biographies. The following will give examples sufficient to demonstrate that. The acts are construed as the power of Jesus at work, and his healing power is portrayed as mediated through his apostles.

The *Acts of Thomas* claims that Thomas is Jesus' identical twin; hence he and Jesus are seen to be working in tandem. Accordingly, in a remarkable story about Thomas raising a dead boy who had been bitten by a great serpent, Thomas says that "Christ will become the physician of your bodies" (38).[8] This serpent comes out of its hole and tells Thomas that he killed the boy because he watched him engaged in loving acts with a woman with whom the snake had also fallen in love. Thomas forces the serpent to suck out the deadly poison from the boy, whereby he gradually returns to life. As the serpent is filled with the poison, it swallows and finally falls dead to the ground. The poison wells out and opens a chasm in the earth, into which the serpent falls. The serpent is identified with the devil, whom Jesus has

---

7. See Aasgaard, *Childhood of Jesus*, pp. 141–42.

8. For this literature in general, see Hans-Josef Klauck, *The Apocryphal Acts of the Apostles: An Introduction*, trans. Brian J. MacNeil (Waco: Baylor University Press, 2008). The translations are taken from Schneemelcher and Wilson, *New Testament Apocrypha*, vol. 2.

come to destroy. The serpent speaks with words taken from Mark 5 about Jesus having come to destroy the demons before their time has come (31). This is a good example of what literary critics call *mis en abyme,* that is, a miniature version of the whole story within which the miniature is found.[9] This *mis en abyme* brings to mind John 12:31, where the whole ministry of Jesus is condensed into the short "now the ruler of this world will be driven out," thus construing Jesus' mission, his death and resurrection as the ultimate and only exorcism.

Thomas is addressed as a "servant of Jesus" (45), through whom Jesus casts out demons and raises the dead. These are the most prominent kinds of healing mentioned here. Thomas prays that "Christ will grant life" (54) to a dead woman who has been killed by her lover. When she is raised she gives a report from Hades, which is indeed an anticipation of Dante's *Inferno.* In chapters 62–67, the devil disguises himself as an older man who takes sexual advantage — this is a recurrent motif in these stories — of a woman and her daughter. For five years they are haunted by this demon, but "Christ will heal them," as it says in chapter 65. A talking wild ass is in this text the "spokesperson" of Jesus, a fact that speaks to the entertaining nature of this text. A serpent and a colt (39–41), both involved in a dialogue with the apostle, and asses who speak to Thomas, all add to the entertaining character of this story.

A fragment (Berlin Coptic Papyrus 8502) of the *Acts of Peter* tells about Peter's paralyzed daughter, who is lying helpless on the ground as her father is healing the blind, deaf, and lame. Someone in the crowd asks why he has not helped his daughter in the same way. The situation takes as its point of departure the New Testament evidence that Peter was married (Mark 1:30 par.; 1 Cor. 9:5), although no children are mentioned there. The *Acts of Peter* therefore reveal an interest in biographical information ripe for spin-offs. Peter assures them that God is able to heal his daughter, and to prove it, he does precisely that: "Rise from your place without any man's help but Jesus' alone and walk naturally before them all and come to me." The crowd rejoices when they see this happen. But Peter then commands his daughter to lie down again and to return to her infirmity, "for this is profitable for you and me." At this point, the story reveals the anti-sex message of many of these texts. It was to the advantage of this young girl to remain paralyzed, lest she became a temptation to men due to her beautiful countenance.

---

9. The term is borrowed from a practice of putting a shield within a larger shield; i.e., a portion that displays the subject of the whole piece; see Jo-Ann A. Brant, *John,* Paideia Commentary on the New Testament (Grand Rapids: Baker Academic, 2011), pp. 151–52.

Chapters 12–29 are devoted to a contest between Peter and Simon. Simon is the opponent figure from Acts 8, who now appears in Rome as well.[10] The contest, announced by a talking dog, is about their capacity as miracle workers.[11] Peter throws a smoked fish into a pool, and it starts swimming, and he brings a seven-month-old infant to rebuke Simon. He also heals several blind widows.

The final test takes place on the Forum in Rome, with all the nobility present; even the presence of the emperor is implied. Both place and audience serve the popular setting of the story. In the first test, Simon is to kill a person whom Peter will then raise up. Simon does his job by gently touching the man. The dead man is then examined by his nostrils to make sure that he is dead.[12] Peter sees this as putting Christ himself to test (26). When the news spreads that Peter raised people from the dead, a mother of one of the senators brings her dead son to Peter, who says: "Do not look at me, as though by my power I were doing what I do;[13] the power is my Lord Jesus Christ. . . . Believing in him I dare entreat him to raise the dead" (28). The dead senator is then brought to him, and this becomes the final test between Peter and Simon. Simon tries to trick the audience into believing he has raised the dead man, but is unsuccessful. Peter, however, raises the man. As a demonstration of Jesus' mercy, he urges the people not to harm Simon in any way, "for we have learnt not to repay evil for evil."

This episode in the Roman Forum also serves to point out that in the apocryphal literature the stories of the apostles' healings often involve nobilities and higher officials. In the *Acts of Thomas* this is evident with the kings Gundaphorus and Misdaeus. In the *Acts of John,* the apostle raises from the dead both the wife of the praetor of Ephesus and the praetor himself (Lycomedes) (19–29). On another occasion, John summons women who are sick and old in the theater of Ephesus; some are lying on beds and others in torpor (30–36). Here the praetor Andronicus is present while John proclaims

10. A contest between Simon and Peter is central also to the *Pseudo-Clementine Homilies.*

11. This plot brings to mind the contest between Elijah and the prophets of Baal (1 Kings 18).

12. This brings to mind Eusebius's *Treatise against Philostratus's Life of Apollonius of Tyana* 26. Eusebius says that the day Apollonius allegedly raised a dead girl was cold, and he observed respiration coming out of her nostrils; hence, she was not really dead. This treatise is found in F. C. Conybeare, trans., *Philostratus: The Life of Apollonius of Tyana,* Loeb Classical Library 2 (Cambridge: Harvard University Press, 1969), not in the new 2005 edition.

13. This echoes Peter's dictum when accused for having healed the man born lame (Acts 3:12).

the gospel and eventually heals the women who have been brought to him. This goes like a reversal of the story in Acts 19 of Paul in the same theater.

This presentation, albeit cursory, of some of the healing stories from the apocryphal traditions occasions some important observations. This literature indulges in miracles and healings that are far more sensational than what we find in the New Testament. Although Jesus and the way he empowers the apostles to perform miracles is not absolutely unique, as Simon's sorcery demonstrates, their miracles are mostly unique, and when they are not they are nevertheless superior. In this way the healing stories serve to set Jesus and the apostles apart more than portray the disciples as continuing the ministry of their master, although this aspect is not entirely absent. The apocryphal traditions convey biographical legends in which healing stories abound. The thriving tradition of storytelling takes as its point of departure that Jesus together with his apostles were remembered as miracle workers. This popular aspect finds no real correspondence in the canonical Gospels and Acts, though there are some possible exceptions in Acts. The entertaining nature of these stories is apparent from their biographical details, sensational healings, talking animals, and the presence of higher officials. They are, moreover, lengthy stories embedded in larger plots of conversion of crowds in well-known ancient cities or in exotic places like India (Thomas). The gospel of sexual chastity that often comes to the surface in these stories is characteristic of the second or third century, when they came into being. Familiarity with apocryphal traditions on healing therefore highlights the sobriety of the canonical Gospels in this regard.

Healing in the Early Church

The aim of the following is to give a survey of how Christian churches of the second, third, and fourth centuries related to the healing tradition, and to what extent this tradition was perpetuated among them. The theme is diverse. It covers a great deal of time and geographical space, and it reveals an ambivalent attitude toward healing. It is not possible here to delve into all this in detail,[1] but some important aspects will be commented on.

Ambivalence

This ambivalent attitude toward Jesus' healings, found even among believers, is due to the fact that pagans viewed them as sorcery or magic. Pagan criticism does not deny that Jesus performed miracles, but they believed that in doing so he showed himself to be a magician. This is voiced most clearly in Celsus's critique of Christianity in the third century.[2] Origen, in responding to Celsus, argued that Jesus was very different from dealers in

1. See Gary B. Ferngren, *Medicine and Health Care in Early Christianity* (Baltimore: Johns Hopkins University Press, 2009); James Carleton Paget, "Miracles in Early Christianity," in *The Cambridge Companion to Miracles*, ed. Graham H. Twelftree (Cambridge: Cambridge University Press, 2011); Andrew Daunton-Fear, *Healing in the Early Church: The Church's Ministry of Healing and Exorcism from the First to the Fifth Century* (Milton Keynes, UK: Paternoster, 2009).

2. See Origen's refutation, *Against Celsus,* in which large parts of Celsus's critique are cited; *Cels.* 1.6; 1.46; 1.48; 2.39; 2.48–49; 3.25–28; 3.31; 3.33; 8.47. For translation see Henry Chadwick, *Origen Contra Celsum* (Cambridge: Cambridge University Press, 1953). See John Granger Cook, *The Interpretation of the New Testament in Greco-Roman Paganism* (Peabody, MA: Hendrickson, 2002), pp. 36–39, 298–300.

magical arts. His healings were not done to show his power as most sorcerers did. Furthermore, magicians do not use their tricks "to call the spectators to moral reformation" (*Cels.* 1.68). He continues by observing that the healings of Jesus were part of a wider ministry. Christians, Jews, and pagans of the second-, third-, and fourth-century Mediterranean world all shared a hesitant or even negative view of magic,[3] which is why, as James Carleton Paget points out, early Christian literature on healing and miracles tends to be defensive.[4] It is therefore important to read this literature against the background of accusations that Christian miracles proved their practitioners as well as Jesus himself to be sorcerers.

Another reason for the defensive nature of this literature is that the healing ministry of Jesus was often seen as fictitious. Quadratus, in a fragment of his *Apology* preserved by Eusebius,[5] argues that Jesus' healings were witnessed by people still alive at his time, thus implying that the reality of the healings was disputed. This is also attested to in Origen's *Commentary on John's Gospel* (2.204). Origen discusses on what grounds faith may come into being. Although he gives pride of place to proof from prophecy, he also includes the working of miracles: "And we must also consider that the prodigious miracles were able to summon those who lived at the time of the Lord to faith, but they did not preserve their impressive nature after many years when, by this time, they were also supposed to be myths."

In other words, whether Jesus really did heal people was a live issue. We tend to think that people of the ancient world were credulous, believing almost anything. Certainly, the Christians lived in a world where miracles, healings, and supernatural inventions were more or less taken for granted. However, it is quite clear that they did not have an "anything goes" mind-set, even in the ancient world.[6]

Jesus at Work

The healings performed by the followers of Jesus were in principle seen as the ongoing presence and power of Jesus or God within the church. We have seen that this is a major perspective, primarily in the Acts of the Apostles.

---

3. It is worth reminding oneself that this is in accordance with scriptural sources, which often depend on the views of an elite.

4. Paget, "Miracles in Early Christianity," pp. 138–42.

5. Eusebius, *Hist. eccl.* 4.3.2.

6. See Paget, "Miracles in Early Christianity," p. 132.

The notion of Jesus' presence in the church is a bridge to the past, and implies that his followers continue his ministry. This notion is stated explicitly, but is also implied in formulations that Christ or God performed healings "through the hands of the disciples"; they are instruments for Jesus, who is still at work. Very often the miracles are also done "in the name of Jesus," which also bridges the past by construing the followers as acting on behalf of Jesus or demonstrating that his authority is at work through them.

Some voices in the ancient church, however, maintained a so-called cessationist position, which held that miracles and healings had ceased after the establishment of the church. In other words, these wonders served the initial period only, as a means of establishing Christianity. In the West, Augustine may serve as an example of this position; and in the East, John Chrysostom. Both of them are concerned with the integrity of faith, avoiding a faith that seeks confirmation in visible things and constantly looks for extraordinary things (Augustine, *On True Religion* 47). Augustine later retracted this position, admitting that miracles still did take place, but not with the same frequency and greatness as they did in the initial period (*Retractationes* 1.12.7; 1.13.5).[7] In the *City of God,* Augustine mentions miracles that occurred in his own time, some of which even he himself had observed, relating in detail an incident he and many others witnessed in Milan. He does insist, though, that contemporary healings are less known, and more limited and particular than those told of in the Gospels (*City of God* 22.8). John Chrysostom shares much of the same view, referring to John 20:29 ("Blessed are they who have not seen and have believed") when he addresses the question of miracles and healings. He underscores the difference between the apostolic age and his own days. The cessationist position is thus aimed at strengthening faith as based on the tradition of the church and not on individual experiences. This development probably served to provide defense against what many saw as heretical subjectivity.

Healing as Supporting Evidence

We have seen that for Paul healing and miracles served to authenticate his ministry and message, most clearly in Galatians 3:1-5.[8] This gives an apolo-

---

7. See Ralph Del Colle, "Miracles in Christianity," in Twelftree, *Cambridge Companion to Miracles,* pp. 237-38.

8. Emphasized also by James A. Kelhoffer, *Miracle and Mission: The Authentication of*

getic function to such reported events. Early Christians took up this apologetic aspect in theology and dogma more generally.[9] The truth of Christian faith was thus generally seen to be defended and confirmed not only by the healings wrought by Jesus but also by those of his followers who still performed such things. Although the apologists focused on different matters, namely, proofs from Scripture, in their writings, their apologetic use of miracles is also evident. Quadratus's fragment, mentioned already, is indicative that even the apologists at times found it beneficial to make reference to Jesus as a healer. The power to exorcise demons is frequently mentioned in support of theological points. The fact that the gospel manifested itself in visible power was a proof not only of the gospel but also of its theological dogmas.[10] Within this perspective, the healees and their needs clearly become secondary.

Mission and Healing

In his book *Christianizing the Roman Empire* (1984), Ramsay MacMullen argues that it was miracles, including healings, that more than anything else drew converts to the early church. Such a conclusion follows in the wake of the classical work of Adolf von Harnack on the mission and growth of Christianity in the first centuries.[11]

The missionary effect of the visible power manifested in healing and exorcisms is recognized by Origen in his refutation of Celsus. The pagan philosopher accused Jesus and the Christians of sorcery, and Origen countered this attack, for example, by pointing to the moral transformation initiated and brought about by such powerful events (see above). From this follows an intimate connection between healing and mission:

Missionaries and Their Message in the Longer Ending of Mark (Tübingen: Mohr Siebeck, 2000), pp. 272–74.

9. Pointed out also by Daunton-Fear, *Healing in the Early Church*, p. 153.

10. See Kelhoffer, *Miracle and Mission*, pp. 317–22; Reidar Hvalvik, "In Word and Deed: The Expansion of the Church in the Pre-Constantinian Era," in *The Mission of the Early Church to Jews and Gentiles* (Tübingen: Mohr Siebeck, 2000), p. 283. A good example is Tertullian's *Apology* 23.4–9, where a test *(demonstratio)* is conducted, aimed at proving *(probatio)* the truth *(veritas)* of Christianity over against pagan religion.

11. Ramsay MacMullen, *Christianizing the Roman Empire A.D. 100–400* (New Haven: Yale University Press, 1984); Adolf von Harnack, *Die Mission und Ausbreitung des Christentums in den ersten drei Jahrhunderten,* 4th ed. (Wiesbaden: VMA-Verlag, 1924), pp. 129–70.

For without miracles and wonders they would not have persuaded those who heard the new doctrines and new teachings at the risk of their lives. Traces of that Holy Spirit who appeared in the form of a dove are still preserved among Christians. They charm demons away and perform many cures and perceive certain things about the future according to the will of Logos. Even if Celsus, or the Jew he introduced, ridicules what I am about to say, nevertheless it shall be said that many have come to Christianity as it were in spite of themselves. (*Cels.* 1.46)

Origen attributes healing acts to the presence of the Spirit. In mentioning the dove, he bridges the gap between Jesus and the Christians of his own day. The missionary effect of exorcism and healing is also stated by Irenaeus: "For some do certainly and truly drive out devils, so that those who have thus been cleansed from evil spirits frequently believe and join themselves to the Church" (*Haer.* 2.32.4). From the wider context (*Haer.* 2.31.2–32.4), we gather that exorcism is closely connected to healing; it occurs together with curing blindness, deafness, and other acts of healing.[12] As James A. Kelhoffer points out, Irenaeus merits attention here because he elsewhere shows little interest in miracles: "This late second-century author could have written much more about miracles if he considered such information important to his treatise against heretics."[13] The clearest example that healing caused curiosity that attracted many to Christianity is to be found in the *Apocryphal Acts.*[14]

In his fascinating book *The Rise of Christianity* (1996), the sociologist Rodney Stark asks: "How did a tiny and obscure messianic movement from the edge of the Roman Empire dislodge classical paganism and become the dominant faith of Western civilization?"[15] In answering this question he points out that the amazing growth of Christianity to a large extent was dependent on the great epidemics in the empire in the third and fourth century: "Had some crisis *not occurred,* the Christians would have been deprived of major, possibly, crucial opportunities."[16] The emperor Julian saw

12. See Kelhoffer, *Miracle and Mission*, pp. 212–14, 322–26.

13. Kelhoffer, *Miracle and Mission*, p. 326. Irenaeus and the heretics he fought ascribed very different importance to the bodily aspect of both Christology and soteriology. In this debate, the healing tradition would be most helpful, but Irenaeus gives priority to the question of unity between the two Testaments.

14. See the *Acts of John* 33–36, 37–45; *Acts of Peter* 12–13.

15. Rodney Stark, *The Rise of Christianity: A Sociologist Reconsiders History* (Princeton: Princeton University Press, 1996), p. 3.

16. Stark, *Rise of Christianity*, pp. 73–94 (quotation p. 93).

that the church's health care, widely understood, had given the Christians an advantage, which he wanted to reverse. He attempted to revive pagan beliefs and to make pagan priests and institutions do equally good works for the sick and poor. "But for all that he urged pagan priests to match these Christian practices, there was little or no response because *there were no doctrinal bases or traditional practices* for them to build upon."[17] The healing tradition, with its emphasis on bodily restoration, paved the way for Christian health care, which had no analogy in its contemporary time.

In his important book *Medicine and Health Care in Early Christianity* (2009), Gary B. Ferngren challenges many views often voiced in this area, some of which are echoed above. He argues that healing by natural remedies had become part of the culture in which Christianity arose and spread, and that Christians mostly embraced this: "They did not attribute most diseases to demons, they did not ordinarily seek miraculous or religious cures, and they employed natural means of healing, whether these means involved physicians or home or traditional remedies."[18] One example Ferngren uses is the advice of 1 Timothy 5:23; here Timothy is urged to take a little wine for his stomach problems. No religion or healing theology is discernible here, simply a drawing on common knowledge. From this he concludes that Christianity was not a religion of healing.

> Probably the majority of Christians continued to seek out physicians or employ home or traditional remedies, while the establishment of hospitals extended medical care to the indigent, particularly to the urban homeless who were previously without the means to obtain it. Christianity was never a religion of healing in the sense that Harnack described it, comparable to the great healing religion of Asclepius and Serapis. At no period was healing central to the early Christian message, and it always remained peripheral to a gospel that offered reconciliation to God and eternal salvation to sinners.[19]

This quotation includes many interesting points worth briefly commenting on. Ferngren rightly makes the point that the establishment of care for the sick implies a fundamental acceptance of natural remedies. Spiritual healing was therefore not seen as the only, let alone the main, means of coping with

17. Stark, *Rise of Christianity*, p. 88.
18. Ferngren, *Medicine and Health*, p. 13.
19. Ferngren, *Medicine and Health Care*, p. 85.

sickness. Care for the sick based on knowledge gained from contemporary medicine was, according to Ferngren, more important than cure as a means of attracting new believers. In other words, philanthropy was more important than healing: "The philanthropic motive of the church was essential to its early success. . . . Indeed, in its development and extension of that role lies Christianity's chief contribution to health care.[20] Christianity's perspective on sickness and health thus marked a dramatic departure from the view held in the ancient world. The sick were not regarded as being responsible for their situation, nor as suffering from some divine punishment, but "as deserving of compassion and assistance."[21] This is a pertinent point, but such changes take place gradually. In my opinion, Ferngren's valuable book suffers from a lack of nuance in his conclusions.

Ferngren depicts early Christianity's attitude to sickness and healing as less religious and more in accordance with ancient medicine. Christians certainly shared both the knowledge and experience of their day, but he hardly accounts for the medical pluralism of the ancient world in his presentation. The multidimensional picture he draws[22] runs contrary to his claim that natural remedies had become a cultural currency. Ancient medicine was indeed a diverse phenomenon. When healing is provided by herb specialists, midwives, religious healers, diviners, exorcists, priests, and physicians of different sorts, it is hardly possible to say that natural means of healing prevailed in general. Ferngren argues that the motif of the "despoliation of Egypt," that is, the biblically founded idea of finding valuable insights among Gentiles, contributed to the adoption of commonly held views on natural remedies.[23] The motif of the despoliation of Egypt was a view embraced by the elite; it is hardly applicable in general, just as it was with regard to education.[24]

Furthermore, Ferngren argues that the motif of the despoliation of Egypt contributed to a rational attitude toward medicine. The problem is that this model elsewhere in early Christianity — with regard to Greek literature, philosophy, and education — aims at distinguishing between what is reconcilable with Christian faith and what runs contrary to it. Ferngren portrays ancient medicine and Christian attitudes as fully compatible, and thus leaves the model of the despoliation of Egypt almost void. This idea was

---

20. Ferngren, *Medicine and Health Care*, p. 139.

21. Ferngren, *Medicine and Health Care*, p. 143.

22. Ferngren, *Medicine and Health Care*, pp. 35-41.

23. Ferngren, *Medicine and Health Care*, pp. 25-35 (more on this below).

24. This is one of the conclusions in my book *The Challenge of Homer: School, Pagan Poets and Early Christianity* (London: T&T Clark, 2009). For this motif, see next chapter.

a means for the ancient church of navigating difficult waters, that is, in areas with potential conflicts. Ferngren, however, does not leave much room for potential conflicts.

Furthermore, Ferngren is critical of the Harnack-MacMullen tradition that healings held pride of place in attracting new believers. He considers this unsubstantiated. His key argument is that healing was hardly ubiquitous in the early Church. The so-called church fathers in the first half of the second century do not include references to miraculous healing. This is not to deny what we have seen above, but a reminder not to exaggerate it. As pointed out by Reidar Hvalvik, there were also other factors, among which the conduct of believers was very important.[25]

---

25. Hvalvik, "In Word and Deed," p. 284.

Toward a Theology of Jesus as Healer

It is time to draw our findings together. This will not be done in an ordinary summary, however. The present chapter casts the net wider by including theological perspectives that grow out of the material that has been examined, and also by taking some initial steps toward the question of present-day relevance. Although the second part of this volume will delve into this in a systematic manner, engaging recent theological works on the topic, some aspects, based particularly on the biblical material, might be anticipated here. Thus some of the theological assumptions at work in the New Testament with regard to Jesus as a healer will be pointed out. On this background, some insights that bridge the remembered Jesus of the past and the present will be developed.

Ruben Zimmermann claims that the problems involved in constructing a theology of healing ("Die Probleme einer Wundertheologie")[1] arise from the stories themselves. He points to the fact that Jesus did not heal everybody, although the summaries may at times give this impression. In this regard, Jesus' words in Luke 4:25-27 ("There were many widows in Israel in the time of Elijah . . . ; yet Elijah was sent to none of them except to a widow at Zarephath in Sidon. There were also many lepers in Israel in the time of the prophet Elisha, and none of them were cleansed except Naaman the Syrian") apply to his own healing ministry as well. It is no wonder, therefore, that Luke in the following verse says that this caused irritation (v. 28), an irritation caused by the unexpected selection and unpredictable nature of Jesus' healings. These stories focus on the concrete and the individual. The

---

1. Ruben Zimmermann, "Grundfragen zu den frühchristlichen Wundererzählungen," in *Kompendium der frühchristlichen Wundererzählungen*, vol. 1, *Die Wunder Jesu*, ed. Ruben Zimmermann et al. (Gütersloh: Gütersloher Verlagshaus, 2013), p. 44.

problem inherent in any healing theology lies in the fact that any attempt at making theology by necessity claims structure, organization, regularity, meaning, and generality for something fundamentally unpredictable in nature. Such theologies run the risk of making regularities and commonalities out of contingent moments of possibilities that transcend human expectations. Healing is by nature a gift received beyond expectation, accessible only through prayer and hope. Any theology of healing must proceed from this "problem," and avoid any attempt at solving the riddle. We must keep this caveat in mind as we now turn to work out theological implications.

Reading or listening to the healing narratives raises the question of what they bring to their particular audience (see below). These stories portray God in a way that brings into question any simple rationalism as the only viable way to look at reality and the world. Thus they envisage possibilities beyond normal expectations and experiences, and become flashes of protest and hope. Not only does the unexplainable come within reach in these stories, but they even justify the possibility of surmounting the impossible. According to Zimmermann, these stories are therefore about hope as well as protest against narrow rationalism.[2] They envisage possibilities beyond the immediate reality and usual expectations.

From Jesus' Healing Ministry to Posterity

The New Testament speaks about Jesus' healing ministry as something that does not solely belong to the past, but as stories that tell about "events that want to happen" continuously.[3] Much present-day teaching and preaching turns the healings of Jesus into illustrations of theological themes, as pointing beyond themselves to something else. In the previous chapters, we have seen that the healing stories do at times include such aspects, but this is always subordinated to and deduced from the effect of the healings, that is, the bodily and individual restoration that takes place (though this is more questionable in John). The tendency to elicit doctrines or meanings from these accounts easily turns them into allegories of various kinds. Any kerygmatic meaning cannot be cut loose from the events in these stories. According to

2. Zimmermann, "Grundfragen," pp. 47–49.

3. I have borrowed this sentence from the English translation in Ulrich Luz, *Matthew 8–20*, trans. James E. Crouch (Minneapolis: Fortress, 2001), p. 58. The following owes much to his *Matthew 8–20*, pp. 52–59, and his *Studies in Matthew*, trans. Rosemary Selle (Grand Rapids: Eerdmans, 2005), pp. 221–40.

Ulrich Luz, understanding the healings of Jesus must "start from their effect." The challenge is to theologically conceptualize precisely this aspect of the healing stories: "What is reported can be rendered unimportant amazingly quickly by simply asking what it means."[4]

The faith that comes out of the New Testament accounts about Jesus' compassion for the sick and needy is not about doctrines or principles, but about a personal relationship constituted by extraordinary and particular events of help and assistance. It is a mistake to address these stories as though they were occasions for philosophizing about natural laws and whether God has the power to dispense with such laws. What Jesus breaks are the shackles of the devil present in human suffering and sickness. No matter the theological garb such philosophizing appears in, it is mistaken if it takes as its starting point the stories about Jesus as a healer.

In Matthew's Gospel the perspective of posterity is found in the last dictum of Jesus: "I am with you always, to the end of the age" (Matt. 28:20). Matthew's story, from beginning to end, is about Jesus' presence among people, including those in the future. This final dictum picks up on Matthew 1:21–23, and thus envelops the whole story. The continuous presence of Jesus envisaged in Matthew 28 stands in continuity with his ministry as reported throughout the Gospel. Luz makes reference to Old Testament texts where the past also becomes the story of individuals and people in the present. What in Deuteronomy 26:5–10 starts out as a story about "my ancestor" gradually involves "us," and is at the end simply "my story." Such merging of past and present finds its classical expression in Deuteronomy 6:20–25: "We were Pharaoh's slaves in Egypt, but the LORD brought us out of Egypt with a mighty hand" (v. 21).[5] Likewise, Matthew closes his story by consciously blurring the lines between past and present.

The considerations made here also proceed from an awareness that *telling* about healing involves more than the mere incident of the story. The act of telling, reading, or passing on always involves some kind of perpetuation; it bridges past and present. When the healings of Jesus were written down and included into narratives that were read aloud to believers, those acts took on a function analogous to what happens when preaching on these texts. The stories about the past concern the present audience and aim at some kind of continuity in terms of attitude and practice.[6] There is a po-

---

4. Luz, *Matthew 8–20*, p. 57.

5. See also Joshua chap. 24.

6. This is emphasized by Zimmermann, "Grundfragen," pp. 47–49; and Wolf-Jürgen Grab-

tential in these stories for hope, for expectations beyond daily routines, to experience God's powerful presence on an individual basis. Thus, passing on these stories has from their very beginning been essential to articulating what it means to have faith in God. How do we perceive of God if he is beyond human physical experience? This leaves us with the "God of the philosophers, not of Abraham, Isaac, and Jacob" (Blaise Pascal).

It follows from this that the healings of Jesus are not proofs, neither of God nor of Christ. Jesus himself voiced his reluctance in this regard. Q has preserved a dictum where Jesus says that no other sign except the sign of Jonah will be given (Matt. 12:39//Luke 11:29). Similarly in John 2:23-24, Jesus is reluctant about those whose faith rests on signs they have seen.[7] The healing stories do not prove anything; on the contrary, they invite the audience to search and pray for God's intervention in our lives.

Faith: Seeking a Gift

What has been said above about healings bridging past and present leads us to focus on the stories about Jesus as healer as equally about faith. Those sick or those carrying their sick to Jesus faced obstacles on their way to find help from him. The friends who brought the paralytic to Jesus had to climb the roof and make a way to lower the sick man down to get Jesus' attention (Mark 2:1-12 par.). Bartimaeus faced attempts at silencing him, but he continued shouting for Jesus' help (Mark 10:46-52 par.). The stories about Jesus' healing call for similar faith even today. It is probably through such actions of faith that Jesus as healer becomes present for posterity as well. The full meaning of Jesus' healing ministry becomes understandable for those who put their hopes in Jesus, who is at the center of these stories.

The way Christology and help are intertwined in these stories has important epistemological ramifications, since this implies that the true experience of healing is revealed in following Jesus. In the end, this is how the stories about Jesus as a healer present an existential perspective. In Mark 1:16-2:28, the call to follow Jesus and his healing of the sick are intertwined throughout. Such linkage is witnessed to throughout the Gospels, and cul-

---

ner et al., "Über Wundererzählungen heute predigen (Homiletik der Wundererzählungen)," in Zimmermann et al., *Die Wunder Jesu*, pp. 159-60.

7. His saying to Thomas (John 20:29: "Blessed are those who have not seen and yet have come to believe") works likewise.

minates in the Fourth Gospel's calling of disciples in chapter 1, where they are told, "You will see greater things than these" (John 1:50).

In his bulky volume *The Miracles of Jesus* (1965), Hendrik van der Loos argues that faith in the healing stories works in the same way as prayers.[8] We have seen that Jesus' healings were not done as answers to his own prayers. However, his healings were done as answers to the prayers of the sick. It is worth noticing that faith and prayer appear in tandem in the well-known dictum found in Mark 11:20-24//Matthew 21:20-22: "Whatever you ask for in prayer, believe that you have received it, and it will be yours." The pleas of the sick are simple prayers, consisting of few words ("have mercy"), cries, or manifest themselves in acts of approaching Jesus. In a wider biblical perspective, the prayers of the sick bring to mind the situation of the righteous sufferer in the psalms. In the midst of various sufferings and troubles, which almost always also affect their bodily well-being, they turn to God in trust and prayer. He is their only helper, and from him they await rescue.[9]

It is worth observing that in some instances the prayers of the sick and needy find an echo in Jesus' prayer at Gethsemane. Especially illustrative is the leper in Mark 1:40-42. He falls on his knees *(gonypetōn)*[10] and says to Jesus: "If you will [*ean thelēs*], you can make me clean."[11] Jesus also fell to the ground, and likewise called on the will of God, hoping that God would provide him rescue. Similarly, in Mark 9:22-23 a man brings his demonic son to Jesus, hoping for his assistance: "'But if you are able [*ei ti dyne*] to do anything, have pity on us and help us.' Jesus said to him: 'If you are able! — All things can be done [*panta dynata*] for the one who believes.'" This sentence is remarkably similar to Jesus' prayer, as it moves from a condition "if" to stating as a fact that God is able. Both these passages echo key elements in the Gethsemane prayer. While the prayers of the sick in the Second Gospel were answered, this did not happen with Jesus. He is cast in the role of the needy who turn to God in a desperate situation. While those who approached him found help, Jesus' own prayer is left unanswered. Two implications may be drawn from this, one of which pertains directly to the present topic. What

8. Hendrik van der Loos, *The Miracles of Jesus* (Leiden: Brill, 1965), pp. 264-80.

9. Here are some examples given according to LXX: Ps 6:5, 10; 21:6, 9, 20-22; 17:7; 30:10, 14, 15-17; 33:18; 37:10, 22-23; 41:6, 12; 42:5; 54:2; 68:14-19; 101:2-3; 117:5-7.

10. This is missing in some mss, most importantly in Vaticanus; hence Nestle-Aland's 28th edition of the Greek New Testament has it in brackets.

11. My own translation aimed at pointing out the similarity with the prayer at Gethsemane (Mark 14:36). NRSV renders "if you choose."

happened to Jesus is a reminder that prayers are just that, requests with no guarantee of finding the wished-for response. Furthermore, the fact that Jesus in the Second Gospel is the only needy person who fails to find God responding to his prayer paves the way for a theology of his passion as altruistic. What he offered to others was denied to himself. Thus Gethsemane is a rehearsal of Golgotha in preparing the readers for his salvific death.[12]

These observations pave the way for some implications for a theology of healing. In the first place, healing may be sought or asked for. In short, it is the object of prayer and trust. Awaiting God's help and intervention is the attitude of trust articulated in prayer; it is not the expectation of exercising a right. Seen from the perspective worked out here, healing is always a gift. It follows from this that God is free to choose how prayers for healing are to be answered.[13] Hence, there will always be an element of secrecy or mystery in this theology, something beyond human explanation. Paul's prayer in 2 Corinthians 12:7–10, which probably involves a wish to have a bodily burden lifted, finds an unexpected answer: "My grace is sufficient for you, for power is made perfect in weakness." Likewise, Jesus prays in Gethsemane as a righteous sufferer, without receiving the answer he hoped for.

A Comprehensive Image of Humanity: Incarnation

Jesus' healings bring out implications inherent in both incarnational and creational theology. His incarnational presence involves a physical body that carries the needs and sufferings of humanity. His concern for people with bodily needs is therefore a manifestation of his becoming human, and also a perpetuation of his humanity. We now formulate this in words taken from Christian doctrine and tradition, but it is nonetheless implied in the New Testament itself. Human beings are intellectual, emotional, bodily, and social beings. The remembrances of Jesus as a healer have preserved a picture that embraces these aspects.

12. This draws on my forthcoming book *Christian Discourses on Jesus' Prayer at Gethsemane* (Supplements to Novum Testamentum 166; Leiden: Brill, 2016).

13. This way of reasoning finds some obstacle in the instances where healings happen according to commands. Healings in these cases are seen as part of a cosmic battle with the devil. From the perspective of the sick, the prayer certainly holds pride of place in the healing traditions about Jesus. A theology of healing that proceeds from rights and commands may be detrimental to Christian faith, because it fundamentally alters the role of the sick from someone who prays to someone who demonstrably claims his or her rights.

In writing that Jesus says to the family or parents of Jairus's daughter after she has been raised: "Give her something to eat" (Mark 5:43), this Gospel brings out Jesus' concern for her entire physical well-being. This piece of information, preserved by Mark alone, brings to mind the resurrected Jesus consuming fish (Luke 24:42–43; John 21:13).[14] The risen Jesus who eats demonstrates an interest in the *bodily* resurrection of Jesus. It is this similar bodily focus that is also at work in Jesus' urging food to be brought to Jairus's daughter.

According to the epistle to the Hebrews (2:14–18; 4:14–16), incarnation is an act of solidarity, culminating in Jesus' unselfish death for human beings. Jesus' sacrificial death for the sins of the people comes as a result of his solidarity with their fear of death. The incarnation thus points to his willingness not only to share in human experiences but also to die for their sins. The author of Hebrews draws on this solidarity to comfort addressees who are both anguished and afraid (Heb. 10:32–39). The same solidarity also forms the proper theological background for his healing activities, encapsulated in his compassion for those in need.

In the ancient churches where the question of the body, be it Christ's own or those of his followers, gradually became a hotly disputed question (Gnosticism), the healing tradition vouchsafed a concern for the body and physical needs. The importance of the physical body is affirmed in these stories. In this way, the healing accounts contributed to the character of Christian faith, and probably also to the ongoing debate on body and soul in human anthropology and soteriology. According to Augustine, that Jesus restored the bodies of those who were sick is intimately connected with Christian faith's proclamation that the physical body will be raised to eternal life (*City of God* 22.8). It is a minimalistic attitude to claim that the only miracle God still does is to give faith.

Jesus' healing on the Sabbath (Mark 3:1–6; Luke 13:10–17; 14:1–6; John 5:1–18; 9:1–14) instructively shows the bodily concern involved on Jesus' part. These healing stories became prime examples of christological significance for posterity in the faith, stating his authority over against the rules of the Sabbath. But the significance of the events told in those passages is not thereby exhausted. The day of the Sabbath epitomizes God's life-saving will in all its aspects, including the giving of rest to weary bodies (Exod. 23:12; Deut. 5:12–15), and takes God's own rest as an example (Gen. 2:2–3; Exod. 20:11). Healings on this particular day are as physical as are the intentions

14. A Johannine atmosphere in Luke 24 has long been noticed.

of the Sabbath rules, namely, to provide physical restoration.[15] It is this idea Jesus picks up on when according to Mark and Luke he asks: "Is it lawful to . . . heal/restore life [*psychēn sōsai*] or to kill?" (Mark 3:4; Luke 6:9). His Sabbath healings thereby perpetuate the very purpose of this day. In a wider New Testament horizon, the use of *sōzein* here takes on a wider perspective (cf. Luke 9:24), implying that Jesus brings the purpose to its fulfillment not only in healing people from sickness but also in giving forgiveness to sinners (Mark 2:17 par.). Thus the healings become symbolic acts whose significance at times transcends the immediate help they provide for their beneficiaries (more on this below).

"From the Beginning": Restoring Creation

In words reminiscent of the creation narrative, the bystanders in Mark 7:37 say that Jesus in healing a deaf and mute man "has done everything well." This places Jesus the healer within the framework of God's restoration of the fallen world. According to Udo Schnelle, "It is precisely the exorcisms and healings that have a dimension of creation theology: they aim at restoring the state of the world as God created it."[16] The vision in the book of Revelation about the "new heaven and the new earth," where neither tears, mourning, nor death is present (Rev. 21:1–5), is a great recapitulation of the creation, now renewed and transformed. This final vision of the Bible forms an *inclusio* with Genesis 1, and also forms a theological framework for Jesus' healings, as they are very much relevant to the renewal envisaged in Revelation. The vision of humankind as freed from sufferings is preceded by all evil powers, including death, being thrown into the lake of fire. Thus fighting evil and restoring the world to its intended order are two sides of the same coin.

Jesus' healings belong within this universal renewal but are at the same time only a partial and anticipatory manifestation of it. Because the Gospels, and Mark's narrative style in particular, convey a picture of Jesus healing wherever the need existed, the partiality of his healings should be pointed out. As mentioned above, the theological frameworks used to make sense of Jesus' healings carry with them exaggerations and generalizations that

15. See Michael L. Brown, *Israel's Divine Healer* (Grand Rapids: Zondervan, 1995), pp. 220–22; see also Annette Merz, "Der historische Jesus als Wundertäter im Spektrum antiker Wundertäter," in Zimmermann et al., *Die Wunder Jesu*, p. 119.

16. Udo Schnelle, *Theology of the New Testament*, trans. M. Eugene Boring (Grand Rapids: Baker Academic, 2007), pp. 127–28.

cannot be taken to mirror what happened in a one-to-one scheme. Jesus' healings are told within parameters prone to enhance this particular aspect and also to make them unique.

In discussions on healings, the issue of divine intervention and supernaturalism is high on the agenda. To what extent are Jesus' healings contrary to nature? This philosophical question was raised by David Hume. His question will be addressed later in this volume.[17] However, at this point it is pertinent to point out that the question of whether Jesus' healings imply a restoration of creation has some repercussions for how we may reason about them theologically. To claim that Jesus' healings are in principle an intervention contrary to nature endangers this biblical perspective, which in fact envelops the entire Christian canon, from creation in Genesis 1 to the new Jerusalem in Revelation 21–22.

Prophetic Symbolic Acts

The healing stories find themselves on the edge of the present, pointing toward a re-created world. They are acts in between "already accomplished" and "not yet complete." They manifest the tension between "the kingdom has come" and "the kingdom is to come." They are simultaneously manifestations of God's saving presence and prophetic actions that carry a symbolic meaning about the future. There is a long-standing biblical tradition of making spiritual sense of bodily weaknesses. In the New Testament, blindness appears to be particularly useful for this purpose. It here suffices to point to Revelation 3:17–18: "'You do not realize that you are wretched, pitiable, poor, blind, and naked. Therefore I counsel you to buy from me . . . salve to anoint your eyes so that you may see.'" In John's Gospel, the signs are embedded in such theological metaphor-making (John 9; 11), but this is not without antecedents in the Synoptic tradition, albeit on a much smaller scale.

In accordance with prophetic traditions, Jesus at times performed his message in symbolic acts.[18] In the passion narrative, the entrance into Jerusalem and the cleansing of the temple together with the last meal are such acts, which provide keys for unlocking the ministry of Jesus. Basically, symbolic

17. See also the extensive discussion in Craig S. Keener, *Miracles: The Credibility of the New Testament Accounts*, 2 vols. (Grand Rapids: Baker Academic, 2011), pp. 107–208.

18. Morna D. Hooker, *The Signs of a Prophet: The Prophetic Actions of Jesus* (London: SCM, 1997).

acts performed by the prophets consisted of an act/performance and its interpretation; the two are connected by a transitional phrase ("this means/ is" or the like) whereby the interpretation proper is introduced (Isa. 20:3; Jer. 18:6; 19:11–12; Acts 21:11). However, prophetic acts are characterized by an analogy between performance and interpretation, thus implying that the symbolic act in its very form carries the interpretation *in nuce*. When Isaiah appears naked in the city, it is a message of disaster (Isa. 20). Broken pottery made anew promises a new beginning (Jer. 18), and a broken jug signifies judgment (Jer. 19). Paul's hands and feet bound with a belt pave the way for an utterance about his forthcoming arrest (Acts 21). Thus the interpretation brings out more explicitly what is already available in the performance, albeit not always equally explicitly. Formally speaking, none of the healing stories follow this basic structure. But this analogy is still helpful for grasping the full meaning of the healings in the Gospels.

Let me take two examples. In Mark's Gospel it is obvious that seeing and hearing include the dimension of understanding or grasping the proclamation of Jesus (8:18–21, following the tradition of Isa. 6:9–10). Immediately after Jesus has spoken of blindness and hearing in such terms follows the story of his healing of a blind man (Mark 8:22–26). This juxtaposition adds a metaphorical dimension to the healing story in a manner that paves the way for what is fully developed in John 9 and the signs in the Fourth Gospel.

Matthew has gathered the bulk of his healing stories in chapters 8–9. It is worthwhile looking at them from the perspective of symbolic acts. According to Matthew 9:2–8, Jesus healed a paralytic and also forgave him his sins. Jesus has the authority *(exousia)* to do both. The authority of Jesus is an issue in these chapters. He has power over sickness, sin, nature, and demons, all demonstrated through a series of stories. Hence, together they portray Jesus' unique power at work. Thus the healings are to be found among christological demonstrations of Jesus' identity. The healing of the paralytic, however, also becomes an action that visually demonstrates Jesus' power to forgive sins. Jesus' "making firm the feeble knees" (Isa. 35:3; cf. Heb. 12:12–13) is a symbolic act of his complete restoration of the man. Hence, the question of sin continues in the immediately following text (Matt. 9:9–13): "Those who are well have no need of a physician, but those who are sick. . . . For I have come to call not the righteous but sinners" (vv. 12–13). All this finds corroboration in Matthew's special interest in forgiveness of sins (Matt. 1:21; 26:28; cf. 20:28).

Furthermore, in three citations from the Old Testament (Matt. 8:17; 9:13, 36), Matthew conveys that Jesus' healings are fulfillments of what has been promised. The fulfillment formula in 8:17 attracts attention here: "This was to fulfill what had been spoken through the prophet Isaiah, 'He took [*elaben*] our infirmities [*astheneias*] and bore [*ebastasen*] our diseases [*nosous*].'" This citation from Isaiah 53:4 is close to the Hebrew text, but distant from the Septuagint's metaphorical interpretation.[19]

The above citation corresponds exactly to the situation, and there is no doubt that physical healing is intended here. Since the text from which Matthew quotes is elsewhere in early Christian texts associated with Jesus' atoning death (1 Pet. 2:24; 1 John 3:5; Rom. 4:25), the question that arises is whether physical healing and health are included in the atoning death of Jesus. Did Jesus carry our sickness on his crucified body? It is justified to ask how much can be made of this citation. As pointed out by many scholars, there is no mention of vicarious suffering at this point in Matthew's text. Nor do the verbs in themselves imply a substitutionary action; they may simply refer to an act of removal. The servant who takes on himself the suffering of the sick is hardly implied. Thus no particular nexus appears between the suffering of Jesus and his healing ministry.[20] Can the entire servant theology and substitutionary suffering of Isaiah 53 really be implied here? To suggest as much would be a fallacy very much on the order of James Barr's famous "fallacy of totality transfer" with regard to how the meaning of a given term is to be decided by the immediate context rather than by including all options listed in dictionaries as relevant for all its occurrences.[21] The scope of Matthew's citation is much more limited, and simply points out that the biblical prophecy is now coming true.

Nonetheless, it is clearly implied elsewhere in the New Testament that Christ's death and resurrection subdued all evil powers (Eph. 1:21; Col. 2:15),[22] and hence also resulted in redemption of the body (Rom. 8:21-23; 1 Cor. 15:43, 49, 53; Phil. 3:21), and therefore also an end to all bodily pains

---

19. It is possible that *eirēnē*, traditionally rendered "peace," in Isa. 53:5 may mean "health" as it may also in Isa. 57:18-19; Jer. 6:14; Judg. 18:15 (B); and Sir. 38:8; see Louise Wells, *The Greek Language of Healing from Homer to New Testament Times* (Berlin: De Gruyter, 1998), pp. 106-7. For the terminology of Isa. 53 as referring to healing, see Sigurd Kaiser, *Krankenheilung: Untersuchungen zu Form, Sprache, traditionsgeschichtlichem Hintergrund und Aussage zu Jak 5,13-18* (Neukirchen-Vluyn: Neukirchener Verlag, 2006), pp. 91-95.

20. See John Nolland, *The Gospel of Matthew*, New International Greek Testament Commentary (Grand Rapids: Eerdmans, 2005), pp. 361-62; Luz, *Matthew 8-20*, p. 14.

21. James Barr, *The Semantics of Biblical Language* (Oxford: Oxford University Press, 1961).

22. Central to this idea is also the use of Ps. 110, the most frequently cited text from the Old Testament in the New Testament.

(Rev. 21:4). In a wider New Testament perspective, therefore, the healings become tokens of what Jesus will one day accomplish also for haunted bodies. This brings us back to the topic of restoring the intended creation. In their partiality, the healing stories are symbolic acts of what the future will bring in full.

The preceding chapters have worked out that the healing ministry of Jesus provided more than the means of cure. The healings are enveloped in a cosmic vision of redemption that involves coping with suffering at large. Amanda Porterfield points this out in saying that "along with the actual healing that might be stimulated by faith in a higher power, this imputation of meaning to suffering has itself been a tonic."[23] Relief from suffering is a sign of the power and meaning of faith, and provides images of hope even when cure does not occur. This aspect of Jesus' ministry has also stimulated care for the sick and dying on a general basis, including the use of current medicine. Thus the healing ministry of Jesus holds together the vision of redemptive care that has made Christianity "a religion of healing."[24]

Jesus the Healer — Exclusive?

The theological parameters within which Jesus' healing activities are understood above may be taken to support his uniqueness as healer.[25] He is then also likely to be seen as the only healer, just as God was seen as Israel's only healer according to a number of passages among which Exodus 15:26 holds pride of place: "I will not bring upon you any of the diseases that I brought upon the Egyptians, for I am the Lord who heals you [LXX: *ho iōmenos se*]."[26] Such exclusive dicta pave the way for contrasting Jesus' healings to medicine in general. The story of Jesus' healing the hemorrhaging woman (Mark 5:25-34 par.) may likewise be used to present Jesus in opposition to contemporary medicine. According to Mark 5:26, the woman had suffered much from many physicians, and spent all her money on them, but "she was

23. Amanda Porterfield, *Healing in the History of Christianity* (Oxford: Oxford University Press, 2005), p. 4.

24. Porterfield, *Healing in the History of Christianity*, p. 2. Thus also Adolf von Harnack, *Die Mission und Ausbreitung des Christentums in den ersten drei Jahrhunderten*, 4th ed. (Wiesbaden: VMA-Verlag, 1924), pp. 129-50, speaks of "Religion der Erlösung" in a context where healing is addressed.

25. See pp. 21-24 above.

26. See also Gen. 20:17; Deut. 32:39; Job 5:18; Hos. 6:1; Jer. 17:14.

no better [*mēden ōphelētheisa*], but rather grew worse." In Luke it says: "and though she had spent all she had on physicians, no one could help her" (Luke 8:43). This piece of information primarily serves to enhance her helpless situation, but an implicit critique against physicians may also be extracted from it. It is worth noticing that in many manuscripts, this Lukan verse is missing, for example, in Papyrus 75 and Vaticanus. Hence, this sentence is bracketed in Nestle-Aland's 28th edition, thus indicating doubt regarding its authenticity. The manuscripts in question date from a time when it was a well-established tradition that Luke's Gospel was written by Luke the physician.[27] It is possible that the relatively poor attestation for the bracketed text is an indication that this piece of information was deemed by many to be inappropriate in a physician's Gospel. It follows from this that the text in question had the potential to be used critically against physicians, and thus to substantiate the view that Jesus was the only healer. It is, however, also clear that some copyists found this exclusive view to be questionable.

This raises the question of how exclusively Jesus' healings are to be understood. Were they, and their perpetuation among his followers, the only option for remedying sickness? Or were God's healing powers also available in healing practices provided outside the church? This is, of course, a question with historical implications: What did the Christians actually do when they fell ill? Most likely they did not act in the same way as pagans. However, at the present, the aim is to address this question from a theological angle.

The talmudic tractate on idolatry (*Abodah Zara* 55a) renders a story from the Diaspora in which a Jew is troubled by what he observes at a pagan temple, most likely a temple dedicated to Asclepius, the god of medicine and health in the Greco-Roman world. He watches people who arrive sick at the temple precincts and in due time leave restored to health. This bothers the pious Jew, and his observation becomes an occasion for instruction on the matter. The base level of the argument is that demons have power, including the ability to heal, an explanation in keeping with the main perspective of this tractate, namely, idolatry. This brings to mind the pattern discernible in Mark 3:22 and parallels: Jesus heals, but he is thought to be assisted by Beelzebul. Many Christians' attitudes to their surrounding society were similar. Since the available means of healing were woven into the very fabric of religion, medical treatment outside the church was dismissed as idolatry. Such debate is documented in relevant Jewish texts.

---

27. See "The Muratorian Canon," in *After the New Testament: A Reader in Early Christianity*, ed. Bart D. Ehrman (Oxford: Oxford University Press, 1999), p. 311.

The society in which Jesus lived and worked had witnessed debates on what it meant that God was Israel's healer. How exclusively was this to be understood? In two recent studies, Maria Chrysovergi has demonstrated that Jewish attitudes to emerging rational medical art (Hippocratic medicine) varied, from rejection to embrace.[28] Contemporary medicine included questions of diet, pharmacy or herbs, and surgery as described by Celsus, a contemporary of Paul, in his *De Medicina* and in works of Galen and Soranus, both first to second century. These works do not necessarily represent conventional knowledge and practice of their time, but knowledge of them is certainly assumed both in Jewish and Christian writings of antiquity. It is equally witnessed that the medical art did not always bring healing.

In the book of Tobit, Tobit sleeps outdoors under the roof of his house. Because of the heat, his head is uncovered, and some sparrow droppings fall into his eyes, causing white spots to form on them. This text is found in two Greek versions, a shorter and a longer one, as well as in Latin and Syrian.[29] I here confine myself to rendering the two Greek versions.

> Shorter version (G1): "I went to physicians and they did not benefit me [*ouk ōphelēsan me*]" (cf. Mark 5:26).
>
> Longer version (G2): "I went to physicians to be healed, but the more they anointed me with the medicines [*ta pharmaka*], the more my vision was obscured by the white films, until I became completely blind" (Tob. 2:10).

The treatment Tobit receives by the physicians blinds him completely, and for four years he is unable to see. His healing in this story is intimately intertwined with finding a remedy that will offer protection against demon possession. The angel Raphael instructs Tobias, Tobit's son, to cut open a fish he has

28. Maria Chrysovergi, "Attitudes towards the Use of Medicine in Jewish Literature from the Third and Second Century B.C.E." (Ph.D. diss., Durham University, 2011, http://etheses .dur.ac.uk/3568); and also her "Contrasting Views on Physicians in Tobit and Sirach," *Journal for the Study of the Pseudepigrapha* 21 (2011): 37-54. According to Pliny, "Physicians acquire their knowledge from our dangers, making experiments at the cost of our lives [*experimenta per mortes*]. Only a physician can commit homicide with complete impunity" (*Natural History* 1.29.8, 18). This is a reminder that we should not think too highly of the rational experimental medicine at this time. In *Natural History* 1.29, Pliny gives a lengthy and detailed presentation of ancient medicine and treatments. The picture rendered here is more complex than Gary B. Ferngren's emphasis on naturalistic medicine in his *Medicine and Health Care in Early Christianity* (Baltimore: Johns Hopkins University Press, 2009) (see the previous chapter).

29. Chrysovergi, "Attitudes," pp. 109-14.

caught, and to take out the gall, heart, and liver (Tob. 6:5). The medical value of this is that any evil demon will flee from the smoke when the intestines are burned. Furthermore, the gall can be used as an ointment to heal eyes with white spots (Tob. 6:7–8),[30] thus giving him a cure for his father's blindness.

Two observations are important for interpreting Tobit's view on ancient medicine. In the first place, the appearance of Raphael, the angel,[31] is clearly a divine intervention. Thus the recipe is given as revealed medical knowledge. It is stated explicitly in Tobit 12:14–15 that Raphael acts on divine instructions. In the second place, Tobias is portrayed as a pious Jew, devoted to his ancestral traditions, which also make him an opponent of any kind of cultural exchange that amounts to syncretism. This is the backdrop against which the whole story must be read. "In this way, the physicians' pharmacological treatment could by no means have been efficacious, as they did not stem from God."[32] The only successful remedy is prescribed by God and revealed by Raphael. Thus God is the only true healer.

The praise of the physicians in the book of Sirach represents a contrastive view, where the idea of God as Israel's healer (Sir. 38:2) is interpreted in light of a creation theology deeply rooted in Old Testament wisdom thinking.

> Honor physicians for their services,
>   for the Lord created them;
> for their gift of healing comes from the Most High,
>   and they are rewarded by the king.
> The skill of physicians makes them distinguished,
>   and in the presence of the great they are admired.
> The Lord created medicines out of the earth,
>   and the sensible will not despise them.
> Was not water made sweet with a tree
>   in order that its power might be known?
> And he gave skill to human beings
>   that he might be glorified in his marvelous works.
> By them the physician heals and takes away pain;
>   the pharmacist makes a mixture from them.

---

30. Chrysovergi, "Attitudes," pp. 145–47, has collected medical texts in which these ingredients are considered helpful.

31. "I have come" (Tob. 5:5) is indicative of a divine mandate.

32. Thus Chrysovergi, "Attitudes," p. 154.

God's works will never be finished;
    and from him health spreads over all the earth.
My child, when you are ill, do not delay,
    but pray to the Lord, and he will heal you.
Give up your faults and direct your hands rightly,
    and cleanse your heart from all sin.
Offer a sweet-smelling sacrifice, and a memorial portion of choice flour,
    and pour oil on your offering, as much as you can afford.
Then give the physician his place, for the Lord created him;
    do not let him leave you, for you need him.
There may come a time when recovery lies in the hands of physicians.
    (Sir. 38:1–13)

Sirach claims divine origin for the medical profession. Through his creation, God is the ultimate source of medicine, and thus also of the cures provided by physicians. That God "created medicines out of earth" most likely refers to rational herbal medical treatment as opposed to magic or religiously inspired means. Herbs[33] are divine gifts that are helpful in bringing healing, and this knowledge is part of divine providence. Prayer and seeking help from those with medical skills are not contradictory to Sirach. While Tobit saw healing as exclusively connected to God, and thus considers Hippocratic medicine as prone to syncretism and idolatry, Sirach views healing from a creation-theological perspective in line with the first sentence in his writing: "All wisdom is from the Lord" (Sir. 1:1). This implies that all wisdom, wherever it is found, owes its existence to the creator God.

The physicians' skills in using plants, trees, and herbs are properly seen as the work of the Creator. Additionally, it must be pointed out that the methods of the physicians described here find no real correspondence in the rituals used by Jesus in the Gospels, which are more mysterious than these. According to Sirach, the work of the physicians is God's ongoing work, which does not cease when illness occurs. However, since medicine in antiquity was so often interwoven with religious practices, traditional healing and contemporary medicine were intertwined and not easily separated. Physicians often operated within a context that was in some way religious, and hence labeled by some Jews as idolatrous. This caused, as we have seen, two fundamentally different views on medicine.

33. For the use of plants, herbs, and other ingredients in medicine, see Pliny's extensive presentation in *Natural History* 1.23–32.

In my book *The Challenge of Homer* (2009) I demonstrated that early Christianity staged a similar debate, not on medicine, but on Greek learning and philosophy.[34] One of the dividing lines here was the issue of whether knowledge was received through revelation or creation. Those who argued that Christians should relate exclusively to knowledge revealed in Christian beliefs, as found in the Bible, paved the way for Christians to withdraw from the intellectual legacy of society.[35] Other Christians reasoned in ways very similar to Sirach above. Due to the belief that "the earth and its fullness are the Lord's" (Ps 24:1 = 1 Cor. 10:26), useful and helpful knowledge was thought to be found even within paganism.

A creation-theological perspective paves the way for looking at ancient medicine in a similar way, even when it is embedded in religious contexts. Knowledge given through creation may be labeled the "despoliation of Egypt," or "the silver and gold of the Egyptians." This phrase is taken from Exodus 11:2–3 and 12:35–36, and became in early Christian interpretation a slogan for both the necessity and legitimacy of finding and making use of what was beneficial in paganism.[36] As I demonstrated in *The Challenge of Homer,* this slogan proceeds from the conviction that God as Creator is at work outside the church as well; hence God's work in caring for his creation is not exclusively bound to the church. This biblical story of "the silver and

34. Karl Olav Sandnes, *The Challenge of Homer: School, Pagan Poets and Early Christianity* (London: T&T Clark, 2009).

35. Andrew Daunton-Fear, *Healing in the Early Church: The Church's Ministry of Healing and Exorcism from the First to the Fifth Century* (Milton Keynes, UK: Paternoster, 2009) mentions Tatian in his *Oration to the Greeks* (*Orat.* 18.1–3). Tatian, student of Justin Martyr, urges a contrast between medicine *(pharmakeia)* and the power of God. He considers medicine to be a power of demons. To seek help from *pharmakeia* is to Tatian equal to distrust in God. Medicine is, according to Tatian, among the "things of this world." A somewhat different, but still related, view is found in Arnobius (late second century), *Against the Nations* 1.48 and 3.23. He says that physicians often bring more harm than help, most likely an experience that sometimes found substantiation. The first text is more interesting, however. With reference to the fact that Jesus healed with commands or touching, he claims that Jesus was distinct from contemporary healers or gods associated with healing. He does not deny that herbs, diets, walking, resting, or abstaining from certain things — all common medical advice — are helpful. On the contrary, he assumes the helpfulness of these things, but claims the superiority of Jesus' healings over against all this: "It is a disgrace to a god that he is not able to effect it of himself, but that he gives soundness and safety *only* by the aid of external objects" (ANF 6:426).

36. Christian Gnilka, *CHRÊSIS: Die Methode der Kirchenväter im Umgang mit der Antiken Kultur,* vol. 1, *Der Begriff des "rechten Gebrauchs"* (Basel: Schwabe, 1984); Joel Stevens Allen, *The Despoliation of Egypt in Pre-rabbinic, Rabbinic and Patristic Sources* (Leiden: Brill, 2008); Sandnes, *Challenge of Homer.*

gold of the Egyptians" served as an encouragement to make use of the best in paganism, while simultaneously sifting the good from the bad. The classical example of this is that some of "the silver and gold of the Egyptians" became building material for the golden calf, the sin par excellence, while some of the same valuables became vessels in the holy temple. It all depended on how these valuables were used. Although this reasoning in early Christian sources is not applied to contemporary medicine, it is nevertheless likely that arguments ran according to these dividing lines. Furthermore, these debates are, in the present context, primarily of interest as hermeneutical aids.[37] It is also worth noticing that Augustine, based on the idea of "the silver and gold of Egypt," developed the concept of knowledge *found/discovered* or *produced,* be it within or outside the church. He even takes this into the field of medical herbs (*Doctr. chr.* 2.110).[38] The healing power of herbs is found or discovered by human beings, but not established by them. This power is the Creator God at work. From that perspective, medical art is divinely given knowledge, and not in itself to be contrasted with Christian faith. There is, says Augustine, a great difference between suggesting that someone suffering from a stomachache should eat a certain herb, and advising them to hang the same herb around their neck for magical purposes. From this follows that creation and redemption are not to be played off against each other, as often happens in questions of healing among Christians. Hence, it is also natural to assume that Jesus is at work as a healer in a way that encapsulates both creation and redemption, to use theological currency that reaches back to the last chapters of the Christian canon, Revelation 21–22.

37. Ferngren, *Medicine and Health Care,* p. 13, argues likewise.

38. Sandnes, *The Challenge of Homer,* pp. 227-28. It is worth noticing that even Tertullian, elsewhere known as antagonistic vis-à-vis knowledge derived from pagans, in his *The Crown* 8 explicitly mentions medicine in tandem with letters and music as useful necessities that provide help for human beings. This applies, he says, even if Asclepius is seen as the one who discovered the cures.

PART II

Jesus as Healer and Contemporary Theology

Jan-Olav Henriksen

Approaches to Healing and Related Topics
in Science and Theology

"He received them, and spoke to them of the kingdom of God, and healed them that had need of healing" (Luke 9:11). This short verse may stand as a headline over the ministry of Jesus, as the New Testament records it. In the previous part of this book, we have highlighted some of the main elements related to Jesus' healing practice as it was perceived in the memory of the early church, and we can conclude that one of the main aspects of Jesus' ministry is clearly that he was a healer. Against the backdrop of this conclusion, we then have to ask: What is the enduring theological significance of the fact that Jesus was a healer?

There are several presuppositions behind this question: First and foremost, the question assumes that it is an important challenge to discern the possible contemporary theological significance of understanding Jesus' historical ministry as a healer. We shall see, however, that in the tradition no obvious and immediately accessible theology has been developed around this theme. In different ways, both historical and contemporary sources seem to complicate the conditions for the understanding of the significance of Jesus as healer, be it due to historical, theological, and/or medical reasons. Second, the fact that Jesus was a healer cannot be seen as an immediate attestation to his divinity per se, as one often sees in more popular religious interpretations of his healing ministry. Other people also seem to have access to healing powers, both in the time of Jesus[1] and today. This is true of both people who belong to the Christian tradition and of people outside it. Accordingly, the relation between the claim to Jesus' divine status and the human possession of healing powers needs to be scrutinized and considered more carefully with regard to the articulation of their possible theological implications and conditions.

1. See for this also the material in the previous part of the book, pp. 22–23.

Taken together, these reflections imply that even the basic conditions for establishing the theological implications of understanding Jesus as a healer cannot in any way be taken for granted. In this part of the book, we will discuss the conditions for this theological significance with respect to how they may be established in a way that is both in accordance with the previous part's presentation of the biblical material and in relation to contemporary theology and contemporary knowledge about healing in general.

Before presenting an outline of relevant positions and the discussion of topics related to a systematic interpretation, let me make a note on the material used in this section of the book: There are few predominantly systematic-theological accounts or discourses about Jesus as healer in contemporary theology. We have many presentations of healing in the Bible (e.g., Gaiser, Darling, Wilkinson), and also some of healing in the history of Christianity up until recently (Porterfield). Among the more contemporary-oriented studies, scholarly works on the practices of spiritual healers dominate (Parsons, Pattison, Lindström). And more than anything, there is a vast literature on testimonies of healing from people involved in actual practices or ministries of healing (MacNutt, Parsons, Keener, et al.). Much of this literature has been reviewed in preparation for this book, and is to some extent also tacitly incorporated in the reflections that follow. At times, I also engage more directly with these studies. To the extent that healing is a theme in contemporary systematic-theological discourse, it is most commonly seen as a part of the *miracles,* which have been debated since the Enlightenment. In much of this discussion, healing as such is therefore not the main topic, but rather the assumed miraculous character of the healings. This situation has led to a general de-emphasis of the theological significance of healing as such, though not in all contexts and not without exceptions. As the reader will see, we find the whole discussion of healing as miracle somewhat misleading, and we suggest that the close relation between the notions should be dissolved.

Given this situation in the scholarly literature, a more robust systematic approach is called for — but an approach that is also informed by the existing literature and the perspectives already present there. I should also say from the outset that the approach here is shaped by my own experience with reports of healing as practiced in a more private, though not completely unchurched context. Previous work of a more ethnographic character relating to such reports[2] has thus also led me to insights into some of what

---

2. See Jan-Olav Henriksen and Kathrin Pabst, *Uventet og ubedt: Paranormale erfaringer*

is going on in the contemporary world with regard to healing. It is against the background of these previous studies and experiences that I find it important to develop a more comprehensive and contemporary theological understanding of Jesus as healer.

In order to establish a contemporary context for assessing the theological significance of Jesus as healer, we must, first of all, get a better grasp of what healing is and how it may be understood. It is only against this backdrop that we can then in turn discuss contemporary and historically given positions with regard to healing, and evaluate their possible gains or shortcomings. Accordingly, from the outset, there are several separate, although interrelated, issues that we need to address in order to provide a grounded understanding of Jesus as healer.

1. How should we understand healing in light of contemporary knowledge? Only after having answered this question may we in turn ask:
2. In what way should we apply the notion of "miracle" to phenomena that involve healing? Only on the basis of a discussion and clarification of these issues are we then in turn able to ask the following:
3. What kind of significance does Jesus as healer have for theology, both in historically given positions and when it comes to a theology that is relevant for Christian believers today?

The first question, what is healing? also opens onto contemporary discussions about healing in a wider and interreligious context, and for understanding healing in relation to placebo and more general issues of medicine and health. The second question then opens up issues related to philosophical understandings of laws of nature, as well as to understandings of what it is to be a human being who is more than a physical and biological organism. Finally, addressing the third and most comprehensive question, we will turn to help from contemporary literature within theology and other disciplines.

---

i møte med tradisjonell tro (Unexpected and uninvited: paranormal experiences encountering traditional belief) (Oslo: Universitetsforlaget, 2013).

What Is Healing?

Healing Researched under "Scientific" Conditions and in Contemporary Discussion

There exists no agreement about what healing is. You can ask people in the medical profession, people confessing the Christian faith, people who have a background in the New Age movement or in African traditional medicine, and they could all provide you with different answers. What is not in question, though, is the fact that "healing" serves as a notion of puzzle, controversy, and wonder. It often seems to denote experiences of health improvement, restoration, or recovery that are not easily captured by the established parameters of modern Western thought and a science based on controlled empirical data, and that cannot be explained with reference to the causes described by and investigated in such science. The notion of "healing" thus describes experiences or alleged experiences that people are aware of, and that some also try to learn more about. Accordingly, due to the conceptual and empirical problems related to the phenomena described by the category of healing, one is probably well advised *not* to offer a brief definition of healing, as this might in turn contribute to eliminating important aspects from one's attention. Instead, we should look at actual experiences of what people call healing, and develop an understanding based on those experiences.[1] In the present section, I will present and discuss some of the work done in order to interpret and clarify the phenomenon of healing from the point of view of psychology, science, and theology.[2]

---

1. See Stephen Pattison, "Healing: A Flight from Definition," in *The Challenge of Practical Theology: Selected Essays* (London and Philadelphia: Jessica Kingsley Publishers, 2007), pp. 125–32.

2. The ambiguity of the notion of healing can also be found in church documents that

From the outset, then, it seems important to state that healing does not seem to be only one "thing": healing takes place in various shapes, forms, practices, and contexts. This makes it harder, of course, to delineate one comprehensive concept of healing, or to describe healing as *one* phenomenon. Also, when we look at the practices of Jesus as reported in the New Testament, healing was sometimes performed by the laying on of hands, and at other times he undertook what contemporary researchers may call "distance healing." Jesus sometimes used some medium or material to heal, but at other times he did not. In the light of contemporary works on healing from a psychological and anthropological point of view, this is not surprising. Healing is not easily assigned to one category of practice, or only present in one specific type of effect.

The phenomenon of healing has often been met with suspicion by those working from the perspective of biomedical science. The reason is evident: healing is a phenomenon that cannot be studied exhaustively from the reductionist approach of established medicine. Furthermore, healing often seems to depend on an interplay between the physical, psychological, social, and environmental conditions of human existence. In the following quotation, anthropologist Thomas Csordas describes healing almost poetically in a manner that allows for a multilevel investigation that enables us to see its different dimensions:

> Healing at its most human is not an escape into irreality and mystification, but an intensification of the encounter between suffering and hope at the moment in which it finds a voice, where the anguished clash of bare life and raw existence emerges from muteness into articulation. An understanding of healing as an existential process requires description of the processes of treatment and specification of concrete psychological and social effects of therapeutic practices, as well as determination of what counts as an illness in need of treatment in particular cultural contexts, and when it can be said that a cure has been effected. However complex, this task constitutes an essential problem of meaning in anthropology, for it is concerned with the fundamental question of what it means to be a human being, whole and healthy, or

---

seem to include various phenomena, from psychotherapy and healing of memories via medical treatment to forgiveness and more alternative modes of therapy, as healing. See, e.g., the report of the Church of England, *A Time to Heal: A Contribution to the Ministry of Healing; A Report for the House of Bishops on the Healing Ministry* (London: Church House Publishing, 2000).

distressed and diseased. The interpretive dimension of the problem is highlighted by the fact that many forms of healing are religious in nature, which requires accounting for the role of divine forces and entities. Given the prevalence of religious healing and the global interrelation of religion and healing, the category of the holy may in its own way be fundamental to our understanding of health and health problems. A complete account of religious healing per se would then have not only to examine the construction of clinical reality with respect to medical motives, but also the construction of sacred reality with respect to religious motives.[3]

Accordingly, healing has in recent years been studied from the perspectives of the humanities (including theology and religious studies), social sciences (including anthropology and sociology), and psychology. Different research paradigms have been involved. It is also important to recognize that faith is always involved in some way or another in these studies, although faith does not produce or constitute the results of the research. Faith may in some way or another be relevant for what one looks for and is able to detect, and is also relevant for the perspectives one chooses in order to interpret the data in question. Craig Keener comments wisely on this:

> Those who start from theistic assumptions may view all recoveries as divine grace, whether demonstrably supernatural (i.e., not readily admitting naturalistic explanations) or not. By contrast, as I have noted, those who start from antisupernaturalist assumptions sometimes rule out all supernaturalist explanations even if no purely natural explanation is readily available, by merely postulating that a naturalistic explanation may be possible when more is known about nature or about the particulars of the recovery. Antisupernaturalists and antitheists should be clear, however, that they are filtering information through an interpretive grid no less than the theist is. Those who do not a priori rule out supernatural factors, awaiting some evidence, will neither dismiss nor endorse all cases. They will find some cases more compelling than others and thus need to critically evaluate claims on a case-by-case basis.[4]

3. Thomas J. Csordas, *Body/Meaning/Healing* (New York: Palgrave Macmillan, 2002), p. 11.

4. Craig S. Keener, *Miracles: The Credibility of the New Testament Accounts*, 2 vols. (Grand Rapids: Baker Academic, 2011), p. 743.

Keener's dichotomy between supernatural and antisupernatural positions may be too strong. As I will argue later, these notions are not the most fruitful for entering the field. However, his main point, about how one filters information and considers relevant possibilities based on what kind of worldview one has, remains important. One of the main challenges to a more open-minded contemporary investigation of healing is a dogmatically assumed biomedical paradigm that is not able to recognize any relevant data outside its own established parameters. This is perhaps the most important restriction that Keener's reflection can make us aware of.

LeShan's Study of Healers

Among the groundbreaking works on healing, Lawrence LeShan's study *The Medium, the Mystic, and the Physicist: Toward a General Theory of the Paranormal* (1974)[5] is often mentioned. LeShan's study takes its point of departure from psychology, but moves quite openly into other fields as well. Although some of the theoretical assumptions behind his *interpretations* may seem speculative, the most important element in his studies is that he has conducted scientifically rigorous experiments and observations. On the other hand, he also addresses critical attitudes toward phenomena like healing on the contemporary scene, whether they come from a more scientific or scientistic[6] point of view, or from the ranks of the religiously orthodox who hold that all that matters is the proclamation of God's words and the right distribution of the sacraments. In such cases, LeShan says, one is confronted with three options: (1) To say that things like these do not happen and that any reports of such events are fake, fraud, and so on; (2) to acknowledge that they happen but try to ignore them and hope they will "go away"; or (3) to accept that they happen, but relate to them only as entertainment, without engaging seriously with them (p. xiii). Almost forty years later, it is not hard to see that we are still often confronted with these very options in this area of research. Furthermore, as LeShan says, none of these attitudes are very constructive from a scholarly or scientific point of view (p. xiii).

5. Lawrence LeShan, *The Medium, the Mystic, and the Physicist: Toward a General Theory of the Paranormal* (New York: Viking, 1974). References to this work are in parentheses in the text until further notice.

6. For a critical examination of scientism in contemporary thought, also in fields related to religion, cf. Mikael Stenmark, *Scientism: Science, Ethics, and Religion* (Aldershot, UK: Ashgate, 2001).

LeShan sees the reluctance to study phenomena such as healing more seriously as an expression of the effects and the status of the success of modern science. Such science has undoubtedly been of huge importance for the development of the modern world, and there are good reasons for holding on to whatever ideas have made this success possible. Against this backdrop, the rejection of healing (and other phenomena that are difficult to explain) by contemporary scientists can be seen as based on a perception that they may weaken the status of causality and law in science, and thereby undermine the very foundation of the modern world. Concomitant to this observation is the belief that if such undermining takes place, the "way will be opened for the introduction in thin disguise of all the magic and superstition which they have fought against so hard and long" (p. 198). In other words, the reluctance to seriously address phenomena like healing, especially from a scholarly point of view, may have to do with the desire to not have to relate to worldviews and experiences that may challenge the foundations of science. This is, one may say, a fairly irrational approach if one really believes that science and scholarly work may enlighten us about what happens in the world. It should be possible to discuss and study healing without having to give up the gains and advantages of the modern world. It should, moreover, also be a phenomenon that it is possible to accept as having a place in many peoples' experience, without necessarily having to accept a given religious understanding of it. It is with these considerations in mind, then, that the primary goal of the following is, first, to address some of the scholarly work on healing as such, and second, to look into the theological and religious significance that can be attributed to it.[7]

Many scholars refer somewhat dismissively to stories about alleged healing both in the contemporary world and in history as "anecdotal evidence." This is not surprising, given the uncontrolled and everyday character that such stories often (but not always) exhibit. However, the fact that the stories are anecdotal is in no way a reason to dismiss them as unimportant for analyzing and understanding the phenomenon of healing. But as stories, they may be more easily studied from the point of view of the humanities and the social sciences than from that of natural science and medicine. This being said, there are other forms of evidence than the anecdotal that can

---

7. This is, admittedly, not an uncontroversial position. Some healers might object that faith is needed for healing to become an actual reality. There is, however, no evidence that this has to be the case or is a necessary condition. There are healers without any specific faith, just as there are healees with a rather skeptical approach to the phenomenon.

be presented with regard to the phenomenon of healing. LeShan divides the evidence for such phenomena in scientific journals into two types: anecdotal (events that happened to occur, in or out of the laboratory) and experimental (carefully planned and supervised under specified conditions in the laboratory) (p. 17). Furthermore, he holds that even some of the "anecdotal" evidence, of which he was trained to be skeptical, has some bearing on how we address and relate to these phenomena (pp. 17–18). This is, in turn, the reason why LeShan is especially relevant to our task of finding out more about the phenomenon of healing as such, because he has conducted supervised experiments on healing.

After having studied the phenomenon under controlled circumstances, LeShan divided the healings he could observe into two categories, Type 1 and Type 2. He describes them as follows: In Type 1, which he holds to be the more important, "the healer goes into an altered state of consciousness in which he views himself and the healee as one entity." Here the point is to unite with and tune in to the other (p. 106), and to focus on them with love and care. There is not one "subject" and one "object" of healing; instead, the unity between the two opens up to the biological processes necessary for healing (pp. 107–8). This unity does, however, heavily depend on the consciousness of the healer. In order to enable this united consciousness, healers use different "techniques." LeShan reports:

> Some prayed, some attempted to look at the healee from God's view-point or to see him as he looked from the spirit world, and some were able to describe what they did without much of an explanatory system. All agreed, however, that there must be intense caring and a viewing of the healee within a framework in which healer and healee could become one entity in a larger context without either of the two losing their individuality. Indeed, both would have their uniqueness enhanced by becoming one as do two people who fall in love. (p. 108)

LeShan interprets the unity between healer and healee as one in which the healer takes part in a clairvoyant reality, and thereby in resources that are somehow transmitted to the healee. It is hard to assess such claims, but there is one significant effect here that has scholarly as well as potential theological implications: No matter how one considers these metaphysical assumptions, the treatment helps the healee to return and find one's place in reality again, and to feel at home in the universe. They are no longer cut off from reality due to their own sickness. This is an experience in which the healee's "being," their "uniqueness," their "individuality" is enhanced. Under these conditions, positive biological changes sometimes occurred, he reports (p. 109). Furthermore, LeShan writes that "The healers — and this is particularly true of those with a Christian approach — make this statement quite clearly. They view 'wholeness' and 'holiness' as having the same meaning, as they did in the original meaning of the words" (p. 109).

We may detect the potential theological significance of this if we look at what happens when Jesus heals: The restitution of the healee is not only biological in character but also has social and spiritual implications. By being included in community with Jesus and his followers, the healee can experience a new unity that makes healing an experience with different layers: biological, social, psychological, and spiritual.[8] To "reduce" healing only to biological causes, or to biological effects, would therefore be misleading. Healing also has the biological effects that LeShan and others write about — and thus cannot be reduced to "mere psychology." Here, one may in fact see healing against the backdrop of what is theologically possible to identify as the cooperation of nature and grace (a distinction I will return to later).

The other type of healing that LeShan identifies in his studies, Type 2, is different from an experiential point of view. Here the healers may perceive a pattern of activity between their palms, or "flows of energy" from them: "The hands are so placed — one on each side of the healee's pathological area — so that this 'flow of energy' is perceived to 'pass through' the troubled area" in ways that the healer conceives as "healing energy" that "cures" or "treats" the sick area. The healee often experiences this as different forms of heat. LeShan says that about 50 percent of the healers he researched have experiences of this kind, whereas a smaller percentage (about 10 percent in his research) "report a sensation of a great deal of 'activity' in the area and very few report a sensation of 'cold'" (pp. 112-13). When the healer's hands are held on each side of a healthy area, no similar responses are reported (p. 113).

Because LeShan distinguishes so clearly between Types 1 and 2, he is also able to describe their different features by saying that in Type 1, the healer unites with the healee, whereas in Type 2, the healer tries to *cure* the healee. Some healers see themselves as the *source* or the origin of their healing powers; others as *mediators.* These differences nevertheless have no consequence for their practices or from the way they experience their work. LeShan also learned how to perform such practices himself, and he

---

8. Cf. the presentation and discussion of the works of John J. Pilch and John D. Crossan in the previous part, esp. pp. 26-33.

concludes: "This much I learned from reading the works of the serious heal-ers, but I could not understand what was going on. Even now I do not have the faintest idea what Type 2 is all about or how it 'works.' And it frequently does 'work,' that is, produces positive biological changes in the healee. I know how to 'do it,' to 'turn on' my hands and teach others how to 'turn on' theirs. It seems perfectly reasonable to me that we may be dealing with some kind of 'energy'" (p. 113).

What LeShan describes seems quite similar to two other practices that are discussed in the literature, namely the so-called Therapeutic Touch[9] and Reiki. In the latter, the healer learns how to regulate the healing energy and to pass it on to the healee. Reiki as a form of healing emerged in Japan in the nineteenth century.[10] From the descriptions of these practices, it seems rea-sonable to think that some of the same conditions and effects are at work in the healing practices LeShan researched. This observation may at least partly contribute to justifying the above claim that what takes place in instances of healing is not just *one* practice and *one* phenomenon, but rather a variety of practices with effects that may have something in common without being completely identical.[11]

LeShan is typical of an approach to healing that Charles Bourne and Fraser Watts find more common in secular circles than in religious ones: here one assumes that people can *train* to become healers. But in a Christian context one may also find examples of people who think that healing can be learned. Among these is the famous American healer Agnes Sanford. According to Bourne and Watts, she found that "it was not just the gift of healing that she needed to pray for, but also the gifts of knowledge, wisdom and other things that she felt were required to use that gift of healing to the best effect."[12] On the other hand, Christians may be reluctant to accept that training is possible in order to develop a capacity for healing, especially if they see it as a charismatic gift. But they may be "more likely to accept that there is a place for personal and spiritual development. In this, Christian

9. For therapeutic touch, see Dolores Krieger, *Therapeutic Touch as Transpersonal Healing* (New York: Lantern, 2002).

10. See on Reiki the description by Charles Bourne and Fraser Watts, "Conceptualiza-tions of Spiritual Healing: Christian and Secular," in *Spiritual Healing: Scientific and Religious Perspectives*, ed. Fraser Watts (Cambridge and New York: Cambridge University Press, 2011), pp. 78–79.

11. For the problem of defining healing, with critical remarks on some of the attitudes toward it in religious circles, see also Pattison, "Healing: A Flight from Definition," pp. 125–31.

12. See Bourne and Watts, "Conceptualizations of Spiritual Healing," p. 79.

healing is quite close to Reiki." Furthermore, "The healer needs first to experience being totally at the disposal of God, and healing is then seen as being dependent on this internal reaching for God."[13]

Bourne and Watts's recent work also critically discusses LeShan's interpretations of his findings. LeShan saw Type 2 as the result of an energy process, but he also suggested that it was a failed attempt at Type 1 healing. Bourne and Watts, however, suggest that "it is equally possible to take the opposite view and to suggest that Type 1 is actually a variant of Type 2, but one in which the healer is too closely identified with the patient for the passing of energy to be experienced."[14] Furthermore, they find that his approach "dichotomizes healing too sharply into two types." They also refer to how "healing in secular settings often emphasizes the more active Type 2 healing, but in Christian settings there is often the opposite emphasis, with healing most commonly being conceptualized as a Type 1 process."[15] This allows them to interpret LeShan's categories in a way that accommodates Christian healing more precisely.

> In the Christian environment the primary focus is on God: prayer and attunement to God give rise to the experience of oneness that characterizes Type 1 healing. In the secular environment it is possible that the healer may also focus on God (although not necessarily the Christian God). However, this focus, being a private matter, may not play an explicit role in either the training or the practice of healing. Though there is a difference of emphasis between secular and Christian environments concerning how far healers see their work in an active or passive way, it would not be appropriate to make the dichotomy too sharp.[16]

The diverse approach to practices in the Christian tradition is also apparent in Bourne and Watts's discussion of the practice of the laying on of hands in a church context. This may from the outset be seen by some as an example of Type 2 healing in LeShan's typology, and this is in accordance with how several other authors perceive what happens during the laying on of

13. Bourne and Watts, "Conceptualizations of Spiritual Healing," p. 80. For more on the overlap and nuances between Christian healers and others, the whole article by Bourne and Watts offers a good overview.

14. LeShan, *The Medium, the Mystic, and the Physicist*, pp. 113–14; Bourne and Watts, "Conceptualizations of Spiritual Healing," pp. 84–85.

15. Bourne and Watts, "Conceptualizations of Spiritual Healing," p. 85.

16. Bourne and Watts, "Conceptualizations of Spiritual Healing," p. 85.

hands.[17] Then the laying on of hands may be used diagnostically to discern hot and cold areas. On the other hand, the laying on of hands is sometimes seen as a symbol of the invocation of the healing power of God, "and so is not critical to how God's healing power is mediated. In this view, it is prayer that is crucial, and the laying on of hands is only symbolic."[18]

When we compare these "Christian" practices with Reiki, both Type 1 and Type 2 seem to be involved. In Reiki, however, it is affirmed that "the position of the hands is not crucial for healing. The energy is intelligent and goes where it is needed."[19] Reiki is also among those practices which hold that healing can be done from a distance[20] (a point that may also be relevant in interpreting some of the New Testament material), a fact that may in turn suggest that healing is not totally dependent on the activity or placing on of hands (despite the fact that this often seems to be the preferred Christian practice, supposedly for both symbolic and experiential reasons).

It is also worth noting that the healers whom LeShan researched did not have any mass gatherings (healing rallies).[21] In this regard, they are in consonance with Francis MacNutt and others who prefer to see healing as an intimate relation and not as something spectacular. Furthermore, we should also note here that while some healers are initiated into their practice by others (as would be the case with Reiki, some traditional healers,[22] and Therapeutic Touch), others may discover their gifts more by accident, or receive them as a result of specific events that have taken place (in the latter case, they may also, e.g., by Christians, be seen as a charism, i.e., a gift from the Holy Spirit, and not as a "natural" capacity).

In a nuanced conclusion to their comparison of Christian and secular

17. Bourne and Watts, "Conceptualizations of Spiritual Healing," p. 85.

18. Bourne and Watts, "Conceptualizations of Spiritual Healing," p. 86. They find the latter view represented in the Church of England report *A Time to Heal,* p. 242.

19. Bourne and Watts, "Conceptualizations of Spiritual Healing," p. 86.

20. For more on this, see Marilyn Schlitz, "Spirituality and Health: Assessing the Evidence," in *Spiritual Healing: Scientific and Religious Perspectives,* ed. Fraser Watts (Cambridge: Cambridge University Press, 2011), pp. 140–52, for reports on distant healing intention (DHI), pp. 145–48, and in support of its efficiency, p. 148.

21. For such healers, see Pavel Hejzlar, *Two Paradigms for Divine Healing: Fred F. Bosworth, Kenneth E. Hagin, Agnes Sanford, and Francis MacNutt in Dialogue* (Leiden: Brill, 2010). The more quiet approach is also reported in Meredith B. McGuire and Debra Kantor, *Ritual Healing in Suburban America* (New Brunswick, NJ: Rutgers University Press, 1988).

22. See for these the studies of Csordas in Thomas J. Csordas, *The Sacred Self: A Cultural Phenomenology of Charismatic Healing* (Berkeley: University of California Press, 1994); Csordas, *Body/Meaning/Healing.*

healing, Bourne and Watts spell out more clearly some of the implications for Christian theology of the understanding of healing.[23] Let me summarize them briefly:

- As for *results*, "The variable results of healing may be due to a wide range of factors, related not only to the nature of the healing itself, but to the environment in which it takes place and the ability of the patient to understand and accept the healing process." An important note in this regard is that they see the Christian environment as potentially "better equipped to deal with the mental and spiritual aspect of healing" as it can place healing "within the wider context of spiritual well-being" (p. 88).

- As for a *common culture* of healing across religious and other boundaries, they hold that there exists more "common ground between secular and Christian understandings of healing, both in practices and assumptions" than what one would think at first sight. I think this is an important observation, given the rather antagonistic and sometimes even hostile relation that the media sometimes portrays between Christian groups, other, secular groups, or groups with alternative spiritualities. In all contexts, "healers show broad agreement in assuming that the ability to heal is to some extent a natural part of everyone, but requires special development in those preparing to be healers" (p. 89).

- This common culture also comes to the fore in the *terminology* used. "Terms such as God, spirits and energy might seem very distinct and specific, the distinctions between them may not be as clear-cut as might at first appear. A surprisingly wide range of terminology for the source of healing can be found in both Christian and secular healing circles, indicating that there is no complete consensus about healing in either group" (p. 89). In their review of contemporary research, Bourne and Watts find that "virtually all conceptualizations of healing that are found in the Christian environment have parallels in how healing is understood in the secular environment, even though some may receive greater emphasis in Christian circles" (p. 89).

- As for *practice,* the difference between Christian and secular healers may suggest that "it is at least possible that the differences are more technological than substantive." Accordingly, although healing may in

___

23. Bourne and Watts, "Conceptualizations of Spiritual Healing." In-text references in parentheses are to this article until otherwise stated.

some sense be "performed" in different ways, these differences do not necessarily reflect fundamental differences in the interpretation of the process and practice of healing (p. 89).

Against this backdrop, Bourne and Watts observe, "It seems justifiable to suggest that Christian and secular forms of healing are part of the general family of spiritual healing rather than being two wholly distinct forms of healing." They call for "an appreciation of the parallel understandings of Christian and secular healers, and encourage a willingness to explore the possibility that they may have more in common than is often assumed" (p. 89). This is a recommendation that we acknowledge and that forms a basis for this book.

Spiritual Healing in a Scholarly Perspective — Some Further Notes on Religion, Science, and Placebo

There are presently many different studies on how healing relates to different strands of scientific knowledge. Among these are LeShan, whom we discussed above. These studies testify to how the modern mind-set seeks validation for experience in what can be scientifically interpreted and related to established knowledge. Among these are also studies of remote prayer. Amanda Porterfield points to how "the interest and controversy generated by these studies illustrate how scientific thinking can frame contemporary religious expression."[24] Furthermore, she writes,

> Today's interest in scientifically validating the therapeutic effects of religious faith grows out of several centuries of effort to establish a relationship between religion and science in which religious claims about spiritual reality can be made to harmonize with scientific claims about nature. Within Christianity, Protestants have been the most eager to square religion and science because of their confidence, prior to the late nineteenth century at least, that because God created nature, scientific investigation of nature should confirm God's existence and complement scriptural revelation.[25]

24. Amanda Porterfield, *Healing in the History of Christianity* (Oxford: Oxford University Press, 2005), p. 162.
25. Porterfield, *Healing in the History of Christianity*, p. 162.

Although the media sometimes describes the relation between science and religion or theology as a conflict, there are no good reasons for upholding this conflict metaphor as the basic pattern of interpretation in this context. This image seems to separate the two more than necessary, and to place religious experiences of healing as totally outside the realm of the "natural." There are many reasons to question this approach, and to suggest a more positive one, in which religion and science are both seen to relate to some of the same experiential phenomena. If not, theology and religion are easily assumed to be about some type of "supernatural reality" devoid of experiential content.

One of the most common responses to Christian healing from a scientific point of view claims that such healings are the result of a placebo effect.[26] It is worth noting that this effect (basically seen as a combination of a good and compassionate relation between healer and healee or doctor and patient, and a well-established faith in the effects of healing practices or medicine) does not deny the healing effect itself. But it is a challenge to believers who see healing as an effect of supernatural powers. Instead, the placebo effect reveals healing as a "natural" phenomenon, originating in the capacities for self-healing in the human organism when they are set free through the interaction and the mental orientation of the healee/patient.[27]

There is no doubt that the so-called placebo effect may play some part in individual instances of the phenomenon of spiritual or religious healing, but it would be misleading to see this effect as the only working cause behind such healing.[28] Among those who discuss this phenomenon is Stephen Parsons, who points to how results of different studies indicate that the placebo effect, which I do not describe in detail here, does not only take place due to psychological and imagined processes, but has a real and positive effect on the bodily processes of people.[29] Placebo seems to stimulate the

26. See the presentation of Gerd Theissen in the previous part of this study as well as the critique offered there, pp. 149-50.

27. For this effect, see the thorough discussion in T. J. Kaptchuk, "The Placebo Effect in Alternative Medicine: Can the Performance of a Healing Ritual Have Clinical Significance?" *Annals of Internal Medicine* 136, no. 11 (2002): 817-25.

28. For an overview of the development of the understanding of the placebo effect, with specific reference to the potential religious dimension and aspects, see Porterfield, *Healing in the History of Christianity*, pp. 13-18.

29. Other scholars who are favorable to the possibility of religious healing also discuss the placebo effect, as, e.g., Keener, *Miracles*, pp. 636ff. See also the discussion in the previous part of this book, above pp. 51-55.

body's self-healing mechanisms. However, one does not fully know, from the point of view of the mechanistic and biological model of Western medicine, what is really going on when such phenomena occur. Parsons also goes on to describe other types of healing mechanisms that show a strong interaction between mind and body, and where special mental practices serve the purpose of improving health, up to the level of hypnosis. A generic way of describing these different techniques is to say that they show beyond doubt that the mind is able to change the reactions of the body and spark or initiate healing processes that engage the body's own self-healing system.[30]

Porterfield also points to how recent studies, although not complete and sometimes limited in scope, nevertheless "make it easier than ever before for a wide range of people, believers and nonbelievers alike, to consider and appreciate the salutary biological effects of Christianity. In other words, it is now possible, as never before, to take religious healing seriously as a real and important biological phenomenon. This is not to claim that biological discourse is able to comprehend the fluidity and multivalent character of religious experience, but simply to say that *biological researchers* have made religious healing more comprehensible."[31] I think her point here is important, because it serves to recognize that what one calls spiritual or religious healing are not phenomena that are set off from or exist in compartments totally separated from what takes place in the experiential and researchable realms of human life.

Furthermore, Porterfield points to how the scientific discussion of the different problems related to the understanding of the placebo effect may also open up to more appreciation of how difficult it is to isolate the therapeutic effects of religion from other factors. Because religion is part of culture and is hard to separate from culture, it is not easy — if at all possible — to separate religious healing from its social and cultural components. Nor can one easily capture what may be the more specific aspects of religion at work in healing, compared to other cultural and social components that may also condition such phenomena.[32] She continues this line of reasoning thus:

> If attempting to isolate religion from culture is impossible, attempting to separate the biological effects of religious belief and practice from other

30. Stephen Parsons, *The Challenge of Christian Healing* (London: SPCK, 1986), p. 98.
31. Porterfield, *Healing in the History of Christianity*, p. 12 (emphasis added); cf. p. 17.
32. Porterfield, *Healing in the History of Christianity*, p. 17.

biological factors may be equally so. Religion may work to strengthen the immune system in many individuals, but how could this ever be conclusively proved? How could any research design completely isolate the effects of religion on the immune system from the effects of exercise, diet, and DNA, or from a constitutional tendency to optimism and healthy-mindedness?[33]

From this discussion, Porterfield draws two important conclusions: (1) The confluence of biological, religious, and cultural factors is more an important discovery than an unsolvable problem. Therefore, (2) this discovery "could be taken as evidence of the inseparability of mind and body and of the biological rootedness of both religion and culture." This is important also because it further underscores the point about how religion can be seen as deeply rooted in common human experiences that reach back in history and have always played a central role in human life.[34]

Porterfield also refers to cultural anthropologist Thomas Csordas's critique of placebo as an explanatory mechanism for religious healing. Csordas describes the placebo effect as a kind of "black box psychic mechanism" and as "nothing more than a label for a poorly understood process of therapeutic efficacy, a rhetorical device that obscured the mysterious nature of religious healing by subsuming it under a name — as if naming it was an explanation."[35]

In his anthropological work, Csordas has defined religious healing as "a restructuring of cognition and memory,"[36] and has emphasized how religious performance restructures the healed self. Csordas's work underscores how the therapeutic relationship is central in Christian healing, as the symbolic element itself does not produce healing. Porterfield has also pointed to how "the sensory engagement in a relationship with a person or force that is simultaneously beyond and within the self must occur for the symbols to have the kind of impact, or make the kind of difference, that people associate

---

33. Porterfield, *Healing in the History of Christianity*, p. 17.

34. She writes: "To admit this rootedness hardly implies that religion is either trivial or simple. Biological approaches to religion are a long way from anything like an adequate understanding of religion's complexity, fluidity, or historical development." For a more extensive discussion of this view of religion as rooted in human biological evolution, from the point of view of Christianity, see Jan-Olav Henriksen, *Life, Love, and Hope: God and Human Experience* (Grand Rapids: Eerdmans, 2014).

35. Porterfield, *Healing in the History of Christianity*, p. 17.

36. See Csordas, *The Sacred Self*; Csordas, *Body/Meaning/Healing*.

with divine power."[37] She goes on to claim that "this kind of engagement with God begins to describe the transforming agency that Christians have often associated with healing."[38]

Summing up this discussion, there are several things to say about the "placebo explanation" in relation to the understanding of healing:

1. One does not know what precisely placebo is.
2. The placebo explanation does not rule out theological interpretation, only some versions of such interpretation that exclusively assume "supernatural causes" to be at work in healing.
3. Placebo cannot explain healing of persons who are not aware of being prayed for, or who in other ways are subject to healers' treatment without their conscious knowledge.

Accordingly, we find that it is difficult to see reference to placebo as having more than restricted value when it comes to explaining what takes place in healing. Furthermore, many make reference to placebo in ways that ultimately dismiss the basis for a spiritual dimension. This view is just as mistaken as interpretations that are not willing to consider anything other than "spiritual causes" behind healing. What the placebo phenomenon nevertheless suggests is that it is problematic to maintain a sharp division between body and mind, just as it is problematic to maintain a sharp division between the human immune system and the nervous system.[39] In the following chapter, we shall see how these considerations are also relevant against a wider backdrop of observations than those that we have presented so far. We will start with looking somewhat further into some of the studies conducted in the last fifty years, and by pointing to relevant elements in a more general discussion about the phenomenon of healing.

37. Porterfield, *Healing in the History of Christianity,* p. 18.
38. Porterfield, *Healing in the History of Christianity,* p. 18.
39. See Anne Harrington, "The Placebo Effect: What Is Interesting for Scholars of Religion," *Zygon: Journal of Religion and Science* 46, no. 2 (2011): 267 and passim.

Christian Healing and Spiritual Healing

Basic Features

For a working definition of *Christian* healing, we will, until further notice, use the one offered by Lars Lindström, who on the basis of his empirical study suggested the following: Christian healing is "the full salvation of the entire man, body, mind and spirit through the re-integration of a life founded on a new relationship to God as a loving Father."[1] This is a definition with a clear theological scope, and it comprises the experiential dimension I called for in the previous chapter as necessary for theology.

Important Christian "healing movements," as well as other groups or institutions concerned with "spiritual healing," have developed in both the United States and in England during the last century. These movements have partly been related to individuals with a Pentecostal background and partly to individuals who have realized their calling to such a ministry in other ways. In England concerns about healing have been taken up in the Anglican Church and led to the development of the so-called healing ministry of the church, an initiative backed by a significant report to the bishops in 1958 (*The Church's Ministry of Healing*), and followed up decades later by the report *A Time to Heal* (2000).[2] On both sides of the Atlantic, scholars have looked into the more spiritual dimensions of healing as well as the medical ones. They have thereby treated the phenomenon with more seriousness than the

---

1. Lars G. Lindström, *Christian Spiritual Healing: A Psychological Study: Ideology and Experience in the British Healing Movement* (Uppsala: Academiae Ubsaliensis, 1992), p. 170.

2. For the United States, see Pavel Hejzlar, *Two Paradigms for Divine Healing*; for the UK, see Stephen Parsons, *The Challenge of Christian Healing*, and Morris Maddocks, *The Christian Healing Ministry*, 3rd ed. (London: SPCK, 1995).

media images, where more spectacular proponents of healing occasionally appear and "perform healing miracles." In the following I will look into some relevant observations from a collection of essays published by Fraser Watts that may help us get a firmer grip on the religious dimension related to the phenomenon of healing.

Watts himself uses the notion of "spiritual" in order to identify the more-than-medical dimension of healing processes. He points out the following different ways of understanding "spiritual" in the notion of spiritual healing:[3]

- Healing in which spiritual practices play a role
- Healing in which the spiritual aspect of the human person is presumed to be involved
- Healing that is explained in terms of what are presumed to be spiritual processes (p. 1)

The first of these interpretations is very open, and is one in which the spiritual dimension does not seem to play any *constitutive* role in the practice itself. For example, here spiritual practices are seen as practices that can enhance healing processes. They may not be used on their own but in conjunction with medical or surgical interventions. Watts points to research indicating "that the effectiveness of ordinary treatments can be enhanced by the explicit use of spiritual practices; medical and surgical treatments tend to work better when a 'whole-person' approach is taken" (p. 2). The increased recognition of the importance in psychotherapy of addressing religious issues constructively also points in the same direction.

This view on spiritual healing, where it plays an "auxiliary role" according to Watts, need not imply any strong or difficult ontological assumptions. "On this view, healings might be deemed to be spiritual simply because of the spiritual practices involved. That would neither invoke any kind of spiritual ontology of the human person, nor require any kind of spiritual explanation" (p. 2). The reason is that such explanations can be grounded in present knowledge about psychosomatic processes. This may provide "an adequate account of at least some of what is regarded as 'spiritual' healing. It is also likely that psychosomatic processes play at least some role in all cases of spiritual healing" (p. 2).

---

3. Fraser Watts, "Conceptual Issues in Spiritual Healing," in *Spiritual Healing: Scientific and Religious Perspectives,* ed. Fraser Watts (Cambridge: Cambridge University Press, 2011), pp. 1–16. In-text references in parentheses are to his work until further notice.

Spiritual healing, Watts claims, is possible in religious and nonreligious contexts alike, at least when it comes to the first category he describes. It can happen both within and outside explicitly religious contexts. Furthermore, "healing that takes place in a recognizably religious setting may or may not involve spiritual practice. Surgery can be undertaken in a hospital with an explicitly religious ethos." This observation allows him to say that from a conceptual point of view "the religious context of healing and the role of spiritual practice in healing are . . . independent" despite the fact that they are often closely associated in practice (p. 3).

Watts undoubtedly points to an important dimension of spiritual healing in his description of the first category, one that should not be disregarded if we are to understand the processes of healing. It is also worth noting that his description here confirms a point that we have already touched on, namely, that healing involves other dimensions than the medical one. This point is further enhanced in his description of the second category, where the spiritual dimension of the person is in some way seen as conditional for the process itself. His arguments concerning this latter category of healing thus suggest a more far-reaching understanding of the human being than what is usually assumed by the so-called biomedical model or a psychological approach, one that more explicitly opens up to the spiritual dimension of human existence.

Watts assumes an emergentist view of the mind in the development of his argument. This view holds that mental powers emerge from the physical body: "In a similar way, spirit can be seen as emerging from body and mind" (p. 5). In this view, neither mind nor spirit can be seen as substances that are separate from the body. I want to highlight Watts's understanding of these matters, as his way of phrasing them provides us with the opportunity for an updated and more holistic view of human life that is not based on any Cartesian mind-matter distinction. In his view, the mind is "best seen in adjectival terms, as mental properties or powers, rather than as referring to a thing called 'mind.' Second, though there is a conceptual distinction between mind and brain (or body), they cannot actually be separated or divided; . . . distinctions do not imply divisions. Third, though mental properties and powers are real enough, they arise from body and brain, and do not have a separate origin" (p. 5). This understanding of the human, which overcomes the body-soul divide, in turn has significant implications for the understanding of healing:

There can be healing that is psychological (i.e. healing that can be explained psychologically), and such healing can be formulated in a way that is consistent with all the above assumptions about mind. It does not imply healing by a mind that is separate from the body. On the contrary, the concept of psychosomatic medicine is remarkably holistic, and built on the idea that psychological processes are closely intertwined with physical ones. Psychosomatic healing does not rest on a flight into radical mind-body dualism. (p. 5)

Given that soul and spirit cannot be separated from body and mind, Watts holds that "mind and spirit are distinguishable aspects of the human person, but not separate entities" (p. 5). Accordingly, his interpretation of spiritual healing as he describes it in his second category above "does not assume that 'spirit' is something separate and distinct from the rest of a person" (p. 5). Although the spiritual aspects of the person are significant here, this does not mean that healing is exclusively spiritual. As he says, "It makes no sense to suggest that healing could be purely spiritual" (p. 5). So far, though, spiritual healing "can in principle be understood entirely in anthropological (human) terms, even though spiritual healing may make use of human processes that are not yet well understood" (p. 5).

The third and last category Watts suggests does not in a similar way understand healing on mere anthropological terms. Here Watts interprets healing as something that involves "transcendent resources, and which requires an explanation in spiritual terms" (p. 5). However, this concept of spiritual healing, which involves a power or energy external to the healee and which is therefore constitutive and indispensable to healing, does not necessarily make a *theological* explanation necessary, although most people involved assume a transcendent power of some sort at work here. As we saw with Lawrence LeShan, healers often assume that they are channels or mediators of healing energy that transcends them. And often, this energy is interpreted as "spiritual." Watts points to the similarity in the assumptions made by both Christian and secular healers when it comes to this: as channels of a healing power that transcends them, different healers do not see themselves as the source of the healing power, but they acknowledge its dependence on transcendent resources (p. 6). Some see this source as God, whereas others simply conceptualize it as "healing energy."

If we look at Watts's categories in the light of LeShan's different types of healing, there is no doubt that the type of healing LeShan has in mind in his presentation of Type 1 and Type 2 belongs to Watts's third category. The description of energy, as well as the close relation between healer and healee that unites them, is not in the same way necessarily present in Watts's category one and two. However, when we look at Jesus' healings, they may belong in all of Watts's categories: Some may be aided by psychosomatic effects, effects not yet known to us, or by more specific types of "energy healing."

Watts opens up a theologically relevant discussion by pointing to how important it is not to "confuse the question of whether or not transcendent resources for healing are conceptualized in theological terms with the quite separate question of whether or not healing depends on the grace of God" (p. 6). That spiritual healing takes place outside explicit frameworks of religious belief does not make it theologically legitimate to say that it happens without God: "A Christian theologian would surely recognize that all human efforts at healing take place within God's created order and are in accordance with His purposes. That is as true of secular spiritual healing as it is of medical science. Secular healing may be outside faith or theology, but it is surely not outside God" (p. 6). This also underscores the point that a specific religious or spiritual context of healing in no way needs to be a constitutive requirement for healing to take place — a point we can also see made implicitly in the New Testament material.

Furthermore, Watts places the discussion of healing in a much wider framework, namely, that of the relationship between theology and science. Within the context of this discourse, several topics are up for discussion; not only the already-touched-on understanding of the emergent capacities of humans, but also the question of natural laws and the possibilities of God's intervention, as well as the whole issue about God's action in the world as such. Some of these questions will be dealt with more extensively in the next sections of this part of the book, whereas others are worth touching on already here. I specifically want to draw attention to how this topic can be discussed within the wider context of the dialogue between science and theology.

In order to have a thorough discussion of these matters, one cannot reject the fact that spiritual healing can occur. Moreover, one also has to rely on the testimonies of those who have experienced such healings as pointing toward a transcendent source of energy or healing powers, be it as a healer or as a healee. There are sufficient witnesses in anthropological and other types of literature to back up such an assumption. Watts's question is then, "How does spiritual healing in that sense relate to a scientific worldview?" (p. 8).

It is important to point to the fact, as Watts does, that those who seek healing for themselves or for others "often use spiritual practices such as laying on of hands to bring healing about" (p. 8). This allows us to see healing as a result of the combination of human initiative and presumed divine action. Given this premise, however, "it is a mistake to ask whether spiritual healing should be understood scientifically or theologically. They represent complementary perspectives on spiritual healing" (p. 8). Accordingly, Watts holds that "spiritual healing can be understood more adequately when it is approached both theologically and scientifically, rather than by either discipline alone" (p. 9). I concur, but in doing so, I also want to indicate that this moves us away from a reductionist approach, and implies a move which acknowledges that reflective resources in religious traditions may influence the way we understand phenomena that are also investigated from a scientific point of view. Like Watts, I hold that "a sharp distinction between healing phenomena that are amenable to naturalistic explanation, and other 'spiritual' or supernatural healing phenomena that are not so amenable" should be avoided.[4]

Watts suggests that it is more apt to view healing "in terms of a subtle interpenetration of the natural and the spiritual, rather than in terms of a sharp disjunction between them" (p. 8). Another way of articulating this theologically would be to view healing as an instance of the cooperation between nature and grace. Then it would be possible to interpret healing as "an enhancement of what normally happens under the laws of nature rather than an overturning of those laws" (p. 8). The reason why this approach recommends itself is that it is open to profound theological interpretation at the same time as it is also open to how science gradually increases our knowledge about what takes place in ways that may eventually pave the way for an acceptance of such exceptional phenomena (pp. 8–9).[5]

---

4. Watts continues, in a way that will be discussed below in the chapter on miracles, that such "a distinction arises from a rigid view of what the laws of nature permit and, historically, it is only since the scientific revolution that a rigid view of the laws of nature has been widely considered. I suggest that there are no good reasons for regarding the laws of nature as invariant laws to which no exceptions are possible. Only if we believe that we know the full range of phenomena permitted by the laws of nature can we presume to identify certain phenomena as 'natural,' and other phenomena as lying outside them and therefore 'supernatural'" (p. 9).

5. This can be elaborated further with reference to an example Watts names later in his essay. There he points to the work on grace by the Jesuit psychoanalyst William Meissner (1987). Meissner "proposes a theology of grace, indebted to Karl Rahner, in terms of relationship with a transcendent God, who is the source of grace. However, alongside that, he proposes a psychological account of how grace works itself out at the human level. There is no contradiction between those two accounts, but they answer different questions. The theological account is more about what grace is; the psychological account is more about how it works. In the same way, a theological account of healing might focus mainly on God as the source of healing, and a psychological account on how healing works" (p. 13).

To understand healing from this angle is accordingly not only to say that we need *complementary* scientific explanations. (Watts mentions quantum mechanics and mind/brain research where complementary approaches are needed.) What we need are *accounts from different disciplines,* from both theology and science. Given this approach, "the key question is not whether spiritual healing is to be understood scientifically or theologically, but what the relationship should be between theological and scientific accounts," which address questions of how and why respectively (p. 11). Watts illustrates how theology and science may share these tasks by listing the following examples:

Theology can place healing within the purposes of God, in ways that may be both revelatory and pastoral. Here Watts, referring to John 9, includes the purposes of events that lie outside the scope of healing and deliverance, namely, in the revelation of the glory of God. Furthermore, for Watts healings can be "signs of the wholeness that God's kingdom brings," of "what human qualities they depend on (faith, urgent desire), and what principles they illustrate (*e.g.* that healing is more important than keeping the Sabbath)" (p. 12). Although it is hard to disagree with this list of suggestions, one may nevertheless ask if God does not also have specific purposes regarding the health and well-bring of those who experience struggles with their health, and intend to do something about their concrete abilities to partake in and enjoy life in its fullness. Watts's interpretation, as it now stands, seems to suggest a more "spiritual" direction that doesn't see the spiritual significance of healings as clearly linked to the embodied existence of the healee. In this way, Watts's suggestion may contribute, though probably unintentionally, to a disembodied view of Christianity and the Christian theology of healing — a point we will critically develop further in relation to Calvin below.

When it comes to the scientific approach to healing, the questions are different. Watts suggests that they "can conveniently be subdivided into outcome and process questions" (p. 12). Among these questions the most basic is whether spiritual healing actually takes place. As I have indicated earlier, there is no reason to think that healing events do not take place; the question is more about how to interpret them and their causes.[6] I agree with Watts, however, that more interesting questions may be found among what he calls the process questions — those that ask *how* healing takes place. He mentions an example that points to the relevant topic here:

6. Watts holds that this fact also "calls for the careful keeping of records, for information about the nature of the problems that are presumed to be healed, and for a comparison with what remission might have taken place without spiritual healing" (p. 12). I concur.

If pain is alleviated by spiritual healing questions arise about exactly how the pain reduction occurred. It is possible in principle to compare how pain is alleviated through spiritual healing with the effects of medication on pain. If pain relief occurs at all, it must be possible to address such questions scientifically, and it is hard to see why that should be resisted, unless it is thought that theology and science are so radically irreconcilable that a theological approach to spiritual healing renders a complementary scientific account completely inappropriate. (p. 12)

So far, it is not hard to agree with Watts's position. However, when it comes to the inferences he draws from this example, I think he offers too much credit to theology as it has traditionally operated. He states that "it rarely, if ever, happens that scientific data rule out a theological approach; keeping science and theology in dialogue influences the details of how the theological approach is worked out" (p. 12). This is to say too much. Theological accounts of healings that can now be determined to have taken place due to the placebo effect or because of therapeutic interventions for conversion neurosis may suggest that previous interpretations of such effects as miraculous can be regarded as superfluous. Where this is the case, theology cannot maintain an interpretative framework that upholds claims about the miraculous. Furthermore, to say that "dialogue between theology and science generally leads to a process of mutual revision, rather than the acceptance or rejection of theological positions" (p. 12) is also a statement in need of further clarification. Theology does not usually influence science in terms of offering theological *explanations* of unexplained phenomena, but rather in urging science to keep an open mind and to continue to investigate on its own terms what is still not possible to understand, but which are nevertheless important phenomena in religious and spiritual contexts. Having said this on a more critical note, though, I agree with Watts that when it comes to the need for a full understanding of healing, "we will normally need to offer both theological and scientific accounts" of it (p. 12), and even more so in light of an anthropology that aims at overcoming the Cartesian divide between mind and matter (or spirit and body).

The view on science and theology discussed here also allows us to address a basic assumption made by Christians involved in spiritual healing, namely, that "special divine action is more likely to be involved in spiritual healing than in medical or psychological healing" (p. 13). This assumption is misleading. Watts holds, and I think correctly, that "both arise within the general providence of God." Furthermore, if one is to make a distinction between different types of healing and their relation to God, one would probably be better advised to see healing as being provided through various means that all have their source in God rather than singling out some as more God-related than others. Any clear-cut distinction would only be able to operate on the basis of a clear separation of the spheres of nature and grace, creation and salvation, and that is not recommendable. However, for both Watts and LeShan, spiritual healing "involves a deliberate seeking of divine action, and special divine action seems more likely to occur when God is acknowledged, sought and invoked. It is in the nature of God to work with people, rather than independently of them, and the most significant cases of special divine action arise when humans are explicitly open to God and are co-operating with him" (p. 13).

The theological accounts that result from such considerations are not only important in the way that Watts articulates them, but also in order to articulate and interpret the constitutive dimension of healing that sees it as the workings of the divine more than as a result of given human capabilities. Watts writes that although "a general theological explanation can be offered of all healing," in relation to medical healing,

> the naturalistic account of how healing takes place is primary, in the sense that it is this that guides the actions of doctors and surgeons, even though it is possible to offer a more general theological view of how medical healing is embedded in God's creation and purposes. In contrast, with spiritual healing the theological account is the primary one in the sense that it is the one that explicitly guides the actions of those involved. It is also possible to offer a naturalistic version, for example of how the alleviation of pain is mediated when spiritual healing takes place. With spiritual healing the theological explanation is primary, whereas for medical healing it is the naturalistic one. Complementary versions are possible in both cases, but the priority attached to them is reversed. (p. 13)

We see here how a fairly open, though simultaneously scientifically oriented approach, may in fact provide interpretative space for theological accounts of healing. Justin Meggitt offers an example of the need for a complementary approach. He discusses Jesus' miracles in a psychosocial context, and thereby opens up space for a nuanced and multidisciplinary approach to Jesus as healer.[7] Furthermore, Meggitt's analysis is actually an example of

---

7. Justin Meggitt, "The Historical Jesus and Healing: Jesus' Miracles in Psychosocial Context," in *Spiritual Healing: Scientific and Religious Perspectives*, ed. Fraser Watts (Cambridge: Cambridge University Press, 2011), pp. 17–43.

how a theologically based understanding may in fact criticize a presumably scientific one, as Watts suggests above. Meggitt points to how New Testament scholarship has established beyond reasonable doubt that "Jesus was considered by his contemporaries to be an effective healer and exorcist — both by critics and supporters."[8] Furthermore, and although there is limited information about it in the Gospels, the disorders that Jesus encountered most likely do not seem to have predominantly psychosomatic etiologies. Their sheer number seems to suggest that. Meggitt summarizes the New Testament evidence as follows:

> The earliest records that we possess of Jesus' healing ministry do not indicate that he gained his reputation by only healing a small percentage of those that came to him. Yet, it is clear that if the success of Jesus was limited to those individuals presenting with symptoms that have a psychosomatic basis alone surely such a pattern should be discernible in the records. However, only in the tradition about Jesus' healings in Nazareth do we get the indication that Jesus could only heal a few of those that came to him (Matthew 13:58; Mark 6:5). The sources also emphasize that a number of the ailments that Jesus cured had been suffered since birth (Mark 9:21; John 9:1) so they cannot have had a psychophysiological aetiology.[9]

Here not only does Meggitt problematize "scientific explanations" and New Testament scholars' interpretations of the reported healings of Jesus that seem to be in line with "placebo" or more psychosomatic explanations. But he also tacitly indicates that too quick a leap into already established patterns of explanation for interpreting Jesus as healer may not serve their purpose, namely, to establish a sound scholarly interpretation of Jesus as healer that takes into account the whole range and diversity in the material we have about healing.

Some Features of How Healing Has Been Understood in the History of Christianity

Amanda Porterfield's aforementioned study of healing in the history of Christianity is a valuable resource for achieving insights into the diverse ap-

8. Meggitt, "The Historical Jesus and Healing," p. 17.
9. Meggitt, "The Historical Jesus and Healing," p. 31.

proaches to healing in the Christian tradition. In her study, she points out that healing practices are described as provocative and challenging already in the Gospel accounts. These provocations were probably considered thus not only due to their extraordinary character and their existence outside the order of commonly accepted everyday knowledge, but also because of their potential disruption of the existing social order. By performing healings, "Jesus and his followers engaged in performances of exorcism and healing that dramatized the restoration of healthy communal life and challenged scriptural interpretations advanced by priests, scribes, and Pharisees who defended Israel's ruling elite."[10] Furthermore, she holds that Jesus' healing practice "embodied the connections that earlier prophets had drawn between sin and suffering, forgiveness and healing, and righteousness and health."[11]

Although Porterfield acknowledges that we need to see Christianity as a diversified phenomenon (she even speaks of "many Christianities"), she nevertheless ends up with an argument that — apparently also to her own surprise — implies that "attention to healing reveals remarkable similarities among different cultural expressions of Christianity."[12] She also claims "that healing has been a driving force in the construction of Christianity as an ongoing historical tradition."[13] Despite the fact that she initially makes this claim from her point of view as a historian, there are nevertheless reasons for applying this perspective to a broader field. Her observations may be used about different religions as well: They are all concerned with health and healing practices in some way or another, and many of the practices involved show remarkable similarities across cultural and regional boundaries.[14]

Like many other contemporary writers and scholars who look at the topic of healing, Porterfield therefore also emphasizes the widespread and generic character of the phenomenon of healing in diverse religious traditions. While acknowledging that "Christianity is not the only religion in the

---

10. Amanda Porterfield, *Healing in the History of Christianity* (Oxford: Oxford University Press, 2005), p. 35.

11. Porterfield, *Healing in the History of Christianity*, p. 35.

12. Porterfield, *Healing in the History of Christianity*, p. 4.

13. Porterfield, *Healing in the History of Christianity*, p. 4.

14. A contemporary example of the widespread healing practices among different religious traditions: one of us visited China a few years back, and a Chinese scholar in the Daoist tradition told us that healing practices like the laying on of hands, as well as distance or remote healing, are well known in that tradition, and practiced in ways that seem to overlap significantly with what we know of such practices within a Western and Christian context. For more on these similarities, see also the anthropological work of Thomas J. Csordas, *Body/Meaning/Healing* (New York: Palgrave Macmillan, 2002).

world concerned with healing," she points to how most religions go "a long way in explaining why tendencies to be religious, and capacities for religious feeling and ideation, seem to have evolved as instinctive parts of human nature."[15] This is an important reminder, as it locates the concern for health and healing closely to the main concerns that constitute a religious way of being in the world. In this way, the messages of religious practices and doctrines relate to experiences important for all human beings. It is important to note that this connection is not one of belief and doctrine only, but is affirmed in the concrete practices of Christians. She writes:

> Even in the context of long-standing, worldwide demands for religious healing, Christians have distinguished themselves. Often borrowing techniques and ideas from other religions and from numerous forms of medicine, Christians have time and again disseminated their religion as a means to healing and eternal good health. Christianity's success as a world religion has much to do with its attractiveness in this regard and with its effectiveness in promoting a whole range of salutary benefits and behaviors.[16]

Given this acknowledgment of the generic character of healing in different religious traditions and as a vital component in much religious experience, one has to ask: What is the distinguishing mark of Christian healing? Porterfield's answer to this question is worth reflecting on in relation to the main theme of the present work: she sees this distinctiveness in its "appeal to Christ as the transcendent source of healing and prime symbol of personal and social integration."[17] This understanding of Christ as the center and source of healing allows a great diversity of *healing practices,* whereas "the basic dynamic that begins to explain how Christianity has actually worked to make people feel stronger and find relief and comfort is the personal relationship that believers experience with Christ. As a person embedded in the memories, imaginations, and thinking habits of Christians, as well as more objectively described in scripture, community, liturgy, prayer, song, visual art, and the lives of saints, Christ has motivated countless people to understand themselves in relation to his likeness."[18]

15. Porterfield, *Healing in the History of Christianity,* p. 8.
16. Porterfield, *Healing in the History of Christianity,* p. 8.
17. Porterfield, *Healing in the History of Christianity,* p. 9.
18. Porterfield, *Healing in the History of Christianity,* p. 9.

Porterfield here points to how healing is related to different experiential realms of human life. Healing affects not only physical or psychological well-being but also cultural and collective resources related to shared memory and anticipation. Furthermore, this experience is not only a matter of belief but is also, as I read her, primarily to be understood as a religious *practice*. Doctrine and belief are secondary, and for some, belief is not an effective power for receiving healing at all. This suggests that Christian healing cannot simply be understood as a sophisticated version of the placebo effect, but has to be understood within a more comprehensive and nuanced interpretative framework. But, as indicated, the central figure in Christian healing experience is Christ: "The experience or anticipation of union with Christ is a religious practice and only partly a matter of belief. Christian healing is more about a sense of relationship to a divine person than about doctrine, although doctrine has been important in preserving and stimulating this sense of relationship and defining its boundaries. If many have been healed because they believed, others believed because they had been healed."[19] This multilayered and dialectical way of understanding healing and how it works and where it may originate points to the need for a nuanced and comprehensive (holistic) understanding of the human being that I will develop later. Here I only want to point to the need for seeing that interactions between different realms of experience are involved in healing processes, and that healing should not too quickly be identified with something that only has to do with the somatic or the psychological realm of human life.

From the viewpoint of Christian theology, it would be reasonable to see the understanding of healing as an important element in the desire to see God as manifest in creation. However, throughout history, this has not unambiguously been the case: The Protestant emphasis on the gospel as the gift through the Word of God has been accompanied by a concomitant critique of all practices that might suggest that Christian life also has a practical side related to rituals involving healing or elements that could be considered magical. Where emphasis on practice could be seen as an indication that salvation could be experienced through the participation in specific (heal-

---

19. Porterfield, *Healing in the History of Christianity*, p. 10; cf. p. 19: "Depictions of Christ, his saints, and his Spirit are diverse, but their status as persons, or as agencies of persons, persists even as their more specific aspects vary. A sense of relationship with Christ goes a long way in defining what people, over centuries and across geographic space, have meant when they have claimed to be Christian. As any insider to Christianity knows, even the name Jesus Christ carries emotional impact and has a remarkable tendency to elicit confessional feeling and talk. He is the divine person felt by many to touch and adumbrate their humanity."

ing) practices, such practices were condemned. Such condemnations were due, alongside rooting out magic and superstition, to the interest in keeping pure the doctrine of justification by grace alone without works. This move in turn probably led to a marginalization of popular healing practices and to the deterioration of a religious language that could interpret such practices in an affirmative way.[20] A prominent example of this approach to healing, which is also underpinned by significant philosophical assumptions, is to be found in John Calvin.

According to Porterfield, Calvin saw healing as no longer relevant for the interpretation of the content of Christian life. She claims that he demonstrated a "sweeping, almost offhand dismissal" that "removed healing from the list of Christian ministries, not even stopping to argue the point."[21] For him healing belonged in the category of "extraordinary gifts of the spirit bestowed on Christ's earliest followers to reflect the momentous events of his actual appearance on earth, not ongoing practices of Christian life."[22] Thus Calvin appears to be a strong cessationist. He saw the contemporary presence of such practices as leading to the corruption of true Christian faith and as an expression of the superstitious stories about the healing powers of saints that had crept in to corrupt Christianity in its Roman Catholic version.[23]

As mentioned above, Calvin's and other Protestant Reformers' skepticism of magic was related to the concern for true belief and was a shield against false doctrine. They here stand in a long line of theologians and others who exhibit an ambiguous or outright dismissive attitude toward magic

---

20. For this, see Meredith B. McGuire, *Lived Religion: Faith and Practice in Everyday Life* (Oxford: Oxford University Press, 2008); but also Charles Taylor, *A Secular Age* (Cambridge: Belknap Press of Harvard University Press, 2007).

21. Porterfield, *Healing in the History of Christianity*, p. 95.

22. Porterfield, *Healing in the History of Christianity*, p. 95.

23. See Porterfield, *Healing in the History of Christianity*, p. 95. Porterfield also refers to research that points to how Calvin's uneasiness about present miracles is related to his metaphysical presuppositions: "Calvin acknowledged that miracles accompanied the world-changing revelations God made through Moses and Jesus, but he emphasized that these miracles were not part of the natural scheme of things. Although most Christians assumed they were part of nature, Calvin rejected that assumption" (p. 95). She quotes historian Carlos Eire, saying that "Calvin's denial of miracles in the material sphere is the capstone of his metaphysical assumptions. Uneasy with any intermingling of spiritual and material, he takes the miraculous out of the ordinary and moves it into the realm of revelation" (p. 96). Porterfield continues: "To expect miracles of healing as part of Christian faith would be to seek God in creation, and that, for Calvin, was the essence of idolatry" (p. 96).

and popular piety in Christianity.[24] The Reformed emphasis on salvation by faith would almost by default also lead to the rejection of forms of healing that could be associated with magic. However, this emphasis in turn also paved the way for a more modern and skeptical approach to healing, miracles, and religion in general. Porterfield claims that

> in denouncing belief in ongoing miracles and equating it with belief in magic, Calvin and other reformers winnowed the field of divine activity in the world as it had never been winnowed before. Ancient and medieval Christians had rejected magic as inferior to Christian practice — if not downright evil — but generally acknowledged its existence and power. In the sixteenth and seventeenth centuries, skepticism about the existence of magic coincided with skepticism about miracles, and these tendencies to disbelief invited skepticism about the spirit world, and even about the existence of God.[25]

On the other side, as Porterfield suggests, the condemnations of superstition and magic also "contributed to new interest in the human side of religion and stimulated new affirmations about the need for Christ-like behavior in ordinary life."[26] In the affirmation of ordinary life that shaped the early modern commitment to Christian life in the world, "Jesus' own life acquired new importance as a model for human behavior," and a new focus on the earthly life of Jesus emerged. However, as Porterfield says, "This quest for the historical Jesus did not immediately lead to interest in his work as a healer,"[27] as the rationalist spirit of the Enlightenment as well as Protestant interest in the internal nature of faith tended to ignore the features related to these dimensions as irrelevant, or even unreal. Porterfield thus claims that "well into the twentieth century, historical studies of Jesus only strengthened the development of earlier tendencies in Luther, Calvin, and other Protestant Reformers to downplay religious healing and marginalize miracles."[28]

---

24. See the story told in Acts 19; see also Hans-Josef Klauck, *The Religious Context of Early Christianity: A Guide to Graeco-Roman Religion,* trans. Brian J. MacNeil (London: T&T Clark, 2003), pp. 153–54, 209–31.

25. Porterfield, *Healing in the History of Christianity,* p. 105.

26. Porterfield, *Healing in the History of Christianity,* p. 25.

27. Porterfield, *Healing in the History of Christianity,* p. 25.

28. Porterfield, *Healing in the History of Christianity,* p. 25. Calvin's position on healing can also be seen to influence a long row of Protestant thinkers, especially in North America. As a "cessationist" he also came to see illness as something in accordance with God's plan, thereby

It is now increasingly recognized in historical scholarship that the witch-craft trials of the late medieval and early modern period may not be inter-preted as a simple continuation of medieval superstitious beliefs. Instead, they may be understood as a result of the combination of the Reformation's rejection of practices not constitutive for, or contrary to, true belief, in con-junction with the emerging modern skepticism of religion in general and especially of folk practices. All these features played together with and were fueled by the increasing rationalism that was seen as the potential basis for a new social and religious order. The traditional belief in demons now ap-peared in new contexts that made belief in and practices of healing appear more dangerous than they had previously. The witch hunters were not the premodern, ignorant, and superstitious ones, but the scholars and learned men who were at the forefront of the development of modern attitudes to-ward the study of nature, and who wanted to eliminate the remaining super-stition expressed in popular practices, including those of healing.[29]

There is one more consequence of the Reformation's affirmation of true faith as based on belief and not on practices that could serve as confirmation of religious status. Whereas belief in justification by faith is about something that belongs to an invisible realm and can only be grasped in faith, healing and health are very much related to this world in its embodied and material character. As Porterfield argues,

> Through their insistence on the believer's direct and immediate relation-ship to God, reformers criticized the materialism of Christian art and ritual, the lore associated with saints and their healing powers, and the validity of devotional practices surrounding sickness, death, and healing. In lieu of these materialistic expressions of Christianity, reformers urged people to focus on the transcendence of God and to trust in God alone for the antidote of transforming grace that would combat the sickness of sin and the fear of illness and death that resulted from sin.[30]

Thus not only the practices themselves but also the material and embodied context for the experiences related to healing were deprived of religiously

---

explicitly ruling out the need for developing a stronger theology of healing for his own time. See Hejzlar, *Two Paradigms*, pp. 80–81, 83–84. See the quote about Christ as "appointed not to cure bodies, but rather to cure souls" referred to in Hejzlar, *Two Paradigms*, p. 82, which contributes to the disembodiment of Christianity, which we will address critically in the present work.

29. See Porterfield, *Healing in the History of Christianity*, p. 32.

30. Porterfield, *Healing in the History of Christianity*, p. 106.

relevant content and affirmation. This development continued even further, sponsored by the increasing attempts to read the Bible in light of historical criticism and to judge its claims on the basis of historical analogies. One could, in hindsight, say that the Reformation contributed to the elimination of possible analogies in people's ordinary practices to the healings that were reported in the Bible. This in turn allowed for a critical consideration of these biblical stories from the point of view of critical scholarship — a situation that has continued more or less until the present day.

The Modern Embarrassment regarding Healing Miracles — and Overcoming It

Owing to the development outlined in the previous chapter, much of modern Protestant theology has rejected (or at least been skeptical toward) the historicity of Jesus' reported healings, or tried to interpret the texts about them in ways that do not fully take the historical (including the physical) claims implied in them into account. But recently, as indicated in the previous part of this book, this picture has changed. New Testament scholars are now able to see Jesus' healings within a wider framework of healings in general, and the way he influenced his contemporaries more specifically. The utilization of anthropological research in New Testament studies has especially contributed to this change. One could perhaps say that the increasing awareness of occurrences of healing that are impossible to explain with contemporary medicine (at least up until the present) has also contributed to the plausibility of seeing Jesus as a healer in a way that seems closer to the biblical narratives than were the interpretations of earlier generations of scholarship.[1]

---

1. The most significant contribution to this development recently is Craig Keener's monumental work on miracles, which testifies to the enormous number of such experiences. It is an impressive and well-documented study of such events, both ancient and contemporary, claiming that even apart from any theological agenda, it is possible to say that "the kinds of miracle claims most frequently attested in the Gospels and Acts are also attested by many eyewitnesses today" (Craig S. Keener, *Miracles: The Credibility of the New Testament Accounts*, 2 vols. [Grand Rapids: Baker Academic, 2011], p. 6; cf. p. 206). However, there are two problems with his presentation, from our point of view: First, he has no clear definition of miracle. Second, he describes such events as (potentially) supernatural, without defining what he means by that (admittedly, he also indicates that one could use paranormal — meaning not ordinary — or extraordinary, but both these as only preliminary concepts for defining some events as supernatural in the end; see p. 3). Both of these features tend to place such events in a compartment of reality separated from other events, a compartment that is in some way or

However, it does not follow from this recently altered picture that there is nothing to learn from the more thoroughly critical reflections in modern theology when it comes to the conditions for, and significance of, Jesus' healings. Therefore, I will in this chapter present some of the theologians who have dealt with these issues, in order to highlight some of the valuable considerations of their works. As will be apparent, most of the following discussion is concentrated around how one should interpret so-called miracles, healing being included in that category by the writers in question.

Friedrich Schleiermacher

The major interest in Schleiermacher's interpretation of miracles — including healings — is that divine intervention should not be seen to exclude natural elements or be totally independent of them. In *The Christian Faith*[2] §47, he states that "it should never be necessary in the interest of religion so to interpret a fact that its dependence on God absolutely excludes its being conditioned by the system of nature" (p. 178). This is a point that may be read as being in accordance with the considerations about the relation between nature and grace that I will develop more in detail below, and that suggests that when God works in, with, and under nature, nature is involved in, and not outside of, the sphere of grace.[3]

Schleiermacher especially applies the above statement to events related to the origins of Christianity. Although he does not say that he rejects or denies the possibility of miracles (and is, accordingly, no cessationist), he insists that one should try, as far as possible, to interpret every event with "reference to the interdependence of nature and without detriment

---

somehow more "spiritual." Thereby, Keener contributes to the dualistic interpretation of events that we argue should be avoided, e.g., by suggesting a distinction between "supernatural" and "natural" causes rather unmediated (see pp. 3, 19, and passim).

2. Friedrich Schleiermacher, *The Christian Faith*, ed. H. R. Mackintosh and J. S. Stewart (Edinburgh: T&T Clark, 1999). References in parentheses in the text are to this work until further notice.

3. A somewhat more critical interpretation than the one I am offering here is found in Keener, who says that "Schleiermacher's influential critique simply presupposed the naturalism that he claimed to prove," and his arguments thus "beg the question by excluding God or other nonphysical entities as legitimate causative metaphysical options. Schleiermacher accepted Jesus's miracles but by claiming that we simply do not understand the dynamics of matter and spirit; what made events miraculous was the subjective wonder they evoked and he warned believers not to expect God to intervene today" (Keener, *Miracles*, p. 178).

to that principle" (p. 179). This is a fairly common approach, and one that is recommendable also in modern theological scholarship. However, in his elaboration on miracles, Schleiermacher clearly testifies to what I would call the embarrassment of modernity when it comes to things that cannot be scientifically explained. He spells out his position against several other different positions.

First, he argues against those who see miracles as special instances of God's omnipotence, as it is not clear why and to what extent omnipotence is greater in the suspension of nature than in the creation of its original order. Rather, the need to change the natural order would, as he sees it, be an admission to the fact that there is a fault in the original order of things. Thus Schleiermacher construes an argument in which God is played out against God if God performs or orders specific miracles to happen. Schleiermacher's alternative position and main argument is that the more we know of nature and the conditions under which it works (i.e., natural laws), the more reverence for God is possible in our experience.

Second, a slightly more subtle argument in favor of miracles would be to see them as something God performs in order to compensate for the effects of free causes (i.e., human beings) in the course of nature and in "direct contact with the world" (p. 179). Against this position, Schleiermacher claims that it presupposes not only "a wholly lifeless view of the divine preservation" (p. 179), but also sounds as if free causes were not part of the divine preservation and were not absolutely dependent on God. More serious in his view, however, is the fact that this position presupposes an opposition between the mediate and the immediate activities of God, an opposition that cannot be conceived "without bringing the Supreme Being within the sphere of limitation" (p. 179). Schleiermacher's own view of nature thus does not exclude God from the natural world but sees God's activities in and behind the interaction of what he calls "nature-mechanism and free agents" (p. 180).

This differentiation of the social and the natural world implies, furthermore, that he can evaluate the biblical miracles as "too isolated and too restricted in content" to provide us with an indication of how they function to restore "in the nature-mechanism what free agents had altered" (p. 180). Christ's mission aims at "the restoration of what free causes have altered in their own province, not in that of the nature-mechanism or in the course of things originally ordained by God" (p. 180). Basically, his argument here is that the causes of Christ's work of restoration are more related to what he calls free causes (human beings) than to the order of nature (p. 180). Or to put it in more contemporary terms: the miracles and the restoration implied in them have more to do with personality and subjectivity than with the forces of nature.

Schleiermacher discusses two further reasons why one might want to hold onto a suspension of the interrelatedness of nature and humanity in miracles: answers to prayer, and the regeneration in the new creation that goes beyond what is comprised in the system of nature. As for the first, he sees both prayer and what takes part in the continuation of it as a consequence of divine preservation (the original divine plan). Thus he considers it "wholly meaningless" to consider prayer and its fulfillment or refusal as anything other than parts of this plan. As for the second, he sees the revelation of God in Christ as not absolutely supernatural, and accordingly we should not be bound to consider it as such: revelation and what "flows from it" are part of this world, and work on the presuppositions that this world works on (pp. 180–81).

Moreover, the idea that miracles *break* the natural order might abrogate the whole conception of nature as we know it, because it seems to alter either the former order on which the world works or the future order of the world on the same previously established principles — which would in turn also imply that God works against God in making them happen (pp. 181–82). This is a common argument. It supposes that when miracles happen, natural laws are suspended — but as we shall see very few more recent thinkers seem to hold such a position today.

It is clear from this presentation that Schleiermacher's view on miracles is based on two main principles: The rejection of so-called supernatural causes as the foundation for an argument for miracles, and the recognition of the status of natural science when it comes to circumscribe what can count as possible. As for the former, he holds that natural science and religion have a common case in abandoning "the idea of the absolutely supernatural because no single instance of it can be known by us, and we are nowhere required to recognize it" (p. 183). He qualifies this statement by admitting that the limitations of human knowledge when it comes to the principles on which created nature works are "continually growing," and therefore "we have not the least right to maintain that anything is impossible and also we should allow, in particular (by far the greater number of New Testament miracles being of this kind), that we can neither define the limits of the reciprocal relations of the body and mind nor assert that they are, always and everywhere, entirely the same without the possibility of extension or deviation" (pp. 183–84). Therefore, we are in principle justified in holding to the possibility that what we now see as unexplainable may be understood in the future (p. 184).

The main achievement of Schleiermacher's position is his insistence that the divine cannot work totally independent of the natural. Accordingly, he opens space for a framework in which Jesus' healings are not in principle supernatural but should be considered to be happening under, or in relation to, conditions that belong to how the world works as ordained by God in creation. Furthermore, his insistence on the fact that we have limited knowledge of the interaction and relation between mind and body points forward to more holistic understandings of healing, and to more contemporary positions that also stress the limitations of a mere naturalistic approach. Finally, and more critically, he mainly restricts his argument to elements that take their point of departure in the natural world perceived as a "mechanism," and thus he ignores the interrelation of the natural world and the social and cultural and psychological world.

When we now turn to look at the interpretations of Jesus' miracles in the theology of the two giants of dialectical theology, Karl Barth and Rudolf Bultmann, we get a good impression of how differently this topic is interpreted in modern scholarship. Furthermore, they both illustrate how much their *theological* positions determine how they relate to Jesus as a healer in the historical sense.

Rudolf Bultmann

Rudolf Bultmann's account of the miracles performed by Jesus mainly focuses on their theological significance rather than on their actual historicity. This significance is spelled out in his treatment of the theology of the New Testament, especially in his treatment of John's Gospel. His approach nevertheless offers us a wider range of interpretation of the significance of Jesus as healer than the one we get by simply looking, for example, at Schleiermacher's or Barth's position.

Bultmann points to John's interpretation of Jesus' miracles as specific "signs." These signs have a double function: they reveal Jesus' glory, but they also reveal the disbelief of those who refuse to be convinced by the miracles. Hence, the meaning of the miracles does not lie in their occurrence as such but in what they reveal. Bultmann finds support for this interpretation in John's critical reports of those who were seeking Jesus because of such events. Bultmann writes, under the heading "The Offense of the Incarnation of the Word":

As "signs," the miracles of Jesus are *ambiguous*. Like Jesus' words, they are misunderstandable. Of course, they are remarkable occurrences, but that only makes them indicators that the activity of the Revealer is a disturbance of what is familiar to the world. They point to the fact that the Revelation is no worldly occurrence, but an other-worldly one. They are pictures, symbols. Therefore, what is this-worldly in the reports of miracles as such, are really attempts to convey the symbolic meaning of the revelation in Jesus of food, light, and life, respectively.

Hence, Bultmann seems to reject the historicity of the miracles of Jesus, including the acts of healing, by interpreting these stories as having a deeper message.[4] However, on this point he does not seem to be fully consistent (see below).

Unlike other interpreters, Bultmann does not find that the miracles provide Jesus with legitimating credentials. This approach may be seen in line with his insistence on their ambiguity as noted in the above quote. His point is that in John, if these events are not interpreted as signs, they are an offense. In a perceptive reading, Bultmann shows how the ambiguous character of the events is displayed in how "the healing of the lame man and the cure of the blind man both elicit enmity and persecution" and how "the raising of Lazarus brings Jesus to the cross."[5]

Bultmann does not rule out the possibility that Jesus performed any miracles, however. This becomes clear in his statement about how these miracles for many might have been "the first shock that leads them to pay heed to Jesus and so begin to have faith — for this purpose, miracles are, so to speak, conceded; nevertheless, for the leaders of the people, the representatives of 'the world,' the miracles are the offense that leads them to condemn him to death."[6] Such an interpretation cannot be made unless one allows for at least some events to be interpreted as miracles. But their status remains somewhat obscure, because Bultmann mostly focuses on how they are construed within a text that is based on theological rather than historical concerns.

The fact that the miracles appear as ambiguous also underscores that they are in need of interpretation: As signs, they can be both understood

4. Rudolf Bultmann, *Glauben und Verstehen* (Tübingen: Mohr, 1952), 2:44. This reminds us of Augustine's approach when he found that the Genesis account was offensive if taken literally, thus concluding that it was in need of symbolic interpretation.

5. Bultmann, *Glauben und Verstehen*, 2:45.

6. Bultmann, *Glauben und Verstehen*, 2:45.

and misunderstood, a point often made evident in the composition of John's Gospel. As is the case with other elements in the ministry of Jesus, the miracles are not always understood as signs, but are simply understood on the "terms of the world." In other words, the works of Jesus as a healer may not exclusively be understood in their actual significance as works offering new chances for health to those who meet Jesus, but can also be interpreted as signs of what will be the situation in the coming kingdom of God.

As Philip Clayton[7] has recently pointed out, Bultmann holds that Christians can affirm miracles when they realize that doing so does not require a contradiction of the laws of nature. The subjective dimension of miracles grounds them in the language and life of faith — which Bultmann like the rest of dialectical theology sees as incompatible with, and accordingly also in tension with, science. A stronger and ontologically based notion of wonder or miracle is impossible for us today because we understand the processes of nature to be governed by law. Here Bultmann works on the premise that a miracle is a violation of the conformity to the laws that govern all of nature, and that this idea is no longer tenable. Clayton summarizes Bultmann's position thus:

> Bultmann introduced a new sense of "wonder." A wonder in his sense is an event that is not in contradiction to the laws of nature but is seen, through the eyes of faith, to be an act of God. If we replace the out-of-date notion of miracles with the idea of wonders, "it is really possible for the Christian *continually to see new wonders.* This world process, which to the unbeliever must appear as a sequence of events governed by law, has for the Christian become a world in which God acts." Applied to our topic, this implies that Christians can believe in both physical and spiritual healings, and indeed in ways that are truly "wondrous" (i.e., that utilize the language of divine action), yet without clashing with the laws of nature.[8]

Bultmann's position implies, as a consequence, that he has to distinguish between how Jesus and his disciples understood the miracles and what we can say about them. When he explicitly focuses on the question of miraculous

7. See Philip Clayton, "The Theology of Spiritual Healing," in *Spiritual Healing: Scientific and Religious Perspectives,* ed. Fraser Watts (Cambridge: Cambridge University Press, 2011), p. 54.

8. Clayton, "The Theology of Spiritual Healing," p. 54. Clayton here refers to *Rudolf Bultmann: Interpreting Faith for the Modern Era,* ed. Roger A. Johnson (London: Collins, 1987), p. 267; cf. pp. 256–69.

healings, it becomes clear that Jesus and his disciples saw what happened as something different from what we are able to do on the basis of today's science. Clayton points to how "Bultmann is careful to emphasize that miracles should never be understood as objective occurrences and should never be used as proof of anything."[9] When he sees them as presupposing belief in God he basically says that the notion of miracle is constituted by subjective faith and not by the experienced occurrence.

Of course, a position like this has its philosophical and scientific presuppositions. Taken in extreme with regard to our topic, it could mean that "healing lies in the eyes of the beholder." In one sense this is true; we all filter our information through the worldview we hold. However, I think there is another, and more significant *theological* consequence here, namely that this approach not only de-ontologizes but also disembodies the notion of healing, whether we interpret such events as divine acts or not. Given Bultmann's perspective, healing as an act of God only takes place in the mind of the believer, and not in the embodied reality of both the healee and their physical and social world. This is a consequence that has significant theological repercussions with regard to the whole understanding of incarnation, as we shall see in the closing section of this part. Instead of a deep incarnation,[10] this can be characterized as a weak incarnation — in which God does not really engage with the concrete and embodied manifestations of physical reality.[11]

Karl Barth

Karl Barth deals extensively with Jesus' miracles in general, and more specifically with the significance of his healings, in *Church Dogmatics* IV/2.[12] Barth's elaborations are not rigidly developed when it comes to characteristics and analysis: On the one hand, he can say that the distinctive acts of

9. Clayton, "The Theology of Spiritual Healing," p. 55.

10. I borrow the notion of deep incarnation from the recent work of Niels Henrik Gregersen. See, e.g., N. H. Gregersen, "Deep Incarnation: Why Evolutionary Continuity Matters in Christology," *Toronto Journal of Theology* 26, no. 2 (2010): 173–88.

11. The previous part of the present study has worked out this embodied nature of Jesus' healings in the NT.

12. Karl Barth, *Church Dogmatics* IV/2, ed. Geoffrey W. Bromiley and T. F. Torrance, trans. Geoffrey W. Bromiley (London: T&T Clark, 2010). In-text references in parentheses are to this work until further notice.

Jesus that we might call miraculous have an "extraordinary, alien and, let us not hesitate to say it, supernatural character" (p. 212). On the other hand, he admits that their incomprehensible character need not be the same in every instance, and that "there appears to be the possibility of explaining some of them, many of them, and perhaps even all of them, in a way which is at least approximately comprehensible, seeing and understanding them as one novelty in a series of others rather than the incursion and appearance of something completely new" (p. 212). This rather ambiguous statement seems to imply that even Barth is open to the approach suggested by Schleiermacher, namely that even though we are presently unable to explain these acts, they have analogies and are thus only of a "relatively miraculous character" (p. 212). Barth also points to how such historical analogies seem to have been available to Jesus' contemporaries, a point that implies that the uniqueness and therefore the incomprehensibility of these acts (due to lack of analogy) would be hard to affirm. Hence, Barth also seems to acknowledge that the implicit christological significance of the acts of Jesus as healer cannot be due to the fact that he was alone in performing such acts.

Furthermore, Barth is aware that from the standpoint of modern knowledge many of Jesus' acts "could and can finally entice us to an interpretation in what is either a wholly naturalistic sense, or a close approximation to it" (p. 213). This point notwithstanding, Barth rejects as too crude the critical scholarship that dismisses these acts as fiction. However, he also sees that some of the phenomena recorded (possessions) may be interpreted in light of what we know of mental disorders, whereas others might be worth considering in light of more recent "naturalistic" approaches similar to those we today would characterize as parapsychology (p. 213). However, Barth underscores that even though we may, in the contemporary world, interpret these acts of Jesus according to a naturalist framework, we do not come close to what Barth claims to be most important about them in the New Testament. He holds that the New Testament tradition sees these acts of healing as extraordinary, supernatural actions, and as miracles in a different sense than we see them when we establish their credibility by relating them to other, similar-looking phenomena. Therefore, to interpret the miracles along such lines is something else than "the faith which the New Testament means to demand and waken in us when it recounts them. Indeed, it might well be the last and strongest obstacle to this faith" (p. 213). Barth thereby suggests that their theological significance is different from the significance they would have within other contexts of interpretation. Thus he affirms the basic approach of dialectical theology, which avoids interpreting theological significance in ways that align this significance with that which can be derived from human experience.

This way of reasoning therefore shows clearly how Barth's approach to the theological significance of Jesus as healer builds on elements other than those that can be established on the grounds of common and accessible knowledge from other sources. Barth even goes so far as to say that an approach that tries to see Jesus as healer in the light of other healers and extraordinary events that we know of in the contemporary world may be counter to faith that qualifies as Christian. Hence, he seems to block the road to a more general approach to these phenomena and their theological significance, a move that in turn makes it even more important to analyze his own position and his reasons for taking it.

What makes the healing events recorded in the Gospels theologically significant is the fact that they appear as "absolutely new and different, in their unity with the good news, the teaching, the proclamation and therefore the existence of the man Jesus, from all other human or cosmic occurrence, usual or unusual, ordinary or relatively extraordinary" (p. 215). Barth calls such events miraculous not because they appear as such compared to other normal or abnormal events but because of their relation to Jesus. He can only say this, of course, on the basis of a prior identification of Jesus as distinct from any other and ordinary human being. In other words, it is the faith of Barth and of Christians in Jesus as the Word of God that makes him designate these events as special in the theological sense that he attributes to them. Without this faith, it would not be possible to claim such events were special. One may ask, however, if this claim would be possible at all unless there were something in such events, apart from the faith *(remoto Deo)* that made such identification possible.

Following from Barth's considerations so far, we can thus identify the following three important theological decisions:

1. Barth does not deny the extraordinary character of healings and other miracles as such, nor does he ascribe to them any real theological significance in themselves.[13]

---

13. Clayton comments on this as follows: "Barth's insistence that science and historiography cannot undercut the claims to miraculous healings might at first blush appear to be similar to Bultmann's. But the reason is in fact radically different: the miracle claims of the New Testament are eminently believable. So we have no reason to jettison them in the belief that the worldview of modern science is more plausible." He thereby shows that although they both reason in ways that can be attributed to the mode of dialectical theology, their

2. The theological significance of these events is constituted by faith in Jesus as the Word of God.

3. Jesus' own way of being involved in miracles sets him apart from others who have different aims in terms of therapeutic, magic, or other practices (see below).

However, it may be asked if Barth does not underplay the significance of the events in question for giving rise to the belief in Jesus as the Word of God, as they attest to Jesus' extraordinary capacities in a way that creates faith, hope, and love in those who witness him doing such acts. This criticism notwithstanding, Barth seems right in identifying the theological significance of such works as related to Jesus' preaching of the kingdom of God.[14]

Barth's dialectical method of theology becomes apparent in the way he develops the theological significance of these acts further: The way the so-called miracles are incorporated in the teaching of the kingdom of God implies a rejection of human-made modes of thinking in contrary terms — which he calls antithesis — like the opposition between the "ordinary and the extraordinary, the conceivable and the inconceivable, the natural and the supernatural, the earthly and the heavenly, the this-worldly and the other-worldly" (p. 216), because the new in the kingdom is not related to anything that can be described by such terms. Instead of these apparent contradictions, Jesus reveals another, and very different, antithesis, which it is not possible to describe in the terms already used to identify the different features of this world (p. 216).

As Barth moves this reflection forward his main aim first of all seems to be to establish the non-significance of the miracles as such, and to downplay their theological content. The miracles are, as he sees it, already part of this world and its conditions, and it is thus possible to compare them to already known or observed phenomena. This can be seen illustrated by his claim that Jesus did not have any practice of healing, and did not use any therapeutic technique (p. 216). It is worth noting how he articulates this position: "There is no such thing as a technique of healing in any serious sense. He [i.e., Jesus] did not control any art or craft which he applied in His acts. He did

---

strategy and outcome are nevertheless quite different. Clayton, "The Theology of Spiritual Healing," p. 55.

14. See Barth, *Church Dogmatics* IV/2, p. 215: "According to the proclamation in the Word of Jesus the alien and miraculous and inconceivable thing that takes place in His actions in the world, and in defiance of all human being and perception and understanding, is nothing other than the kingdom of God."

not practice at all in this field, whether as a doctor or magician or, for that matter, as a physician of the soul. . . . Miracles which are characterised by the application of any physical, magical or psychical technique are miracles of a very different type" (p. 216).

In short, Jesus' miracles have the aim of calling people to faith in the kingdom of God. They serve the aim of faith. Hence, Barth can say that "there in an indissoluble connection of proclamation, miracle and faith" (p. 217). The gospel miracle is the real miracle, and any other event or happening is only an actualization of Jesus' own proclamation as call to repentance and faith (p. 217).[15] It is against the backdrop of this theological interpretation that Barth can explain why Jesus commanded many who were healed not to speak of what had taken place: They should not focus on the miracles as such, only on the kingdom they bore witness to. As Clayton has pointed out, this means that "Barth recognizes that spiritual healings are not ends in themselves. Their purpose is not merely to improve someone's physical or bodily condition," or part of some welfare program with spiritual aids.[16] Furthermore, this is why we should not, suggests Barth, equate the miracles of Jesus with the "relative miracles" we can find both in other parts of ancient history and in our own time (p. 218). An understanding of the "absolute miracle" in the miracles of Jesus cannot be established on the basis of a comparison with the relative ones, because the kingdom is something totally new, which does not work on the basis of the conditions of this world. Barth writes:

> The realisation that this is the case depends wholly and exclusively on the insight that we have to do here with the kingdom of God as it has drawn near in Jesus. The actions of Jesus are the miracles of this kingdom, "the powers of the world to come" (Heb. 6:5). And it is the fact that they are miracles of the kingdom which alone characterises them as true and absolute miracles as opposed to those which took place and still take place in our human antitheses. It is this fact alone which is the basis of the distinctive symptoms that warn us against any simple identification. (p. 219)

15. "Barth is a true son of the Reformation in his emphasis that 'their significance [that is, the significance of the New Testament miracles] is only as actualisations of His Word, as calls to repentance and faith.' But for him, unlike Bultmann, the centrality of faith is no substitute for objective truth. Because Christian faith is true, what it entails is also true; and because the revelation of God in Jesus Christ is trustworthy, the miracle claims are more to be trusted than what rests on the authority of science." Clayton, "Theology of Spiritual Healing," p. 55. Clayton is referring here to Barth, *Church Dogmatics* IV/2 (1975 edition), p. 217.

16. Clayton, "Theology of Spiritual Healing," p. 55.

We are now able to add one more significant theological decision to the three already listed above:

4. Jesus is not a healer among healers, but the Word of God. Hence, in order to establish a "high" Christology, Barth's interpretation of Jesus' miracles and Jesus' work as a healer results in a Jesus who is not a healer, but a proclaimer of the kingdom of God. To understand Jesus as a healer would accordingly for Barth mean that one does not understand Jesus' ministry at all.

But if it is the power of God alone that is operative and revealed in the miracles of Jesus (p. 219), in what sense is it the case? Barth's understanding of the power manifest in these events interprets the miracles, including the healings of Jesus, mainly as signs. Their power is a power that "sheds light" on the human condition. In an almost gnostic way, he writes:

> What always takes place in them is that in and with them a completely new and astonishing light — and in all its different manifestations the same light — was cast on the human situation. And in the strict sense it was simply this light, and its shining, and the radiance which it shed, that encountered men as the unconditional power of God in the miracles of Jesus. This light was the genuinely incomprehensible, the genuinely miraculous, factor in these miracles. (p. 220)

In other words, the physical and/or natural phenomena are not manifestations of God's power in the way that Barth is after here. Instead, it is the events' ability to inform us of the new and in-breaking kingdom of God that is the main point. By developing his interpretation of the theological significance in this manner, Barth thus contributes to *the removal of the kingdom of God from the concrete experiential dimensions of human life,* and instead he situates the realization of this kingdom primarily in the context of human reflexivity. It is possible to see his development of this position in relation to the sketch of Calvin's theology presented earlier.

This rather critical comment is nevertheless somewhat outweighed when Barth elaborates further on the different aspects of what it means that Jesus turns to people in their need for healing and salvation. Here Barth develops several theological topics. The first is that Jesus wants to heal humans from the condition of suffering, which places them in the shadow of death. In this way, Jesus invites humans to start living as creatures of God and not only as determined by "cosmic" forces: "His existence as a creature in the natural cosmos is normalised. We must not ignore or expunge the phrase—as a creature in the natural cosmos. It is as such that he is radically blessed by the miracles of Jesus" (p. 222). Furthermore, the important element here is that humans are *sufferers*, not that they are sinners. They suffer under the conditions of the cosmos, and this is why Jesus opens up a new future to them by means of these miracles (p. 223). Thus the healings become signs of the future kingdom of God with all that this kingdom implies. What these healings shed light on when it comes to interpreting the human condition is that God has not forgotten the suffering human being (p. 224). Barth writes: "As Jesus acts in His commission and power, it is clear that God does not will that which troubles and torments and disturbs and destroys man. He does not will the entanglement and humiliation and distress and shame that the being of man in the cosmos and as a cosmic being means for man. He does not will the destruction of man, but his salvation" (p. 225).

Against this backdrop, Barth is able to further substantiate his reasons for claiming that the miracles of Jesus should not be understood on the same terms as other "miraculous" events known to us: As part of the activity of Jesus, they imply a rejection or defiance of the destructive powers in human life. Moreover, they have ethical content, as they are, according to Barth, signs not only of a generic form of omnipotence but also of an active omnipotence shaped by mercy. This ethical character makes God's power hostile to all powers that destroy human life. Hence, for Barth the ethical character of the miracles is not primarily to be found in the actual events that happen, but in the revelation of God as hostile to and fighting these powers. "For what is miraculous and new and incomprehensible in them (from every standpoint, not merely from a scientific but from an ethical and religious and even an aesthetic) is that God is a God who for man's sake cannot stand aside in this matter" (p. 232).

Barth closes his considerations on the miracles and their theological significance by underlining their gracing or graceful character. These events reveal God's actions as free and as independent of any human work or merit. Jesus does not allow the sinful condition of humans to influence his merciful acts of healing. These features of the human condition are, says Barth, at the "extreme margin" of such events: "Jesus is not really concerned with what from the anthropological point of view is the cause of human misery, but only with the misery itself and as such" (p. 232). The focus is, as already said above, on actual suffering, and in Jesus, God places himself in the world to relieve this suffering. "That He does so is quite undeserved by him, the creature, this cosmic being. It is simply and exclusively because this is the good will of God for him" (p. 232). I will return to this motif later.

Jürgen Moltmann

Jürgen Moltmann sees Jesus' ministry as closely related to his work as a healer. He writes: "Together with the proclamation of the gospel, the healing of the sick is Jesus' most important testimony to the dawning kingdom of God."[17] Furthermore, Moltmann sees the works of healing not only as related to Jesus but also as "an essential part of the church's apostolate."[18] Most likely because he writes from a perspective informed by the recent development of the charismatic movement in the Christian church, he identifies such works of healing as belonging to the charismatic experience of life.

The identification of works of healing as part of the essential work of both Jesus and the church does not keep Moltmann from also acknowledging the more general and common character of such abilities. Like others, he points to the commonness of miraculous healings in the ancient world, as we also know they are today.[19] Therefore, he emphasizes the theological context and significance of these healings. At this point, Moltmann sides with Barth and others in seeing how they, in the case of Jesus, are part of and "belong within the context of his proclamation of the kingdom of God."[20]

The healing ministry of Jesus is accordingly a testimony to who God is, and to God's power: It means that God's healing power becomes manifest in God's creation. Moltmann writes: "When the living God comes and indwells his creation, every creature will be filled with his eternal vitality. Jesus does not bring the kingdom of God only in words that waken faith; he also brings it in the form of healings which restore health. God's Spirit is a living energy that interpenetrates the bodies of men and women and drives out the germs of death."[21] Thus Moltmann interprets the healings carried out by Jesus as concrete and manifest experiences of who God is and what God's kingdom implies. And even though he leans on Christoph Blumhardt's notion of these

---

17. Jürgen Moltmann, *The Spirit of Life: A Universal Affirmation,* trans. Margaret Kohl (Minneapolis: Fortress, 1992), p. 188.

18. Moltmann, *Spirit of Life,* p. 189.

19. See Jürgen Moltmann, *Der Weg Jesu Christi: Christologie in Messianischen Dimensionen* (Munich: Kaiser, 1989), p. 124.

20. Moltmann, *Spirit of Life,* p. 189.

21. Moltmann, *Spirit of Life,* p. 189.

events as "miracles of the kingdom," he nevertheless also suggests that one should not emphasize their miraculous character, because,

> In the dawn of the new creation of all things, they are really not "miracles" at all. They are completely natural and just what we have to expect. It is only if this eschatological hope is lost that these "wonders" appear to be miracles in an unchanged world. But in the framework of hope for the kingdom of God, Jesus' healings are reminders of hope. They justify expectations brought to the Spirit of Jesus now, in the present.[22]

This last quotation is important, because it suggests two different approaches to what takes place: One is to see the healing works of Jesus as instances of what can and may take place in this world. Then these works are put on the same level as those of every other healer and of every other event that we may — on the basis of what we know, expect, and may be surprised by — call miraculous or a wonder. But then their impact on faith is lost: for the believer in the kingdom of God, these events are events of eschatological hope, and justifications of what will be a "natural" expectation in a world where God's life-giving powers rule and have conquered the powers of death. Thus, for faith the "healings are signs of the new creation and the rebirth of life."[23] They are portents of the resurrection and the eternal life promised by Jesus. Moltmann therefore also points to the close etymological relation between the notions of "healing" and "salvation" in German (*heilen* and *Heil*).[24] Accordingly, healings are for Moltmann foretokens of resurrection: healing restores people to their life, just as resurrection means that the kingdom of God conquers the powers of death.[25]

Such an understanding of signs is also in accordance with the concept of signs in John's Gospel, where they are closely related to "the time" of Jesus and his manifestation in the glory of the resurrection. It is Jesus' death and resurrection that makes it possible to see healings as more than things "of this world" and to interpret them as signs of the kingdom of God to come.

Like Barth, Moltmann points to the lack of method and possibility for repetition in Jesus' healings. This point notwithstanding, he also holds that healings are a result of the interaction between the expectations in a person's

---

22. Moltmann, *Spirit of Life*, p. 190. See also Moltmann, *Der Weg Jesu Christi*, p. 127.

23. Moltmann, *Spirit of Life*, p. 189.

24. Moltmann, *Spirit of Life*, p. 189.

25. Moltmann, *Spirit of Life*, p. 190.

faith and Jesus' will. Healings are *contingent,* not deliberately produced or contrived. Healings therefore "happen when and where God wills it"[26] — not because they are brought about by human effort. As such, they manifest a character of uncontrolled grace. We can add that as signs, they are not the final manifestation of what is to come: even people who are healed will eventually die, illness may return, or other challenges may present themselves.

At this point I also want to insert a reflection that may have some relevance for the question of theodicy, which I will return to later as well. If we see the healings of Jesus in light of concepts of sign and grace, it is hard to develop any theodicy on the basis of them. The most they can offer is an indication that God will not put up with human suffering forever, and wants to offer humans hope that such suffering will be overcome one day. As grace, healings are signs, and as signs, they are grace.

Moltmann describes the significance of Jesus' healings against the backdrop of some of the shortcomings of modern medicine: Because medicine focuses on the body and on biological functions, and makes the body an object, its concept of healing is restricted to the restored function of particular organs. Contrary to this approach, Moltmann sees in psychosomatic and holistic medicine another and more comprehensible way of accessing the experiences of faith healing, which may in turn make such healings less odd or peculiar. His main point is that when sickness affects the whole person, the whole person needs to be healed. In this way, Moltmann's own understanding of healing points to a more integrated anthropology — and a way of understanding illness which also suggests that healing of the body may lead to the healing of the soul, and vice versa.[27] It is against this backdrop that Moltmann articulates his answer to the question, how does Jesus heal? "Healing consists of the restoration of disrupted community, and the sharing and communication of life. Jesus heals the sick by restoring their fellowship with God. He restores to the sick their community with God through his solidarity with them, and his vicarious intervention for them."[28]

Finally, Moltmann points to how Jesus' power to heal the sick is related to his suffering. Here he refers to the words in Isaiah about the one who carries diseases and through whom "our wounds are healed" (Isa. 53:5). There are two strands in his elaborations here, both heavily reliant on the theological tradition that interprets Jesus mainly on the basis of his relation

---

26. Moltmann, *Spirit of Life,* p. 190.
27. See Moltmann, *Spirit of Life,* p. 191.
28. Moltmann, *Spirit of Life,* p. 191.

to God and his suffering at Easter. Not surprisingly, then, Moltmann claims that Jesus' "passion and his self-surrender on Golgotha are the secret of his healings of the sick."[29] He goes on:

> But how can the wounded find healing in his wounds? In Christ God has become human, and has assumed limited and mortal humanity and made it part of his eternal divinity. He assumed it so that he might heal it. In the passion of Jesus Christ God has assumed sick, weak, helpless and disabled human life and made it part of his own eternal life. God heals the sicknesses and the griefs by making the sicknesses and the griefs his suffering and his grief. In the image of the crucified God the sick and dying can see themselves, because in them the crucified God recognizes himself. Through his passion Jesus brings God into the God-forsakenness of the sick and into the desolation of dying. The crucified God embraces every sick life and makes it his life, so that he can communicate his own eternal life. And for that reason the crucified One is both the source of healing and consolation in suffering.[30]

There are several elements worth discussing in this interpretation: First, one may ask if it was the actual Easter events that allowed Jesus to heal — before his passion at Easter was undertaken. It is more likely to assume that Jesus was — like many other healers we know — very familiar with suffering already, both in his own life and his surroundings, and that these experiences had provided him with a basis of empathy and engagement that in turn made him a healer. Already from his childhood onward, he may have experienced challenges that made him prone to these powers.

Second, when Moltmann sums up the healing powers of Jesus by pointing to how Jesus is the place where God identifies with the human who suffers, this may indeed provide believers with a hope for the future, and a new vision of what is to come in the resurrection. However, this interpretation is on a different level and relates to other themes than those that actually made Jesus a healer in his concrete and temporal ministry. Thus there is a shift in focus here that does not seem to pay full tribute to what made it possible for Jesus to be a healer during his lifetime, whereas it may, on the other hand, help people find comfort and trust in how Jesus, by means of his resurrection, is able to finally overcome the powers of death and offer humans concrete and visible signs of this possibility.

29. See Moltmann, *Spirit of Life*, pp. 191–92.
30. Moltmann, *Spirit of Life*, pp. 191–92.

Recent Discussion about Miracles

The healings of Jesus, as well as of other healers, seem to challenge the world-view of Western society, which is at least partly based on scientific evidence from carefully conducted experiments and observations that are verifiable and repeatable. However, these stories about healing are themselves occasionally challenged by contemporary knowledge. It is against this backdrop that the whole discussion about Jesus as healer relates to the contemporary discussion about religion and science.

Are Healings Miracles? Preliminary Considerations

Spiritual healing is taken by some to be a particular example of a *specific divine action* in the natural world. But is this a necessary assumption? The idea of divine action often seems to be taken to imply a kind of supernatural *intervention* that overturns the laws of nature. This is a perspective that suggests some kind of competition between God and nature. But this division of labor is problematic, as it suggests that God works in certain areas whereas natural laws work in others. This seems to overturn the fundamental notion that God's work is also constitutive for the works of nature. Hence, the idea of specific divine interventions does raise concerns, both theologically (as we saw in Schleiermacher above) and scientifically (how can one specify what it is we are talking about?). Furthermore, this would be to give up the notion that God acts in specific ways with and in nature, which seems to be central to the biblical witness. As Fraser Watts writes, "To eliminate special divine action is to jettison a concept that has been central to the Judeo-Christian tradition."[1]

1. Fraser Watts, "Conceptual Issues in Spiritual Healing," in *Spiritual Healing: Scientific*

Accordingly, we have to ask if healing represents something that is contrary to "laws of nature." Watts summarizes the predicament clearly:

> From a scientific standpoint, "intervention" by God looks improbable, and there appears to be no scientific evidence for it. From a theological point of view it is unattractive because it involves the assumption that God overturns laws of nature that emanate from Him, and which it would be more consistent with his faithfulness and constancy to uphold. It also risks marginalizing God's action in the world to a few occasions when exceptional things occur, and neglecting the sense that the ordinary world depends constantly on God's general providence.[2]

In the following, I concur with Watts's description of this predicament as a starting point for the discussion. However, I also want to make it clear from the outset that this section discusses how and in what sense we can talk of *healing* as miraculous. The main point will therefore not be to discuss the notion of miracle with regard to all the events that are reported to surround the life and ministry of Jesus (e.g., walking on water and the resurrection), although some of what is said may also have bearings on these topics. In order to provide an adequate basis for the problem of how to understand something as miraculous (if at all), I suggest that the best way to start is by adopting a more *phenomenological* approach that asks why we assign some events to the category of a miracle.[3] Only against this backdrop is it then in turn fruitful to discuss scientific and theological dimensions related to this notion. A fairly common way of understanding Jesus' healing work is to assign it to his skills as a *miracle* worker or his acts of power.[4] From such a perspective, his healing ministry is simply categorized as part of the miracles he worked. As a consequence, healing is seen as a miracle. There are several features we should consider before assigning the healings to such a category — or not.

---

and Religious Perspectives, ed. Fraser Watts (Cambridge: Cambridge University Press, 2011), p. 7.

2. Watts, "Conceptual Issues in Spiritual Healing," p. 7.

3. I prefer to use the notion of phenomenology instead of making use of the subjective-objective distinction used, e.g., by Terence Nichols, in his introduction to the *Zygon* 2002 issue on miracles, "Miracles in Science and Theology," *Zygon: Journal of Religion and Science* 37, no. 3 (2002): 703–16.

4. See Hans Kvalbein, *Jesus: Hva ville han? Hvem var han? En innføring i de tre første evangelienes budskap* (Oslo: Luther, 2008), pp. 128–42.

First, because the healings take place in a way that cannot be accomplished by everyone else, or generated as a result of clearly defined (medical) skills, healings appear *extraordinary*. Not only are they not possible to accomplish as a result of common and familiar medical intervention, but they also have an element of the unknown in them: we do not know exactly what happens, how it happens, and so on.

The above is furthered by a second consideration, namely, that healing takes place by the intervention of specific "healers," who have capacities, gifts, or skills that are not common among humans. However, these skills are nevertheless not so rare that people do not know of them — healers are known in different cultures and in different religious and nonreligious contexts. The specific status of healers, including Jesus himself, is probably not unrelated to the fact that they can do something that others cannot, and do so without anyone being able to *explain* in medical or other terms what is happening.

Both these features point to elements that are usually also attributed to so-called miracles: They are extraordinary, unexpected in everyday common experience, and they are not possible to accomplish for all who might wish to make them happen. Furthermore, they are not always a result of clearly delineated practices or skills that have been developed and cultured. There is (often, always?) an element of *gift* behind such events: the person able to work healing has a gift that makes it possible, although this gift may be developed, cultured, and so on. This gift makes the person stand out as special, elected, and/or privileged in specific ways.

Taken together, not all of these features warrant the claim for seeing healings as miracles: that there are unknown processes at work is not a sufficient warrant for this claim. Moreover, that some humans have skills or gifts that others do not have is not in itself sufficient to say that they are miracles. (Think of a child born with perfect pitch or other extraordinary gifts.) An uncommon gift or capacity is not a miracle. (Think of small children with extremely high IQ or a specific talent for music and composing.)

Having said this, however, the *unexpected* character of the healing event against all odds and medically based predictions is perhaps one of the main reasons why people want to ascribe such events to the category of the miraculous. Especially for people who suffer over a long time from severe conditions that cause serious impediments to social life, physical capacities, or other vital functions for flourishing, such events may appear as miraculous because they are so life-changing. We see that this is sometimes the situation for those people who are reported to be healed in the New Testament narratives.

However, the fact that gifts of healing occur and are known in different milieus and cultures may suggest that the events that follow from them would be more aptly described as *extraordinary* rather than miraculous. Of course, there may be overlap between these notions. My point here is simply to suggest that by describing healings in this way, we need not necessarily see them as events that are incompatible with what our reality as such makes possible, although we are clearly considering events that go beyond what is possible to explain by means of the knowledge base of established Western medicine.

The intention here is in no way to play down the importance of Jesus' healing ministry. Rather, it is to indicate that his ministry is not primarily about making miracles, but of opening up the world of experience to more than what is present in ordinary, everyday experience. Furthermore, by seeing the healing ministry of Jesus against such a backdrop, we can see how he is an extraordinary human being, endowed with extraordinary human gifts and capacities working in the service of God, instead of seeing him and his capacities as something that is completely beyond the conditions of this world. The advantage of such a perspective, then, is that the gift of healing testifies to Jesus as fully human, instead of pointing to the exclusively divine character of his being.

Furthermore, this latter reflection is not to say that such gifts do not have a divine origin: they are clearly founded in the gracing and gifting powers of God, who wants his creation to experience life in its fullness. That God works within and on the basis of natural conditions neither makes God's works less divine nor the natural conditions less a part of God's works.

Soundings in the Contemporary Discussion

The view on miracles sketched out above can be developed and confirmed further when we look into the contributions to a specific issue on miracles in the journal *Zygon*, which in 2002 invited prominent scholars from different fields to reflect on the topic. In the following, I will present some of the reflections they offered. One of the advantages of referencing this discussion is that it allows us to see how the topic of healing and miracles is intertwined not only with philosophical and scientific topics but also with important theological ones.

Terence Nichols

A good example of the latter is Terence Nichols, who writes that "nothing could be more repellent, both scientifically and theologically, than a God who capriciously intervenes to heal this person while ignoring that person or who arbitrarily interrupts natural processes to produce a 'wonder' to astonish the multitudes."[5] Accordingly, Nichols argues that to understand miracles as a "violation" of natural laws is misleading. Instead, he proposes to see them as events that are consistent with, but transcend, natural processes.

Nichols further reflects on the fact that the hallmark of empirical science is its impartial openness to evidence. This openness has an important consequence when it comes to so-called miracles, because it means that we cannot see scientific laws as prescriptive, that is, as telling us what can and cannot occur in nature. But they describe what is going on and why. If these laws were prescriptive, however, even empirical evidence that cannot be explained by present scientific theory would have to be dismissed because it cannot be explicated according to current scientific theory. What scientific theories and formulated laws help us articulate are the patterns of events and precedents we have been able to observe. Their prescriptive function is not in saying what *must* happen, but is related to what we ought to expect in light of what has been observed previously.[6]

5. Nichols, "Miracles in Science and Theology," p. 703.

6. Nichols, "Miracles in Science and Theology," pp. 704-5. Cf. for a further elaboration on these points R. J. Berry's article in the same volume, "Divine Action: Expected and Unexpected," where he stresses that "it is not logically valid to use science as an argument against miracles. To believe that miracles cannot happen is as much an act of faith as to believe that they can happen. . . . Miracles are unprecedented events. Whatever the current fashions in philosophy or the revelations of opinion polls may suggest it is important to affirm that science (based as it is upon the observation of precedents) can have nothing to say on the subject. Its 'laws' are only generalisations of our experience. Faith rests on other grounds" (*Zygon: Journal of Religion and Science* 37, no. 3 [2002]: 719). Similar considerations are offered in Keith Ward's contribution in the same issue, "Believing in Miracles," which also suggest some of the procedures necessary for considering something to be miraculous: "In the question of whether miracles occur, then, the prestige and success of the natural sciences is of no avail. The sciences cannot, of themselves, make the possibility that miracles occur more or less likely. In assessing whether a miracle has occurred, we have to pay close attention, first of all, to the reliability and wisdom and knowledge of those who report its occurrence. Then we have to assess the sort of value explanation that can be given of its occurrence. Does it, for instance, contribute to the realization of a good and intelligible purpose that points to a transcending of physical conditions as their fulfilling destiny? Or is it just an odd event that seems to have no particular

With this understanding of natural laws and miracles, Nichols goes on to argue that the present evidence for what are commonly called miracles is respectable and deserves attention, and that it would be unscientific to ignore it. He suggests that "miracles are better understood as signs of divine action, which, like grace, do not violate nature but work through it, perfect it, and reveal its divine ground. Nature is not a closed system but an open system within a larger, divine context; viewed within this context, miracles can be seen as rational and even lawlike events that express the divine ground within which nature exists."[7]

This quote suggests that Nichols sees miracles within a framework where nature and grace cooperate — not unlike what one of the present authors has developed more extensively in another context.[8] Nichols points to different theological traditions' understanding of human nature as being elevated by God's grace, and uses love as an example. Although human beings have a natural capacity for love, it is limited; and "loving one's enemies seems to be beyond our natural capacities. But the love of God, poured into our hearts by the Holy Spirit (Romans 5:5), can elevate this love so that it is no longer self-centered (we love those who love us) but universal, as God's love is."[9] Nichols suggests that something similar may be possible in natural processes: "Just as the human psyche or will can transcend its normal state through the action of grace, so perhaps can the normal healing processes of the body transcend their usual capacities through the action of miraculous grace. Both the normal state and the transcendent state, however, are states of nature."[10] In other words, healing may be grounded in natural causes and enhanced by God's enabling an interaction between different parties that cannot occur in a similar way in any other relation.

This approach takes the embodied character of miracles seriously and

---

spiritual point? If the testimony is reliable, and the event transcends the normal powers of objects, which is disclosive of divine power and helps to realize a divine purpose in a conspicuous way, it is wholly reasonable to accept that a miracle has occurred. The occurrence of miracles, then, will be a proper part of a many-stranded argument for the existence of a personal ground of being, a Creator of the universe" (*Zygon: Journal of Religion and Science* 37, no. 3 [2002]: 748).

7. Nichols, "Miracles in Science and Theology," p. 705.

8. See Jan-Olav Henriksen, *Life, Love, and Hope: God and Human Experience* (Grand Rapids: Eerdmans, 2014). Some of these ways of reasoning are presented in more detail on pp. 231–44 below.

9. Nichols, "Miracles in Science and Theology," p. 710.

10. Nichols, "Miracles in Science and Theology," p. 710.

does not see them as having a purely spiritual content or as caused by spiritual causes only. This is a clear advantage. There is an interplay between Creator and the created here that is of crucial importance for a more holistic understanding of healing as such, and of God's relation to creation in general.[11] As Nichols indicates, his understanding implies that "miracles are never only the activity of God, as if God in a miracle acts alone, nakedly, in place of natural causes. Theologically, a miracle, even an exalted miracle like the resurrection, is always God working through or in cooperation with nature, not against it."[12] This being said, however, he goes on to speculate on how "the unknown-law-of-nature hypothesis" may relate especially to healings, and can be seen as "attributable to some unknown capacity of the mind."[13] He admits that although an "appeal to an unknown does not constitute an explanation," one may still argue that if God works through nature and not around it, "it is likely that the mind is involved in healings."[14] He continues to claim that "it makes sense to think that the best explanation is that somehow, by a mechanism we do not yet understand, divine activity, working through the mind, empowers the healing capacities of the human being in a way that transcends its usual capabilities."[15]

Nichols draws an important inference from these reflections: If a miracle is partly caused by divine activity (whatever "caused" may mean in this context), it will have to appear as an inexplicable event or a mystery that "seems to go beyond what can explained by natural causality. Natural causes will still be involved in the event . . . but it cannot be explained completely by natural causes."[16] This leaves him with a rather firm definition of what can count as a miracle from his point of view. If something is to count as a miracle, it (1) cannot be fully explained by natural causes, and (2) it must take place in a context of faith and prayer, as an apparent response to this prayer. If these conditions are fulfilled, Nichols says — and it is worth noting the careful phrasing here — that an instance of healing, for example, "*may be* a miracle."[17]

---

11. See, e.g., p. 87 above, and pp. 243–44 below.

12. Nichols, "Miracles in Science and Theology," p. 710.

13. Nichols, "Miracles in Science and Theology," p. 711.

14. Nichols, "Miracles in Science and Theology," p. 711.

15. Nichols, "Miracles in Science and Theology," p. 711. He admits, though, that this "would explain only some miracles, not all; it would not explain the resurrection."

16. Nichols, "Miracles in Science and Theology," p. 713.

17. Nichols, "Miracles in Science and Theology," p. 713 (emphasis added).

Keith Ward

A contribution that develops the argument along the same lines as Nichols, but also deepens our appreciation of the conceptual issues related to the understanding of miracles in general, is Keith Ward's article "Believing in Miracles" in the same issue of *Zygon*. The main points for consideration in our context here are the following:

First, like Nichols, Ward suggests that there is no need to see miracles as *opposed* to nature and the natural order. If we understand a miracle as an event that transcends the natural powers of objects as we know them, then a personal creator might well "cause such events in order to achieve a supernatural purpose — bringing creatures to eternal life." From this perspective, when such events happen, they would contribute to disclosing and realizing the divine purpose while simultaneously being "integral to the rational order of nature."[18] Ward's position here has the advantage that it can be integrated into an understanding of the cooperation between nature and grace as suggested by Nichols. The classical expression of this understanding is *gratia non tollit naturam sed perficit*.

Second, and important from a philosophical point of view, Ward rejects the influential view on miracles held by David Hume. He recognizes the importance of upholding the integrity of the natural order, which God does not set aside in his agency in what is called miraculous.

The Humean understanding of miracles presupposes that the laws of nature are absolutely changeless and universally operative, and divine agency would in this view represent interferences with or violations of the natural order. Ward writes:

> The antidote to this view is to see that if there is a personal Creator of all things, the physical cosmos will be partly instrumental in the realization of a purpose that begins with but transcends it — eternal life. Laws of nature are the general principles of intelligible regularity that govern the physical cosmos, but there is every reason for a theist to think that there are higher principles than laws of nature — principles that draw finite persons into conscious relationship with the Creator. Miracles, events that transcend the regularities of nature, result from the application of such intelligible principles. In extraordinary circumstances, and for reasons connected with the realization of the Creator's ultimate purpose, miracles are partial

18. Ward, "Believing in Miracles," p. 741.

completions of the intelligible purpose that underlies the very existence of a physical universe. Insofar as they disclose personal purpose and its foreshadowing in the history of this cosmos, miracles vindicate, not violate, the rational unity of the cosmos.[19]

Ward's position here occasions two comments: First, although he emphasizes physical nature in the above argument, there is no reason to see this argument as only related to God's works and intentions as manifested in the *physical* dimensions of reality. God can also manifest his intentions in *other* experiential realms of human life — a point I will return to later. Second, Ward also suggests that the full content of the divine purpose or what takes place can only be realized when the unity of the cosmos is grasped — something that can happen only when the Creator's ultimate purposes have been realized. This latter point is important to keep in mind in light of objections to miracles that arise out of considerations of the theodicy problem. We cannot at the present stage in history make final decisions as to why things happen according to divine intentions.

Wolfhart Pannenberg

Whereas Nichols along with Ward and others reflects on *objective* conditions for miracles, Wolfhart Pannenberg stresses mostly the *subjective* dimension in the experience of miracles.[20] He recommends that theology avoid purely objective concepts of miracles as occurring *praeter naturam* or *contra naturam*. Most likely he wants to avoid claims about the ontological nature of these events as such that are too strong. Instead, he picks up on Augustine's idea of miracle, which stresses the subjectivity of human experience of nature: "The Augustinian concept of miracle is subjective in that it is related to what we experience as unusual and exceptional in contrast to the accustomed patterns of events. The objective basis of this experience is the contingency of events. Unusual events really happen."[21] This is a more modest approach than the one offered by Nichols, and takes its point of departure in a "weaker" understanding of the events in question,

---

19. Ward, "Believing in Miracles," p. 746.
20. See Wolfhart Pannenberg, "The Concept of Miracle," *Zygon: Journal of Religion and Science* 37, no. 3 (2002): 759-62.
21. Pannenberg, "Concept of Miracle," pp. 760-61.

namely, one that sees the perception of them as "unusual." Compared to Nichols this is a more open approach, but it is also one that allows us to say that such things as miracles do in fact not happen, although Pannenberg himself does not say so. When Pannenberg therefore admits that contingent events take place and appear as contingent because they are not covered by known natural laws, he sees the only challenge in this regard to be that it "only requires us to admit that we do not know everything about how the processes of nature work."[22]

Pannenberg's position can be used for two purposes: One is to provide the basis for a theoretical approach that allows for admitting that unusual things can happen — though this does not in itself provide grounds for openness to specific divine intervention under specific circumstances. The other is that his position can be used as a basis for criticizing modes of scientific hubris that claim we have a sufficient basis for knowing what happens in all unexpected and unusual events.

Ilkka Pyysiäinen

Ilkka Pyysiäinen, a Finnish scholar of the cognitive science of religion, backs up Pannenberg's more subjective approach, but he also grounds his understanding more firmly in recent results from his own area of study. He sees what we call miracles as "counterintuitive phenomena" that are based on the way human cognition works in relation to external reality: "Every now and then we encounter events and phenomena, and hear stories of such events and phenomena, that contradict our intuitions. When such events and phenomena are not simply left unexplained but instead are connected to our already existing beliefs about counterintuitive agents and forces, the result is the idea of a miracle in the strong sense of the term."[23]

It is worth noting here that Pyysiäinen is writing about our *ideas* of what a miracle is, and how these ideas come about, and that he does so on the basis of knowledge about how the mind works more than on the basis of the mind's relation to reality. Against this backdrop, he lists four features that may be seen to cause people to believe in miracles:

22. Pannenberg, "Concept of Miracle," p. 762.
23. Ilkka Pyysiäinen, "Mind and Miracles," *Zygon: Journal of Religion and Science* 37, no. 3 (2002): 738.

1. We experience some real events that contradict our intuitive expectations.
2. We are able to form counterintuitive representations and store in the mind half-understood and meta-represented information.
3. Such representations fascinate us, evoke emotions, and are therefore culturally successful.
4. Our minds are equipped with a symbolic mechanism that treats half-understood information by carrying out searches in the memory, trying to find old representations that fit with the acquired and partly incomprehensible new representations.[24]

It is not hard to see how the features listed here may apply to instances of healing that cannot be explained from the point of view of established medicine and the expectations to which it gives rise.

After having given this explanation of why we employ notions of the miraculous, Pyysiäinen concedes that none of the above features say anything about "the question of whether some counter-intuitive forces and agents, not presently recognized by science, in fact do manipulate known reality in miraculous ways" — a point he admits cannot be decided by science in principle (as that would be a contradiction in terms).[25] There is, however, another reason why I bring his work to attention here, namely, this understanding seems to be in full accordance with Pannenberg's position as stated above, while simultaneously making it clear that the ontological categories at stake are, for both of them, related to the unexpected, the counterintuitive, and the unknown. Accordingly, they do not offer much help in assessing the reality of, say, miraculous healings.

John Polkinghorne

In his *Zygon* article, titled "The Credibility of the Miraculous," John C. Polkinghorne offers some reflections that may help us get a better grasp of the phenomenology of the miraculous in a way that bridges the position of Nichols and Ward on the one hand, and the position of Pannenberg and Pyysiäinen on the other. Polkinghorne starts by asking what causes the human experience of *wonder,* and answers that it arises from three logically different sources.

---

24. Pyysiäinen, "Mind and Miracles," p. 738.
25. Pyysiäinen, "Mind and Miracles," pp. 738-39.

First, wonder arises when the effects of normal human powers are greatly enhanced in a particular instance, as when a five-year-old can compose brilliant music or a ten-year-old graduate from college. Although such occurrences are rare, they are not contrary to nature, although "an exceptional degree of human ability is being manifested."[26] Polkinghorne also applies this understanding to events of healing, and rightly points out that much evidence suggests "that some people possess the power to enable psychosomatic healing in others."[27] Accordingly, to believe "that Jesus possessed this power to a supreme degree would help us to understand at least some of the healing stories that are integral to the Gospel accounts. Such healings would be the results of a kind of enhanced naturalism."[28] We note that this view may also be in accordance with Pannenberg's assertions, whereas it falls short of Nichols's conditions for identifying miracles.[29]

Second, we also experience wonder when two natural and unremarkable phenomena "coincide in a way that produces an occurrence that is perceived as significant."[30] Whereas a neutral observer in this situation would not be able to see more than what Polkinghorne calls a remarkably fortunate coincidence, it is nevertheless possible to assume that God may be active in such events.[31] He suggests that some of the nature miracles in the gospels are such "striking coincidences brought about by divine action." But as he sees it, "these events, though astonishing and powerfully significant, are consequences of God's special providential interaction with creation rather than miracles in the stricter sense of their involving an apparent violation of a law of nature. These events are indeed brought about by God, but they take place within the normal grain of nature rather than in any contradiction to it."[32]

Third, wonder occurs when we are faced with radically *"unnatural"* events that are so "contrary to normal expectation that they cannot be contained within any plausible extrapolation of science's account of the way the world works."[33] The first and most important instance of this is the res-

26. John C. Polkinghorne, "The Credibility of the Miraculous," *Zygon: Journal of Religion and Science* 37, no. 3 (2002): 752.

27. Polkinghorne, "Credibility of the Miraculous," p. 752.

28. Polkinghorne, "Credibility of the Miraculous," 752.

29. Cf. above, pp. 191–93.

30. Polkinghorne, "Credibility of the Miraculous," 752.

31. Polkinghorne, "Credibility of The Miraculous," pp. 752–53.

32. Polkinghorne, "Credibility of The Miraculous," p. 753.

33. Polkinghorne, "Credibility of The Miraculous," p. 753.

urrection of Jesus Christ from the dead. As Polkinghorne admits, "If such an event really occurred, it could only credibly be as the consequence of a direct exercise of divine power in a wholly new and unprecedented way."[34]

With these distinctions in place, Polkinghorne identifies three major theological issues that one still needs to address when it comes to a full-blown theological understanding of the miraculous, and which may also have some relevance for our understanding of healing.

The first issue is divine consistency, which is at root a theological problem: "It is theologically inconceivable that God acts as a capricious magician or conjurer, doing something today that God did not think of doing yesterday and will not be bothered to do again tomorrow. So, the question of divine consistency is the central problem to address in relation to the credibility of the miraculous."[35] In other words, we need to see what are called miracles as events or actions that can be understood within the wider framework of God's actions with and for the world.

A theologically viable framework for understanding such actions can only be developed if we have a proper conception of what it means that God is almighty — of divine power. Here Polkinghorne, along with Keith Ward, finds it necessary to argue on a more sophisticated level than simply claiming that "if God is the Creator of the world God can bring about anything in that world that God fancies, whether it corresponds to happenings that have many precedents or to a miraculous happening that has no precedent at all."[36] Whereas God's actions are not externally constrained by the powers of God's creation, they are constrained by the divine nature itself: "God will neither will nor do anything that is not in accord with the divine character. The good God cannot do evil deeds; the rational God cannot act irrationally."[37]

The second issue is the Johannine understanding of miracles as "signs" *(sēmeia)*, which we touched on earlier. A theological framework for understanding God's miraculous actions from such a perspective identifies miracles as "events that serve as windows enabling us to look deeper into the character of God's will for creation."[38] Here Polkinghorne rightly points to the fact that an "adequate human understanding of divine power and divine intentions cannot be gleaned from everyday experience alone." Against

34. Polkinghorne, "Credibility of the Miraculous," p. 753.
35. Polkinghorne, "Credibility of the Miraculous," p. 753.
36. Polkinghorne, "Credibility of the Miraculous," p. 754.
37. Polkinghorne, "Credibility of the Miraculous," p. 754.
38. Polkinghorne, "Credibility of the Miraculous," p. 755.

this backdrop, their theological significance must be seen as a "component of God's self-revelation, acting not as unchallengeable endorsements but as the indispensable means by which certain kinds of truth can only be conveyed."[39]

The third theological issue in a full understanding of the miraculous is theodicy. As we have already seen in another context, miracles — healing miracles included — open the whole question of theodicy. It is worth returning to this again, as several of the writers critical of attributing divine agency to experiences of healing use this problem as their main argument.[40] Polkinghorne aptly articulates the challenge they pose in this regard when he writes, "Miracles, if they occur, must be rare events. The perplexity remains why, if God does indeed sometimes act in exceptional ways that profoundly manifest divine care for creation, these events are so exceptionally rare. There seem to be so many occasions that cry out for divine action of this dramatic kind. If God can work miracles, why did God not do so to prevent the Holocaust? The problems of theodicy, of which these agonizing queries are a particular case, do not lend themselves to any simple resolution."[41]

We will return to the question of theodicy in the last section of this book. Here we will only note that it cannot — and should not — be ignored when discussing what it may mean, from a theological point of view, to see Jesus as a healer who alleviates the burdens of some of those he encounters, while the world at the same time remains full of people who do not get similar miraculous relief.

So far in this section, we have seen that healing events, instead of being merely miraculous, are more adequately dealt with and interpreted as unexpected events that open up to the reality of God. Contrary to Hume's infamous assumption, they need not be seen as violations of natural laws, but can be seen as events that enhance rather than disrupt the integrity of the natural order and God's intentions for the world. The theologians and philosophers we have presented in this section provide us with a sufficient philosophical and theological basis to recognize the possibility of healing without ending up in either sheer irrationality or claims that healing contradicts what we know about nature.

---

39. Polkinghorne, "Credibility of the Miraculous," p. 755.
40. See, e.g., Stephen Pattison, discussed below.
41. Polkinghorne, "Credibility of the Miraculous," p. 757.

Niels Henrik Gregersen and Divine Action in the World

Niels Henrik Gregersen discusses ways of seeing God's acts that make more sense than a distinction between a deist God on the one hand and an interventionist God on the other, which tend to be the two main contrasting positions in discussions of miracles.[42] Gregersen employs a distinction between special divine action (SDA) and general divine action (GDA).[43] After discussing some of the problems of this distinction and its relation to the question about the status of natural laws, Gregersen suggests that we see God's fundamental actions in the world as the *special* activities of God's doing. This relates to his view that natural laws only have explanatory power if everything is equal.[44] He writes: "What if we take the notion of SDA as fundamental rather than as something added on the top of GDA? On this view, the singularity of divine activities has the ontological priority over against the notion of general divine actions, God's activity is always one and undivided, and yet complex and multifaceted in its manifestations. God is not first creating 'a being' of a thing (GDA), and then perhaps also determining its 'operations' (SDA). *Esse et operari unum sint.*"[45] One of the advantages of this way of thinking is that Gregersen is able to see what we call GDA "as grounded in the divine self-consistency as self-giving love, but actualized ever anew as God's gracious activity from the midst of the material world itself."[46] Then we cannot speak of God's general activity as abstracted from God's singular acts. The world as a complex network of interacting events and processes exists at each moment as created by God *ex nihilo* (out of nothing) and *ex ovo* (out of the potentialities of the past) and for the purpose of letting something new come into being *(ad novum).*[47] As the observant reader will recognize, this approach allows us to see events like healing as actualizations of God's self-giving love in the practice of Jesus, and simultaneously as an expression of God's self-consistency.

---

42. For a theological discussion of the problems with setting up the dilemma in this way, see the discussion of Pattison's criticism of MacNutt in the following section.

43. The following builds on Niels Henrik Gregersen, "Special Divine Action and the Quilt of Laws," in *Scientific Perspectives on Divine Action: Twenty Years of Challenge and Progress,* ed. Robert J. Russell et al. (Vatican City: Vatican Observatory; Berkeley, CA: Center for Theology and the Natural Sciences; Notre Dame: University of Notre Dame Press, 2008).

44. See Gregersen, "Special Divine Action," p. 198.

45. Gregersen, "Special Divine Action," p. 192.

46. Gregersen, "Special Divine Action," p. 192.

47. Gregersen, "Special Divine Action," p. 192.

Gregersen's reconception of natural law, furthermore, makes it possible for him to see how God may be at work in all realms of human life in a way that cannot in principle be addressed by a reductive approach. Because life in its concreteness, as it appears to us in our experience as human beings, is such a multifaceted phenomenon, we need to think of it as prior to law-like descriptions. This, of course, has significance for understanding healing and wholeness as belonging together in the creating activity of God. He writes: "Just as SDA should be given priority over against a homogenized concept of GDA, so the multifaceted phenomenon should be given priority over physical laws."[48] He then formulates the theological importance of this approach in the following manner:

> On this theological account, God is and remains ontologically prior to the laws of nature. At the same time we can at once acknowledge the laws of nature that God actually has chosen for our world (and which science is uncovering for us) and yet be metaphysically open to the diverse canvas of laws that the different sciences present to us — metaphorically speaking — in their different shapes, sizes and colors. The uniformitarian view of a divine action, which always and everywhere repeats itself in accordance with a reestablished principle of nomological universality, is supplanted by a conjecture of a living God, who is constantly in a process of self-donation, both as ordering principle (Logos) and as operational presence (Spirit).[49]

By describing the priority of God's special action over against all the other features that constitute human experience of nature, Gregersen is able to point to how God's healing actions can be understood in a way that is parallel to how we experience the world: first as surprising, chaotic, and irregular, and then slowly moving toward regularity. This may in turn also suggest that we, in order to experience God, first need a special revelation of God and then, against this backdrop, might become able to identify the regularities

48. Gregersen, "Special Divine Action," p. 193.
49. Gregersen, "Special Divine Action," p. 193. Gregersen formulates more hypothetically and tentatively the underlying understanding of God and the laws of nature implied here as follows: "What if most of the 'laws of nature' that we believe inhabit the world of nature, are only '*ceteris paribus* laws,' that is, laws that only have explanatory power 'if everything is equal' — which is never the case? The issue is here to what extent the boundary-conditions may begin to invade the notion of laws, so that we can no longer make a clear distinction between the 'system' and the ever-changing 'boundary conditions'" (p. 198).

of the world as indications of God's faithful caretaking. Thus, we in turn also become able to interpret the world in light of the Logos revealed as Christ. Here, I simply want to point out that Gregersen's approach to the relation between God and nature allows us to uphold the notion of God as prior in a way that simultaneously acknowledges that nature, when experienced by humans, always appears as concrete. This makes his approach preferable to the abstractions that we may find in both metaphysics and in nomologically based accounts of nature that ignore the irregularities present in some of the extraordinary events of healing. From this perspective, events of healing may be part of a larger picture that consists of all God's works. They may, moreover, be events we will be able to learn more about as the world moves further toward the goal God has set for it.

Stephen Pattison's Criticism of Christian Spiritual Healing

Somewhat surprisingly, some of the recent literature we reviewed prior to writing this book addresses why Christians do *not* think healing happens today. Some of the more apologetic contributions do this in a somewhat moralistic sense and see this reluctance as the result of secular modernity's increasing influence on Christianity. Other contributions are more self-critical toward the Christian tradition and the way it has sometimes employed simplistic notions of the concept of miracle in a way that tends to overlook the complications it opens up. We will look at one of these critical contributions in the present section.

The British practical theologian Stephen Pattison[50] suggests that there is no area of human and religious life more important than that of illness and healing. However, he finds that much of the literature that deals with such topics does not do justice to their complexity and depth. Thus he calls for a more critical engagement with this topic — an approach he believes has deserted Christian writing on the theme (p. 1). Pattison's book can be read as a challenging contribution that serves this purpose. He sees the central place these topics have in human existence and in religion as an expression of the fact that "it is when people are ill that their faith is experientially verified or refuted" (p. 7). Accordingly, "A theology which cannot speak to the

---

50. In the following, I refer to Stephen Pattison, *Alive and Kicking: Towards a Practical Theology of Illness and Healing* (London: SCM, 1989), with page numbers in parentheses in the text until further notice.

issues raised by disease and suffering could well seem a theology not worth having" (p. 7).

Pattison does not reject that healing takes place in distinct religious context and forms, but he sees all the ways in which healing takes place as having both strengths and weaknesses. Therefore, they need to be assessed properly, and not be subjected to overgeneralizations (pp. 2–3).

One of the first features Pattison highlights and criticizes is the tendency to speak of disease and illness as *one* thing: in fact, conditions related to these are experienced, perceived, and dealt with in a number of ways. Only by recognizing this diversity does it become possible to say something about what a good and correct healing response would be (p. 4). On the other hand, fragmentation, plurality, and isolation seem to be main features in much contemporary reflection on healing. Many of the present approaches and contributions overlook the complexity of the issues at hand, and this often leads to the wrong idea about only one approach being adequate or spiritually apt (see p. 10). Not only do different healing methods require theological evaluation, but also, says Pattison, "theology also needs the challenge provided by different healing methods with the implicit ideologies and values they promote" (p. 15). It is hard to disagree with these concerns.

While Pattison does not reject in principle the fact that there may be such a thing as spiritual healing, he also thinks (unlike Watts and others) that it is not clear from a scientific point of view that such healing takes place. Nevertheless, like Schleiermacher he is open to the possibility that more light may be shed on the relevant phenomena in the future (p. 15). From a theological point of view, "the main task of Christians is not so much to discover how and whether healing 'works,' so much as to evaluate the significance, implications and values promoted by various healing methods" (p. 15). He then considers the debate about the possibility of Jesus acting as a healer as a dead end, and instead emphasizes that "the point consists in the significance of Jesus' healings; what did they reveal about the nature of God, of human beings and of disease?" (p. 15).

Again, there are valuable concerns in Pattison's statements, but in the above we can also identify the previously addressed tendency to see the contribution of theology as related to the "meaning" and significance of healing rather than to the actual embodied experience of healing. Of course the two are closely related, but Pattison's emphasis on the former easily slides into a dismissal of the latter, where people should not be concerned with the opening up of concrete and experiential spaces of healing in their lives, spaces that are also charged and enabled by religious symbols and traditions.

Pattison highlights a significant point in relation to the "noise" that sometimes surrounds present-day healers and their ministries in "healing rallies." Despite the different interpretations of the ministry of Jesus, there is some agreement that it was not untainted by others' struggle to gain power, to manipulate him, and so on for their own gain. However, the Gospels provide a clear picture of "how the power of Jesus was over the illness or disease, and not one of coercion and manipulation of the healees" (see pp. 18–19); this picture allows us to see his actual healing ministry as opposed to such struggles.

In a review of contemporary theological literature, Pattison identifies several important traits of a viable theological approach to healing: it focuses on the present reality, and "beliefs and perceptions derive their primary significance from what they can tell us about the present" (p. 63). Furthermore, many theologies "are concerned with action to change the world rather than with just understanding the world" (p. 64). Contemporary theology is also anthropocentric, as it is more concerned with humanity than the reality of God as such. Included in this last trait is moreover a concern for how humans live in the material, embodied world (p. 65). After having identified these traits, Pattison uses them as a backdrop for criticizing other, popular contributions to a theology of healing.

> Theologies emerging from and associated with the healing movement may have a great deal in common with practical theologies in their contemporary, anthropocentric concern for relating faith and life in healing action. As yet, however, they are disappointingly attenuated and narrow. In the first place, religious healing is mostly seen as the straightforward application of ancient scriptural truths to present day conditions. There is little attempt to learn from the text of the present in order that the views and practices of the past may be critically evaluated and modified. Instead of a dialogue taking place between the realities of our knowledge about illness in contemporary society and the theological tradition, religious healing is all too often a matter of conforming the present to a very particular religious interpretation of the past. (pp. 66–67)

Pattison continues by saying that this narrow approach also "characterizes the range of understandings regarded as significant and valid by healers," but his claim in this regard lacks substantiating sources in the context where it appears. According to him, "they [the range of understandings] do not draw widely on the resources of philosophy, theology, the social sciences or medical science to develop different practical responses and theological attitudes to different situations" (p. 65). He goes on:

> What could be a very exciting area of practical theological exploration too often becomes a rut of pragmatic fundamentalism. The consequence is that important questions remain unanswered, no new insights into healing or theology emerge and new books on healing simply regurgitate the received "truths" of the past. The whole area of healing and illness is a crucial nexus for the veracity and relevance of Christianity and Christian theology. It deserves a more active intellectual engagement than is presently offered by the religious healers themselves.

The criticism launched here is perhaps apt when one considers when the book was published (1989), but can hardly count as valid today. An increasing number of studies on religious healing have been published; the books of Porterfield and Watts that we have discussed above, for example, suggest that this is no longer a relevant description. Pattison's criticism can nevertheless be regarded as a warning against too simplistic theological approaches to healing, or approaches that do not open up to seeing healings within the wider context of culture, society, and the history of religions.

Who Is the God of Healing? Pattison versus MacNutt

Pattison offers a long list of questions that he would like to see addressed by healers and others engaged in the field. Among these are, To what extent are healing powers inherent in creation or in human nature? Are "secular" ways of healing theologically recognizable, and are they to be regarded as complementary or contradictory to religious healing methods? Although some of these questions have been addressed in the above considerations of this part of the book, the one Pattison deals with at some depth is "the question which lies both at the centre of Christian attitudes to healing and also at the centre of Christian faith, namely, *what kind of God* is witnessed to in this activity?" (p. 65 [emphasis added]). In order to do so, he turns to a critical analysis of the former Catholic healer Francis MacNutt.[51]

According to MacNutt, what is at stake in the so-called religious healing

---

51. In the following I refer to MacNutt via Pattison, but I have also consulted Francis MacNutt, *Healing* (Notre Dame, IN: Ave Maria Press, 2006).

movement is how one understands the nature of God. He asserts that one has to choose between God as a remote abstraction along the lines of the deist movement, or God as an "active, loving father who is known precisely by his particular benevolent interventions in the lives of his children by healing them directly in response to their faith and prayers" (pp. 65–66). When rhetorically asking how we can know that God is a loving Father who cares for us personally, the answer is that we cannot know this unless God acts to save us from illness and death.

Although this may at first sight appear as an attractive and compelling position, Pattison indicates that the only thing worse than a God who does not intervene benevolently and directly in the world, as the deists would assume, is a God who does intervene directly. He says this because he takes issue with the position that we explored, and more or less dismissed, in the previous section, namely, that of an interventionist God. His reasons for this are the following: Although we can see the natural order as having relative autonomy from God, theologically speaking, this is also an advantage, as this order allows for the possibility of belief in a loving God. Pattison then states his version of the problem of theodicy in relation to healing:[52]

> If God does intervene actively in the world he is capable of preventing or averting the evils which afflict human beings. If God is omnipotent, all-loving and interventionist, why does he seem to inflict such misery on his beloved children? It may be argued that the ills which humans suffer are indeed part of God's good purpose, that they are in fact benefits in disguise. But if this is so, they do not appear to be so to those who suffer, and, in the present context this would be a contra-indicator to direct divine healing unless such healing was performed not so much for the benefit of the person healed but to accomplish some wider purpose. And if individual healing only occurs as a means to a wider end, can it be said that God truly loves and respects his children as individuals? The implication of all this is that if God can heal directly, he can prevent suffering directly, and if he is all-loving, he should indeed do so. (p. 66)

It is worth noting here that this argument is based on the assumption that divine intervention is exactly that: intervention, whereas many of the po-

---

52. It is worth noting, in passing, that some of the arguments Pattison uses here are later taken up by and employed in far more critical contexts, e.g., by Christopher Hitchens, in his *God Is Not Great: How Religion Poisons Everything* (New York: Twelve, 2009), pp. 16ff.

sitions referred to above see healing more along the lines of cooperation with natural conditions in a way that makes the rather imprecise notions of "intervention" or "direct healing" problematic. It is also worth commenting that the above does not exclude the possibility that people may in fact be healed in ways we cannot offer a good explanation for or account for, and that healing also happens in contexts that are (not necessarily, though) religiously colored. Accordingly, Pattison seems to be arguing more against a specific interpretation of such occurrences or events than against their fundamental possibility. The same goes for his objection that "the interventionist God of healing miracles can also be arraigned on the grounds that he is arbitrary" (p. 66).

An alternative view that may challenge Pattison's suppositions is suggested by Bruce Epperly. He critically addresses some of the more rationalistic tendencies that seem to preclude Christians from recognizing that healing actually takes place under circumstances we cannot always explain. Among the reasons some people react negatively toward practices of healing, Epperly mentions how "immature, archaic, and destructive images of God as heartless, arbitrary, judgmental, vindictive, and emotionally distant" that are "often inherited from dysfunctional church or parochial school teachers obsessed with hierarchical authority and anxious about the temptations of embodiment" shape an approach to health and embodiment that makes it difficult to combine one's own need for health and well-being with images of "God as loving parent, joyfully seeking abundant life."[53] Such images of God may also correspond with more deistic views that render "intercessory prayer or extrasensory perception an absurdity."[54] Epperly addresses understandings of God that Pattison also criticizes. However, he makes a different argument than Pattison, one that is more open to and accepting of such things happening within a Christian context, although he simultaneously admits that such things cannot be explained or articulated in a formula that allows us to see how the "divine logic" in healing works — if any such logic exists.

The fact that not all people who seek contemporary religious healers are healed provides an empirical argument that problematizes theological interpretations of healing as based on the notion of an interventionist God. The question is how to account for this fact from a theological point of view.

53. Bruce Gordon Epperly, *God's Touch: Faith, Wholeness, and the Healing Miracles of Jesus* (Louisville: Westminster John Knox, 2001), p. 14.

54. Epperly, *God's Touch*, p. 15.

Some people with much faith remain unhealed, while others with little faith are healed. "If God is directly responsible for this distribution of benefits, he is arbitrary to a degree which no human being could contemplate" (p. 67). Such observations lead Pattison to the conclusion that if God was like an earthly loving father who had healing power, he "would make himself available to his children in every way possible." However, "the fact is that the interventionist God of religious healing emerges from these arguments looking less like a loving father who is close to his creation than like an arbitrary despot who may or may not act in an overtly loving manner according to his own lights" (p. 67).

Accordingly, the understanding of the character and being of God that is at stake in healing is related to issues of providence and power, and raises complex questions. Pattison admits that he cannot discuss them thoroughly, but affirms the wisdom in preserving "a substantial relative autonomy for the creation and for human life. Unless this is done, God must be seen as directly responsible for all the evil in the world, human freedom must be an illusion and, as a corollary, humans have no choice about the sort of relationship and response they have to God — they are his vassals, not his lovers" (p. 67).

In light of the above, MacNutt's interpretation of God's sovereign and fatherly love for his children as being manifested directly and anew by the occurrence of divine healing on earth in the present time seems indeed to be in need of further theological development. Pattison does not deny that people are healed by religious means, but the arguments he presents should make it clear "that the attribution of healing directly to the divinity may be a false or dubious one which raises more problems than it solves on both theoretical and practical levels" (p. 68).

Summary of and Comments on Pattison's Criticisms of Healing

Pattison also offers some criticisms of Christian responses to healing and illness that address distinctively religious healing methods. His criticism is overall fairly negative, and therefore deserves careful consideration from a point of view that tries to interpret the significance of Jesus as healer for contemporary theology and the contemporary world. His criticism does not exclude him from holding a position that sees "any method or attitude which actually alleviates human misery and distress . . . to have a prima facie right to be regarded as a good thing; it seems very likely that religious healing methods do accomplish real relief and cure of illness" (p. 69). He especially calls for "a much more vigorous evaluation" of these methods, attitudes, and the values they promote.

We can summarize Pattison's criticisms in the following five points, especially focusing on those elements that are relevant for developing a contemporary theology on healing, and ignoring the more sweeping and generic statements he makes that cannot be put to constructive use for theological reflection.[55]

1. Christian responses to healing and illness lack nuance and are uncritical. This uncritical attitude may go both ways, however: On the one hand, "the sort of healing promoted by charismatic healers contains within it the concept of a directly interventionist God which raises all sorts of complex theological problems"; on the other, it is often expressed that "people can only be healed through the use of 'God-given' modern medicine." In both cases, and similar ones, the problem is that these responses are consistently applied to all circumstances (pp. 69–70).

It is hard not to agree with this point. But as we have learned even more since Pattison wrote his book in 1989, one-sided and exclusive approaches to human health and healing are problematic from many points of view, not just among popular healing theologies. As for the criticism of "divine intervention," the problems related to such an assumption have already been addressed above.[56]

2. The actual effect of Christian healers' work is not clear. Although it is hard to see how God could be submitted to tests like those of clinical medicine, this does not rule out the possibility of conducting scientific tests on people who have been subjected to religious healing. This would provide healers and others with a better instrument for assessing the real value of their work "beyond merely collecting testimonials from their satisfied clients" (p. 70). Pattison backs up this suggestion with the claim that "it often

---

55. Among the latter are statements like these: "Christian responses to healing and illness have been incredibly and unduly narrow. The last chapter revealed the variety and complexity of different ways of looking at illness, and of course, that each different way of looking at illness requires a slightly different response in terms of prevention or healing. Little of this breadth and depth of different perspectives is evident in Christianity. For Christians all illness is illness; it can be understood in a restricted number of ways, e.g., as misfortune, as demon oppression or as the result of sin. It can be dealt with religiously in correspondingly few simple ways, e.g., prayer, exorcism, laying on of hands, anointing" (p. 72; see also p. 73 for further examples of the same kind).

56. Cf., e.g., the approach of Schleiermacher and Ward on divine integrity, which we saw related to this point above on pp. 171, 194.

turns out that therapeutic methods are less effective than their administrators think they are." Hence, "It may be that far fewer people benefit from religious healing methods than is thought by religious healers" (p. 70).

As I read it, this criticism has two parts. One is that we need to assess as thoroughly as possible the value of the work of religious healers. There should, following such investigations, be some evidence for the improvement of health following from their practices. But even though these methods may be less effective than some think on all types of illnesses, this does not rule out that for some people, they are the only means left after they have been given up by modern medicine. Even if spiritual healing is not as effective as occasionally appears, for the people in question it is a valid and important means of improving their health. Having said this, however, an important implication of Pattison's criticism would be to advise healers to be cautious about what they promise and how they phrase their interpretation of the conditions for healing. This advice may also be relevant with regard to the next of Pattison's criticisms.

3. A corollary to the previous criticism is that there may be people who are in fact harmed by encounters with practices of religious healing. Despite the many who witness to their positive experiences, others can tell "stories about people who feel that their hopes have been dashed, that they failed to recover from illness because they had not had enough faith or because they were in the grip of some deep and nameless sin. Such people learn despair and a sense of abandonment by God from their encounters with religious healing" (p. 70). Pattison holds that "if there are more of them than there are people who feel that they have been helped, there is a strong case for changing beliefs and practices in Christian healing as well as for ceasing to practice religious healing altogether" (p. 71).

This criticism, as I read it, comes down to how people are prepared for experiencing the effects of healing practices by the interpretations offered in such contexts. Any "conditioning" of the positive effects on the capacities or qualities of the healee is deeply problematic, be it in terms of the ability to believe, openness or not to the grace of God, or other factors. There are good reasons for seeing his criticism here as a challenge to develop a theology of healing that can actually help people come to terms with the fact that they are not healed, just as some are. More than good intentions are called for. Pattison points out that it is "not sufficient to think that because people do something in the name of a good and loving God" an ill person will experience the goodness and love of God. What is called for in these cases is also thorough counseling and theological work. Similar to how other practitioners must evaluate the fact that they might do harm as well as help, healers also have to self-critically scrutinize their practice. Pattison suggests being conscious of two important questions when encountering any religious-healing response: (1) How do we know that this does not harm people? (2) What measures are taken to ensure that if people are harmed they do not lose the sense of a loving God who remains present with them no matter what (p. 71)? Especially from a Christian point of view that affirms God is actually revealed or manifested in such experiences, these seem to be apt questions to keep in mind.

4. Pattison further claims that Christian responses to illness and healing are often anachronistic and uncritically transport us back into the cultural world of the New Testament — a world where illness is due to sin or the wiles of demons. Although he (rhetorically?) admits that "it may indeed be the case that the old ways are the best ways" and that "methods which have a close superficial affinity to those of the early Christians may have a time-less value" (p. 71) this cannot be taken for granted and needs to be looked into further. More constructively, he states that it would be appropriate for someone who believes in a God who makes all things new and who does new things in the world to overcome the captivity of having to remain in the first century, and to think of imaginative new ways of engaging with illness and healing today. "To attempt timelessness in responding to illness is to ensure contemporary irrelevance. To cleave to the assumptions and practices of the past, just because they come from the past, is to stifle imagination for the present and future" (pp. 71–72).

This criticism seems relevant especially in contexts that see the Christian healing approach as the only valid or the exclusive approach to the challenges at hand. However, once one realizes that Christian healing may be a supplement to other approaches, much of the strength of this criticism is weakened. A nonexclusive approach to disease and illness can recognize the gains as well as the limits of modern medicine, and still be open to other forms of practices that may still be relevant and applicable — especially in cases where other treatments are not accessible. Such a response may also be in consonance with Pattison's claim that in the light of the present knowl-edge of illness and disease, the practice of distinctively "religious" healing methods, "insofar as it does appear to be the manipulation of the supernat-ural for the benefit of suffering humanity" and is based on beliefs "within a mystical enclave," may be an obstacle to a more complex, more difficult, and more authentic witness to healing (pp. 72–73). This criticism is aimed at the conviction that the religious approach is the only one that works and that constructs an opposition between these practices and other ways of providing healing. Pattison does not exclude a more constructive approach that can recognize their theological validity: "Truly religious responses are those which are sensitive to God's ongoing work in the whole of creation and through all people" and do not narrow this work down too much to the specific healing practices of the church (p. 73).

5. Pattison furthermore criticizes the individualistic and sociopolitically naive response to illness in Christian theology. As "Christian healing, like much medical healing, makes the sick individual its object and concern," there is a shortening of perspective, which leads to ignoring political and structural causes. "Indeed, in taking this general line Christianity actually reinforces the idea that illness is a personal matter which cannot be prevented and so passively supports the prevailing social order, whatever its cost in terms of widespread suffering throughout society" (pp. 73–74).

It is not hard to agree with Pattison that "if we know that some things in society promote illness, it is surely better to engage in preventative action rather than reactive healing." However, he also admits that "there will always be sick individuals who require an individualized Christian healing response" (p. 74). In this way, he again rightly opens up to a perspective that sees the practices of healing in a wider framework, which is situated within the struggle for justice and healing in society as a whole. From a theological point of view, this allows an understanding of God as the one "who expresses his love in justice as well as in acts of individual care" (p. 74). Pattison may also be right in his claim that if this is not taken into consideration, Christians involved in healing ministry may, by continuing their individualized healing, "continue to contribute to the ideology of injustice" (p. 74). But it is hard to see that this necessarily has to be the case.[57]

Having observed Pattison's five criticisms, I will argue that some of them can be addressed and met by building on his considerations in the chapters that follow the one in which he made these critical remarks. I develop them

---

57. Similar critique of an individualistic and apolitical approach to healing is voiced, e.g., in Martyn Percy, "Christ the Healer: Modern Healing Movements and the Imperative of Praxis for the Poor," *Studies in World Christianity* 1, no 2 (1995): 113–14. Recent studies by McGuire suggest, however, that individualism is not the main or dominating trait in healing practices — as contemporary healers tend to address the whole situation in which the healees find themselves. See Meredith B. McGuire, *Lived Religion: Faith and Practice in Everyday Life* (Oxford: Oxford University Press, 2008), pp. 151ff. However, such criticism is still valid when addressing healing rallies — which in fact seems to be quite the opposite of the more silent practices that many contemporary healers are involved in.

here, as they also take as their point of departure reflections on the biblical material and the ministry of Jesus. We may summarize these considerations along the following lines.

Jesus' ministry had social, political, and conflictual dimensions. His healings caused much controversy among those who witnessed them (see Bultmann's point above). The conflictual language in which healings, and particularly exorcisms, are described needs to be recalled (p. 80). "As far as we can discern, Jesus appears to have seen himself as being involved in a war against Satan and his Kingdom in the name of the Kingdom of God. It may be that much of the language of war which we use today of the struggle against illness finds its ultimate source in the healings of Jesus. He certainly seems to place healing in a combative light" (p. 80). Recent studies also suggest a similar approach.

> The conflict described in the Gospels concerning Jesus' miracles occurs between Jesus, a Jew, and his Jewish followers on the one hand, and his Jewish antagonists on the other. In other words, this is an intra-Jewish, theological argument. The parties involved are therefore conditioned by exactly the same historical and cultural assumptions about reality. There is no question in this dispute about the possibility of miracles or about how they can be made to cohere with the natural world. The real issue in question concerns whose power is on display in these amazing events. Thus it is a question of what *theo*-logical status they can be said to have. Are they signs of God's covenant, or are they signs indicative of a covenant with Satan?[58]

In the above perspective, Jesus' healing ministry is not based solely on individually orientated compassion but "should be seen primarily as social events which had primary significance for communities rather than individuals" (p. 80). The relevant context here is his preaching of the kingdom of God. Building on the work of Robert Lambourne, Pattison claims that in this perspective, "the healings were acted parables. They provoked a response from those who witnessed them and they would be deeply divisive of communities." This division meant that some could see in Jesus' healings the finger of Satan or Beelzebul, whereas others recognized an "inbreaking

---

58. Stefan Alkier and David Moffitt, "Miracles Revisited: A Short Theological and Historical Survey," in *Miracles Revisited: New Testament Miracle Stories and Their Concepts of Reality,* ed. Stefan Alkier and Annette Weissenrieder (Berlin: De Gruyter, 2013), p. 316.

of the Holy Spirit and chose life, health and healing for themselves and their communities" (p. 80). From a more collective point of view, the healings thus serve as signs of the kingdom, and moreover, the healings Jesus performed "functioned as concrete judgment of the Kingdom on actual earthly communities" (p. 80). Pattison thereby suggests that Jesus' healing ministry was related to social factors, particularly social disintegration, and that "his person, message and technique was strongly influenced by the society and times of which he was a part, that his message and ministry had substantial socio-political content and implications (even if these are now hard to define precisely) and that his healings must be seen against a background of protest and controversy" (p. 81).

Even though it was written more than twenty years ago, this interpretation can still prove its worth for a Christian political theology developed on the basis of some of the concerns Pattison voices: The health-care systems in Western societies, marked increasingly by alienating technology, marginalization of those who are unable to receive a biomedically based cure or who are not able to pay, and providing increasing opportunities for extensive economic profit for the companies involved, are in need of challenge and protest. Christian healers express such criticism when they care for those who fall outside the parameters of this system. The people who benefit from Christian healing are provided with an opportunity to experience their own dignity and worth over against a system that views them as numbers in a queue or as potential consumers of various medical products or as insurance holders. Together with Pattison, there are reasons to say that although we cannot imitate Jesus' ministry exactly, there is still a need to "reclaim aspects of Jesus' healing ministry from the realm of a-political, de-contextualized and individualized benevolence and good will whence it has been exiled so firmly by many Christian practitioners and writers on healing" (p. 81).[59]

Another related issue Pattison addresses is that healing and illness are often implicit in different forms of power relationships. "On the face of it, the ill person is an involuntary victim of forces outside his or her control. S/he is seen as a sufferer. By the same token, the healer is perceived as a benevolent reliever of suffering, a doer of good. I hope to show that these views of illness and healing are, in some situations at least, naive. They may sometimes conceal a very important, if only covertly articulated, dialogue about power and social control" (p. 82). Again, it is difficult to disagree, but

---

59. In fact, the subversive role of many healers over against such a system is also analyzed in the works of Meredith McGuire. See McGuire, *Lived Religion*, pp. 148–50.

the phrases to note here are "in some situations, at least" and "sometimes." The danger of becoming overly critical is just as problematic as the naïveté that Pattison wants to address.

That healing has much to do with power and protest is apparent already in the works of Jesus: his healings confirmed, for many, his authority as a teacher and leader. And he is not alone in experiencing such confirmation: people perceived to be healers in "every society down the ages have been accorded great power and authority which stems ultimately from close contact with the forces of chaos and death which both threaten and energize the social order" (p. 82). On the contemporary scene, this power and influence is given to medical doctors, to a large extent because "their activity is bound up with life-threatening forces." "A relatively large, formally trained and publicly recognized medical profession, which monopolizes healing power by force of law, is largely associated with the rise of industrial societies and of Western biomedicine" (pp. 82–83).

In a religious context it is not training but association with healing forces beyond the reach of ordinary people that contributes to the power and authority of healers. It is important to be aware of this pattern, which is often found in the Christian healing tradition: "By acquiring supernatural powers from outside himself, the healer becomes confident of the legitimacy and authority lying behind his work. He can challenge earthly and supernatural authorities and powers with confidence and impunity. It is within this kind of context of the supernatural acquisition and legitimacy of power that healing can often be seen as an incentive to, or confirmation of, social protest or power" (p. 83).

Finally, Pattison argues that an important part of healing in theological terms is that of *revealing something* (p. 83). The consideration behind this proposal is the following:

> Many healing methods, both religious and secular, may cure people in the sense that they remove symptoms and allow a return to "normal" functioning in society. The question is, is this enough? Surely there should be an element of healing which pays attention to actually helping a person see what sort of situation he or she is in. This enables a person actually to choose how to tackle it, rather than opting for a curative method which may be damaging in its side-effects (and I suggest that methods which strongly encourage people to regard themselves as entirely passive in regard to their own illnesses should be seen as having damaging side-effects). It is true, of course, that there may be circumstances in which a person can

do nothing about their own situation and must be passive while treatment is administered to them by others. Even in these circumstances, though, it is possible to help a person to gain a perspective on things which may help them to have a sense of control, however slight. (p. 101)

Pattison is careful to state that he is not opting for a position where "only methods which enhance individual autonomy and control are valid in healing" (p. 101). We need to note this, as many of those who experience the need for healing seem to be people given up or left behind as incurable cases, people who have no way of thinking about themselves as anything but victims of bad circumstances over which they have no control whatsoever. However, Pattison may himself come close to the position he accuses some healers of: By encouraging those seeking healing to take a more active approach, he ignores those who are not able to be or become active because they are simply too ill. Many people have worked hard to do what he suggests, that is, "discerning the truth of one's own situation, or that of one's group," but are nevertheless unable to provide the result he indicates, namely, a realization of "real choice about healing methods and attitudes to illness," which may in itself be therapeutic (p. 101). His almost scornful comment on this active engagement as certainly demanding "more active human participation at more levels than simply taking tablets or having hands laid upon oneself" does not seem to take the desperation of many of the people in question seriously enough.

Nevertheless, we can agree that practices which "take away symptoms while leaving fundamental causes unchanged might be regarded as no more than 'cheap healing' analogous to Bonhoeffer's 'cheap grace'" (p. 101). This, however, may not be relevant to many of the cases in question, for instance diseases with no obvious cause. When Pattison suggests "that knowledge and discernment with regard to illness, its context, causes and treatment should be the fundamental component of religious healing," one can agree without reservation. However, his reservations and the conditions for attempting the cure may seem to restrict practices of healing more than necessary, as when he says that these conditions are fundamental elements and that they "should *always* accompany attempts to cure" (p. 101 [emphasis added]). To say that "the Christian response to illness and its first step towards healing should be seen in terms of active revelation and discernment of what is going on, rather than in terms of direct action," is in practice a retreat to doing nothing when one has the means to do something — although admittedly not for everyone and not always.

I agree with Pattison in seeing faith as an active and important power in healing processes (see p. 102). But sometimes even to require faith is to demand too much. From a New Testament perspective it is, as we have seen, not always necessary. For people who are ill, faith is impossible to practice as anything other than what he describes negatively as "primarily passive waiting upon God." Others will have to take up the "active struggle for healing and wholeness amidst the socio-political complexities, ambiguities and conflicts of an industrialized society which makes many people sick and deprives them of real hope in the future" (p. 102). Those in need of healing not only need people to heal them — they also need people who can have faith in their healing, and faith in their power to change a society that makes being ill an even heavier burden than it needs to be.

Acceptance of Healing from an Empirical and Theological Point of View

From a scholarly point of view, there seems to be increasing acceptance that healing takes place in ways that are easier to identify with New Testament reports than with those coming from a biomedical paradigm of treatment. In his survey of the development in research, Lars Lindström summarizes this in a way that to a large extent overlaps with my own experience in surveying the material.

> At the beginning of the research era, the phenomenon [of spiritual healing] was certainly considered worthy of scientific investigation although some believed that the phenomenon simply does not exist, *sui generis,* or that it is merely a case of fraud — at the best a case of self-deception, of faulty diagnosis, or the result of the self-restoring powers of the human organism. Others saw it as a matter of vivid imagination, of hysteria, or of suggestive influence with no lasting result. However, the critical voices seem to have become more and more silent. Today, some are even prepared to admit that there might be cases of what may be called "authentic" spiritual healings. These are healing events, where the restoration of health seems to be the result of an application of some spiritual technique, as the healing agent.[60]

60. See Lars G. Lindström, *Christian Spiritual Healing: A Psychological Study; Ideology and Experience in the British Healing Movement,* Acta Universitatis Upsaliensis Psychologia et Sociologia Religionum (Uppsala: Academiae Ubsaliensis, 1992), p. 3.

Lindström, as have others, has also collected a large body of material consisting of interviews with people involved with or having experienced spiritual healing.[61] Stephen Parsons, for example, suggests that it is important to recognize that healing powers are a widespread phenomenon, and that people may develop capacities for healing others by many different methods. Therefore we should not be too skeptical of people of other faiths or contexts who practice healing. Instead, he suggests that a more theologically sound way of thinking about these issues would be to see the notion of healing as pointing to something that belongs to creation as such and, accordingly, that healing can be used for good and for bad. As Parsons writes, to lack understanding of God as creator does not make creation bad — it only makes it less whole: "A gift received with gratitude is more valuable than a gift not recognized as gift. And even though one might not recognize the giver of the gift, the gift itself does not turn evil. Creation in all its dimensions remains good, unless it is purposely used for evil."[62]

Parsons sees it as a problem that healers, historically speaking, have been met with suspicion from the church. This, as we also indicated in the introduction to this book, has led to people going to other places and engaging themselves in other organizations where they found more recognition for their need to use these gifts for others. For the Christian church, this should be recognized as an important challenge, especially if it wants to be conceived of as a place where the gifts and capacities of all its members are understood and made use of.[63]

One of the contemporary features that becomes apparent after this survey of topics and material related to healing is that in healing, wholeness is an important topic. Healing implies that the healee can experience herself not only as one who is ill but also as one who is whole, created in the image of God, and thereby as more than a passive person in need. Furthermore, even in her condition of illness she is one who can witness to the gifts of God, and can receive God's caring love and compassion. The experience of

61. For others, see Morris Maddocks, *The Christian Healing Ministry,* 3rd ed. (London: SPCK, 1995); Stephen Parsons, *The Challenge of Christian Healing* (London: SPCK, 1986); Parsons, *Helhed og Helbred* (Valby Kbh.: Unitas, 1998); Jan-Olav Henriksen and Kathrin Pabst, *Uventet og ubedt: Paranormale erfaringer i mote med tradisjonell tro* (Unexpected and uninvited: paranormal experiences encountering traditional belief) (Oslo: Universitetsforlaget, 2013); Meredith B. McGuire and Debra Kantor, *Ritual Healing in Suburban America* (New Brunswick, NJ: Rutgers University Press, 1988).

62. Parsons, *Helhed og Helbred,* pp. 102–3, quote p. 103, my translation from Danish.

63. Parsons, *Helhed og Helbred,* p. 104.

being created in God's image and of being cared for by God is something that medicine cannot provide. It is in itself a reason for a more holistic approach to healing, which includes an acknowledgment of how spiritual resources are important in making humans become what they are.

The modern experiential approach to health and healing that is adopted by many (also Christians) in the Western world often works together with a metaphysical and rationalistic approach that does not provide a language or the possibility for being open to and accepting of such phenomena. This poses a challenge not only for relating to healing in general but also for establishing an experiential framework that gives people a context for their belief in Jesus as a healer. Despite these attitudes, however, many have found healing in such practices, whereas others have experienced problematic claims and disturbing interpretations of illness and lack of health.[64] The challenge for theology is accordingly to develop a viable and robust theology of healing. As this book indicates, we think this cannot be done without seeing healing within a framework that draws heavily on the theological tradition, and thus develops an understanding of healing as something that can find a place within a christological framework. The last chapter of this book will suggest some trajectories for reasoning along these lines.

64. See Epperly, *God's Touch*, p. 12.

Healing within a Christological Framework

Christianity is not based on doctrine but on the ministry of Jesus Christ, who proclaimed the gospel of the kingdom of God (as promise, exhortation, vision) and who healed those who were sick and included those who — due to sickness or other reasons — were at the margins of society. This statement about Christianity is both programmatic and polemical, directed critically against positions that take Christianity to be primarily about belief or worldview. Christian doctrine is thus secondary, always an interpretation of specific events and practices surrounding the ministry of Jesus. Christianity, then, is about faith in what happens in the concrete practices, experiences, and events that constitute the history of Jesus. Furthermore, Christianity leaves open some phenomena to explanation that may seem hard to explain or grasp fully on the basis of contemporary knowledge. Healing is an obvious example of this, and as we have seen, it has been interpreted or addressed differently throughout the history of Christianity up until today.

To see Christianity as primarily rooted in what happens in relation to the ministry of Jesus also means that as a religion it is firmly rooted in the basic experiential conditions of human life. These experiential conditions are just as diverse as the different approaches we have seen to healing. For the sake of simplicity, we can identify four different experiential realms that may be of relevance here, and that are parallel to how human knowledge is often organized:

1. The physical realm of experience — which is the realm that functions in accordance with laws of nature, and which is basically a realm that would exist even if humans were to not exist.
2. The social and cultural realm of experience — which exists only because human beings are symbolic species that can create a common world of

understanding dependent on the use of symbols and communication. The laws on which this realm functions are based in human decisions (concerning adequate or right conduct and behavior etc.).

3. The inner realm — which is the personal realm of psychological experience, memory, and so on, which is idiosyncratic to each human being, and which is only accessible to ourselves and others on the basis of our ability to use language and memory. The role of other humans in this realm is closely related to our emotional bonds to them.

4. The fourth realm of experience is hard to define — it transcends the grasp we are presently able to establish. Here, things seem to function according to "laws" that are not within the realm of ordinary science. Examples of the phenomena we are talking about include clairvoyance, mystical experience, visions, and — spiritual healing. For lack of other names, we may call this realm the spiritual, but with the addition that from a theological point of view God is not only related to this realm. Accordingly, this is not the "spiritual" realm in the sense of "the only theologically relevant" realm or the only realm in which God works. This realm of experience is not accessible in the same manner to all people, and it seems to be beyond what we can grasp or control through our own initiative.

Arguably, all of these realms are interdependent in our experience; we would not have physical or psychological experiences unless we had a body, nor would we be able to talk about them if we didn't participate in a shared world with others. *This also goes for experiences of healing:* They may involve — in different ways — all the realms of experience listed above, and it would be a mistake to reduce healing to only one of these realms (say, to interpret it from the point of view of psychology, or only as an effect of specific causal functions). Human existence as we know it would not be what it is without taking all these experiential realms into account. Furthermore, these realms are mirrored in the New Testament witness of the ministry of Jesus.

One of the reasons why it seems fruitful to insist on the interaction or interplay of these realms of experience is that it may help in overcoming two related pitfalls: those who want to address healing from either a materialist (biomedical) approach or from a mere spiritual approach. By insisting on the interplay among these realms, we can also recognize the theological significance of people who experience bodily (physical) healing due to (social) practices of spiritual healing. For people who experience healing, these different realms of reality of human existence — all working together and separated — contribute to an experience of wholeness. The experience of this wholeness is crucial to becoming healed in the true sense of the word — whole. This becomes apparent, for example, when regaining physical health allows people to enter the social world again, or to have their faith in God enhanced.

We find a good example of how these different realms are linked together in the Christian interpretation of healing as related to repentance and forgiveness of sins. The connection between repentance and healing goes all the way back to the Old Testament. Its view of life, which links together the blessings of health, fertility, respect, and prosperity, is also related to an understanding of what God's forgiveness implies. Amanda Porterfield holds that the "affirmation of a connection between sickness and sin lies at the root of Christian healing."[1] This connection has nevertheless had an ambiguous status, as it at times resulted in Christians blaming people for being sick, while in other cases they saw illness and suffering as caused by surrounding forces of evil and sin. Already the Gospels show signs of similar patterns of interpretation. As Porterfield says, "Wherever Christians have laid blame, discernment of sin as the cause of suffering has contributed to visions of reality that place human beings and their sufferings at the center and that link relief of these sufferings to the purpose of creation."[2]

If we see sin as that which destroys life and distorts the free flow of life as it articulates itself in the interplay between the different realms of experience, it still seems possible to uphold this understanding of sin — but without blaming it on the one who suffers from illness. Sin is a power that afflicts people even when they are unable to prevent bad things from happening (as, e.g., in consequences of abuse). Accordingly, there are good reasons to see (as does Stephen Pattison) both illness and healing in a context that transcends the mere individualistic approach so often adopted by modern medicine.

As illness is something that afflicts most peoples' lives at some stage, we can say that the experiences of these phenomena provide us with an experiential context in which the message of Jesus as healer becomes both important and relevant. We are now in a position where we can articulate more precisely how this is the case.

---

1. Amanda Porterfield, *Healing in the History of Christianity* (Oxford: Oxford University Press, 2005), p. 5.

2. Porterfield, *Healing in the History of Christianity*, p. 5.

The Status of Jesus: Exceptional or Exemplary?

A fundamental theological decision for the understanding of Jesus as healer is whether we understand the healing dimension of his ministry as exceptional or as exemplary. These two options present us with several opportunities for reflection.

To see Jesus as one of several healers (exemplary) allows us to interpret his healing ministry in relation to that of other healers in the past and present. We are then able to see him as a human being with extraordinary gifts, but these gifts are of a kind that can be compared to and understood along similar lines to the gifts of other healers. In this view, Jesus is a person endowed with special gifts that are a part of his personal calling to help people realize their place and position in relation to God, and as witnessing to God's grace, care, and compassion. We have previously seen that Karl Barth considers this approach as one option for interpreting Jesus, but rejects it. However, from a theological point of view, there may be other reasons for considering this a more viable position than the ones he had in mind.

Within such a perspective, Jesus' gifts of healing will still be given by the Spirit. They can then be seen as something that is used by God, for the sake of the kingdom of God and for the benefit of humanity. Because these specific gifts can also be found in other humans, the ability to heal may be an indication of what is possible at the level of humanity for people whom God decides to endow with specific capacities for alleviating the struggles, pain, and misery of others. Accordingly, these gifts do not work against nature or outside of creation, but they are rare and exceptional for a specific group of people who are called to use them in a specific ministry for others. When used in this way, they contribute to the fuller realization of nature.

Given this interpretation, it is not necessary to interpret the gifts of healing that Jesus was endowed with as an expression of his divine status — although they may make it possible to see him as someone who, partly because of these gifts, had a specific calling from God. An interpretation of Jesus as healer that sees him as one among many healers will have to make specific qualification in addition to the possession and practicing of such gifts in order to back up claims about his divine status. The previous presentation of material indicates that there is widespread experience of healing and healers within different religious traditions (also those outside of Christianity). Given that this is the case, Jesus as a healer is *extraordinary*, as we have already previously described him, but not a singular exception.

However, from a more critical perspective, this interpretation of his exemplary and extraordinary character may concur with those who simply see Jesus' healings as part of his shamanic capacities.[3] However, such an interpretation ignores the specific and important spiritual context in which the New Testament writers place their description of his ministry. To see Jesus as "just another shaman" or healer would be a reduction that fails to bring to the fore the full theological significance of what takes place in Jesus' healing ministry. Wolfhart Pannenberg makes the principled point behind this concern clear: there is no reason to exclude the fact that Jesus was a healer from historical and theological considerations that work on the basis of analogy. Pannenberg stresses that "if the historian keeps his eye on the non-exchangeable individuality and contingency of an event, then he will see that he is dealing with non-homogeneous things, which cannot be contained without remainder in any analogy. Provided that historical science is occupied above all with the particularity and uniqueness of phenomena, its interests must therefore be focused more upon the ever peculiar, non-homogeneous features, rather than the common ones first obtruded by analogies."[4]

Having said this, we have to admit that there is actually no way to decide if the healing powers of Jesus are fully analogous to those of people who possess the gift of healing today. One should be cautious about making too many inferences about how Jesus' healing abilities should be interpreted and what kind of significance should be attributed to them. I say this with reference to two positions in recent literature: on the one hand, the above-mentioned interpretation of Jesus as just another shaman, and on the other hand, a position that sees Jesus' healings as a unique testimony to his divine powers.

We find a more careful interpretation of Jesus as exceptional in a more profound sense in Keith Warrington's work. He suggests that Jesus is to be viewed more as an exception than as a paradigm in which others can also be understood. Among his reasons for this claim is what he calls the biblical report of Jesus as one who healed people instantly,[5] in contrast to many

---

3. As seems to be the case, e.g., in Pieter F. Craffert, *The Life of a Galilean Shaman: Jesus of Nazareth in Anthropological-Historical Perspective* (Eugene, OR: Cascade, 2008), pp. 277-78. Craffert nevertheless offers important contributions to the healing activities of Jesus and their interpretations, as he both suggests that present scholarship explicitly or implicitly assumes a biomedical paradigm for these interpretations and remains "trapped" in this paradigm (p. 251; cf. p. 260).

4. Wolfhart Pannenberg, *Basic Questions in Theology: Collected Essays,* trans. George H. Kehm (Philadelphia: Fortress, 1970), 2:46.

5. This is also pointed out in the discussion on the NT material in this book, e.g., p. 72 above.

present-day healers who emphasize the process and gradual character of healing. More important, however, is his interpretation of the biblical materials as "important vehicles presenting invaluable lessons for the followers of Jesus, including lessons about trust and obedience."[6] In his perspective, the Gospels witness to Jesus' motivation to heal was "his desire to establish important principles regarding himself and the lifestyle of his followers. His ministry is first of all to be understood in the specific context of his Messianic, and therefore unique, mission."[7] Warrington sees these healings as establishing the authority of Jesus, and as having a pedagogical function.

In my view, the interpretative framework Warrington operates within is based more on a specific view of Christianity that emphasizes the spiritual rather than the embodied, and the authority of God rather than the well-being of humans. It seems to ignore how the healings reported in the New Testament to a large extent function as events that are valuable in themselves, and are done for the concrete benefit of the actual healee(s).[8] Warrington's repetitive emphasis on how such events establish *principles* for the interpretation of Jesus or for the practice of his followers deemphasizes concrete, embodied well-being, and even emphasizes the spiritual at the cost of the embodied. As such, his interpretation is similar to the one I criticized in Calvin earlier. It also has some similarities with Barth's position, who acknowledged that it could be possible to interpret Jesus' healings in analogy with those of others, while simultaneously denying that these similarities had any bearing whatsoever on the theological significance of the acts. I will return to some of the general features of this interpretation in the discussion of the healings as signs in the next section.

This criticism notwithstanding, it is, from a theological point of view, important to see the "generic" features of Jesus' healing ministry as something more or something else than what we can identify in the practice of other healers. This has to do with concerns related to Jesus' special calling, and with the way in which his healings actually functioned within the context of his proclamation of the kingdom of God. Taken together, then, it is possible to see the above dilemma, exceptional or exemplary, as a false one: Jesus is both. As I shall also argue later, it is when we see his ministry as reestablishing the integrity of creation with the means of grace that we can

6. Keith Warrington, *Jesus the Healer: Paradigm or Unique Phenomenon?* (Carlisle, U.K.: Paternoster, 2000), p. 29.

7. Warrington, *Jesus the Healer*, p. 29.

8. That being said, there are admittedly indications that the healing tradition was shaped didactically; see pp. 56–57, 62, 81, 94 above.

see nature and grace, the exemplary and the exceptional, as cooperating in his work.

Accordingly, we can conclude that the healings of Jesus, although not possible to establish as uniquely exceptional, nevertheless serve a specific and unique purpose integral (even necessary) to his proclamation of the kingdom of God and its actual content. Their purpose is not only pedagogical, but must be recognized as concrete anticipation of the reality of the kingdom, as well as significant manifestations of God's care, mercy, and compassion for God's creatures.

The implied pragmatic character of the belief in Jesus as healer has been well expressed in the study of Eric Eve. When discussing the question of Jesus' miracles in general, he claims that they "have less relevance to the question of whether or not he was truly God incarnate than is often supposed."[9] His argument for this point is historically based, as he says that "it is most unlikely that any of Jesus' Jewish contemporaries would have regarded the ability to perform miracles (however spectacular) as an indication that God was incarnate in the human being performing them (as opposed to simply empowering the performer), and it would be a theological mistake for us to make belief in the incarnation rest on Jesus' miraculous abilities."[10]

Furthermore, Eve makes a point that is in accordance with my initial statement in this chapter about Christianity's basis on Jesus' ministry and practice, and not on doctrine. He says that "the incarnation is a theological idea that cannot be proved (or disproved) by empirical evidence."[11] Of course, he is right in this, but we also have to add, as he does, that the concept of incarnation is closely related to historical data that in turn "could have considerable bearing on whether Jesus of Nazareth is an appropriate object of faith." Eve stresses that "Christian faith is not primarily a matter of assenting to abstract theological propositions about Jesus, it is rather a matter of living one's life in the conviction that God is most fully revealed in Jesus."[12] In this way, he emphasizes that faith provides people with an orientation and direction for considering how to live and act in the world.[13] If we apply this reflection to the understanding of Jesus as healer, one implication is that Jesus was called by God to heal, and this is something that God calls

9. Eric Eve, *The Healer from Nazareth: Jesus' Miracles in Historical Context* (London: SPCK, 2009), p. 167.

10. Eve, *Healer from Nazareth*, p. 167.

11. Eve, *Healer from Nazareth*, p. 29.

12. Eve, *Healer from Nazareth*, p. 29.

13. See Eve, *Healer from Nazareth*, p. 29.

all humans to do, in multiple ways and in every way and mode accessible to them (this opens up space for a wide notion of healing).

Against the backdrop of this discussion, then, we lean more toward seeing Jesus as an exemplary healer than as an exceptional one.[14] His healings were not only his, but belong to events that humans still can experience — although they are, as exceptional, something that it is hard to claim that people should *expect* to happen. They are, moreover, exceptional in that they also open up to a reality beyond the present and familiar, and as such, may make people open to faith in God.

Healing as Sign: Presence and Revelation of God

What happens to a body cannot be grasped without some kind of interpretation. The encounter between healer and healee will inevitably be attributed some significance by the parties involved, or by others.[15] Hence, although healing can take place in different contexts and be interpreted within different frameworks, for Christian theology it is important not only to recognize this but also to articulate and explicate the framework that is actualized in, with, and during the healings that take place in Jesus' ministry. It is only under these conditions that we can access the theological significance we are trying to articulate here.

The recognition of the need for interpretation means that every healing will also have the character of a sign: it will point to something, mean something for someone in some respect or other.[16] We have seen that the sign character of Jesus' healings has been explicated differently by different theologians throughout history, ever since the time of the New Testament. As sign, or symbol, the healings need some further consideration: I will sug-

14. See Craffert, *Life of a Galilean Shaman*, pp. 277-78, who states that "a number of the healings ascribed to Jesus are not only very similar to the list ascribed to folk healers today, but they are also very similar to those ascribed to other ancient healers like Apollonius of Tyana and Hanina ben Dosa"; see also the chapter on Jesus and other ancient healers, pp. 22ff. above.

15. See for many good analyses of this point Meredith B. McGuire and Debra Kantor, *Ritual Healing in Suburban America* (New Brunswick, NJ: Rutgers University Press, 1988).

16. This way of articulating the sign character implies that there are different levels or dimensions in the process of signification. I need not go deeply into those here. For a full-blown theory of this process within theology, based on the theory of C. S. Peirce, see Andrew Robinson, *God and the World of Signs: Trinity, Evolution, and the Metaphysical Semiotics of C. S. Peirce* (Leiden: Brill, 2010).

gest that Paul Tillich's notion of the broken symbol is adequate as a starting point here. Seeing Jesus' healings as signs or symbols of the kingdom of God allows us to become aware of a profoundly fruitful interpretative horizon. According to Tillich's theory, symbols are able to engage us even while we are aware of their limitations. Symbols relate us to what they symbolize, but in a way that also affirms how they are different from their referent; thus they cannot be understood as a substitute for the reality they relate us to.[17] What makes Tillich's theory so apt here is his understanding of how *religious symbols symbolize the infinite but are themselves finite.*[18]

Applied to the healings of Jesus, we can see them as finite manifestations of the infinite reality of God. As finite, it is possible to experience and relate to and appreciate them as part of our present world. At the same time, however, they point to something beyond what we experience here and now, as they re-present a reality that we cannot fully grasp or understand. Without making any decisions as to when and how we may be able to explain such healings, we can nevertheless affirm that as long as these events are able to point to something beyond the concrete embodied reality for the healee (or the beholder), the healings may have a *revelatory* character: in the concrete, actual manifestation of the healing, the reality of God can be seen to manifest itself. It is important to note, however, that this cannot happen unless some healing actually takes place: the healing is not a *mere* sign of the kingdom, but part of a manifestation of the kingdom, albeit a finite one.

If the healings of Jesus (and others) are then understood as broken symbols in the Tillichian sense, we can — despite the fact that they do not always take place and not everyone is granted the chance to experience them — see them as signs of the kingdom. Even people who are healed eventually die; not all are healed, and some are only partially healed. As Craig Keener writes, "That everyone dies shows that no one, regardless of one's theology, will always be healed. That is, whether remissions are permanent or not, death is inevitable for everyone. Not only are many not healed (as noted above), many have died without healing even in movements that emphasize healing, despite abundant prayer for them. In some movements, a number of persons have even died precisely because, waiting for miraculous inter-

17. For an extensive analysis of Tillich's own theory of symbols, which fully addresses the distinction between finitude and the infinite, see Lewis S. Ford, "The Three Strands of Tillich's Theory of Religious Symbols," *Journal of Religion* 46, no. 1 (1966): 104–30.

18. See Robert Cummings Neville, *The Truth of Broken Symbols* (Albany: State University of New York Press, 1996), p. x, referring to Paul Tillich, *Systematic Theology*, vol. 1 (Chicago: University of Chicago Press, 1967), esp. pp. 239–40.

vention, they neglected medical intervention already available to them."[19] Thus the healings are themselves "broken" as long as the world's present conditions are as they are. In other words, the healings of Jesus should not be seen as an opportunity to escape the conditions of this world, but as signs of a reality that is not yet realized. As concrete and broken symbols, the healings of Jesus testify to and *reveal* the care, compassion, and love of God, which is not yet fully realized in the world. Their finite character warns against any *theologia gloriae,* and they should instead be seen as symbols that orient humans to care for others and alleviate their sufferings in any way possible. As such, the healings are thus also symbols that contribute to the orientation of Christian life in the world: suffering and illness are things one should struggle to overcome, and not accept passively as part of one's fate or destiny. This is what Jesus reveals when he heals people.

The many testimonies to Christian healers today — especially those who serve others in a quiet way — can be seen as a continuation of the ministry and as a continuation of the distribution of signs of the kingdom. However, the interpretation of the healings as symbols suggested here contains a tacit criticism of those who do not see healing as *broken symbols,* but as a manifestation of God's power in the world in an unqualified manner. Such approaches are most likely going to cause frustration, disappointment, and even the loss of faith, if they encourage people to think that one should expect healing as part of the "normal" reality of those who believe in Jesus. To see healing as probable is not the same as seeing it as something that is always possible.[20]

When people pray for healing in the name of Jesus, this can accordingly be seen as a request for a sign of the kingdom that Jesus promised. When healing happens, then, it is a sign that at the same time makes it possible to experience concretely the reality of God in the embodied manifestation of his power. Hence the sign presents God as present in a specific manner. The ineffable character of healings nevertheless suggests that the God present, represented, and signified in such experiences cannot be controlled.

---

19. Craig S. Keener, *Miracles: The Credibility of the New Testament Accounts,* 2 vols. (Grand Rapids: Baker Academic, 2011), p. 605.

20. The position suggested here implies that the present authors find the dispensationalist or cessationist approach to healing unsatisfactory: healings like those of Jesus were not restricted to the first times of Christianity, but have to a different extent followed the church throughout history. Accordingly, a rejection of healing as superstition, magic, or false doctrine seems to miss the point that healing has been and is an integral part of the reality of Christian faith since the beginning until this day.

Thus the sign character is itself multilayered — healing is a sign not only of God's compassion, care, and promise but also of God's ineffable and infinite character.

Healing as Grace

When people are healed, it is not due to their own qualities, their faith, or their own merits. Healing is an expression of the grace of God manifest in the ministry of Jesus. The embodied character of Jesus' healings opens up to considerations about the relation between nature and grace: as nature expresses itself in and through the human body, one can see the acts of grace for the healing of the body as something that engages with, presupposes, but also transcends the capacities of the body. Healing enables the fulfillment or realization of nature in new ways that are beyond the measures and capacities that the body can provide by itself.

Previously, I suggested we can see sin as that which destroys life and distorts the free flow of life that articulates itself in the interplay between different realms of experience. Grace liberates from sin; it enables nature to realize itself more fully, although not yet in a perfect manner.

When Jesus heals, we can see it as a manifestation of how God works by means of both nature and grace. In Protestant theology, nature and grace are often contrasted as opposites, and sometimes they are. When grace works "against" nature, it is not against the basic conditions for health, goodness, beauty, and love in the universe, but against the forces that, for different reasons, impede and destroy the possibilities for these features of experience to occur. In classical theological sources, such as in Thomas Aquinas, nature and grace also work in interplay in a way that may shed light on the phenomenon of healing. In the relationship between nature and grace, grace builds on nature and contributes to and conditions its perfection (*gratia non tollit naturam, sed perficit* — "grace does not destroy nature, but perfects it").[21] At

---

21. Thomas Aquinas, *Summa Theologiae* I, q. 1, a. 8, resp. 2. If understood in this way, a theology of grace, as John Haught suggests, may also "make intelligible the randomness, natural selection, and eons of time for experimentation that form the core of the Darwinian understanding of evolution. The doctrine of grace claims that God loves the world and all of its various elements fully and unconditionally. In its deepest expression, however, love does not absorb, annihilate, or force itself upon the beloved. Instead it longs for the beloved to be self-actualizing, so as to become more and more 'other' or differentiated. Along with its nurturing and compassionate attributes, love brings with it a longing for the independence of

the same time, there would be no grace unless there were a nature in which and by which it could be realized.

Christian faith sees this world as created by a God who loves beauty and goodness and has set for humans the goal of being like God in relating lovingly to the world. Healing is an expression of this love. Natural evolution is a process that allows little consideration for the other in the struggle for survival — and no consideration that is unconditional or agapic with regard to how to relate to the other. To see humans as a composition of nature and grace is accordingly to see us as evolving *out of* natural conditions in partly unpredictable ways. This is a manifestation of grace in nature, as it is this natural process that has offered us the chance and the conditions for experiencing the world as gift, for gratitude, flourishing, and enjoyment. Faith thus opens up to grace and a way of being in the world that is caused by and oriented by more than nature.

A theology that takes seriously God's interaction with the present and evolving world, as this comes to the fore in experiences of healing, needs to see grace as conditioned by and building on, but not fully determined by, nature in its present form. Grace reveals new chances for nature, presenting it with new and surprising opportunities. This perspective is rooted in an understanding of God as the creative source of both nature and grace, and as such God allows for both freedom and independence, for interplay and interaction. The grace implied in healing thus cannot be understood as supranatural, but rather as *intranatural*.[22]

Christian theology that takes creation seriously cannot ignore that the natural conditions of human life are the basic conditions for all that God does and for all that befalls us in different realms of experience. In healing, grace builds on and is related to nature; without nature there would be no place for grace. However, from a more generic perspective, the opposite can

---

that which is loved. Without such 'letting be' of its beloved, the dialogical intimacy essential to a loving relationship would be impossible. Consequently, if there is any truth to the central religious intuition that God loves the world with an unbounded love, then God's 'grace' must also mean 'letting the world be itself.' God's love would refrain from forcefully stamping the divine presence or will upon the world, much less dissolving the world into God" (John F. Haught, *God after Darwin: A Theology of Evolution,* 2nd ed. [Boulder: Westview, 2008], p. 43).

22. According to these reflections, I join with those who see the distinction between natural and supranatural as unsatisfactory for describing religious belief. To see religious faith as belief in supranatural beings is therefore not necessarily adequate. For a nuanced critique of this understanding of religion, with reference to anthropologist Pascal Boyer's reductionist understanding of religion along such lines, see J. Wentzel Van Huyssteen, *Alone in the World? Human Uniqueness in Science and Theology* (Grand Rapids: Eerdmans, 2006), pp. 263 and 291.

also be said: without grace, there would be no nature. Nature as we know it is part of God's gift to creation; it displays a loving and living God who calls creation into love and life. Therefore, it is mistaken to see the healings that liberate nature as mere signs of an otherworldly reality or of the mere spiritual dimension of reality.

Like Thomas Aquinas, we can therefore see divine grace as not working against nature in instances of bodily healing but as God working through and on the basis of nature. Health is internal to nature, but health is also sometimes realized in ways that surpass our actual natural capacities. In this way, it is possible to interpret both nature and grace as ways in which God is manifest in the world and in instances of healing.

John Webster's interpretation of the wonders of Jesus seems to be fitting here. He sees them as

> neither intrusions into processes of nature by a person with extraordinary powers nor a proof for the divinity of Christ in front of those who do not believe. They are the visible presence of the kingdom of God, in which God's good order realizes its shape and where God's final rule over all things is anticipated. It is not the natural laws that are contrary to the wonders, but the destructive forces of sin that will finally be overcome in the Eschaton. This understanding sees wonders as extraordinary acts performed by God in God's freedom, as testimonies to God's plan, and as a confirmation of the ordinary ways in which God upholds the world.[23]

This underscoring of the eschatological character of the wonders is important because it holds together the present and the future in a way that allows for seeing healing as significant in both realms of time. Furthermore, Webster here shares our interest in seeing the present and the future, nature and grace, natural law and the exceptional, as in consonance, as we argued in the section on miracles above.

When we interpret healing from this perspective, we have a solid argument against any devaluation of embodied human reality. Without the graceful acts of God in and with and for the body, the human being will not reach its final and eternal goal *(telos)* in terms of displaying the love, care, goodness, and beauty of God. Jesus' graceful interruptions, on the other

---

23. John Webster, "Wunder, Dogmatisch," in *Die Religion in Geschichte und Gegenwart: Handwörterbuch für Theologie und Religionswissenschaft,* ed. Hans Dieter Betz et al., 4th ed. (Tübingen: Mohr Siebeck, 2005), 8:1728.

hand, always provide new opportunities for this will to become realized. Furthermore, the transforming power of grace in nature should not be underestimated. Grace not only supplements nature, but changes it, as can be seen in how the graceful reception and presence of a mentally challenged child in a small community can open up to new experiences of what it means to be a human for those who hitherto emphasized achievement and cognitive capacities as the only valuable elements in human personhood, or how receiving the gift of forgiveness can change a person's self-perception and the way she orients herself in her social world. *Grace transforms nature and the body.* Theologian Joseph Sittler articulates one of my main concerns when he suggests that "if grace is to be an intelligible word of redemption, and if the human person to whom the word is addressed defines himself in ever more profound, precise and fateful transactions with the world-as-nature, then the place of operation of this existence cannot be excluded from whatever redemption is to be meaningful."[24]

As suggested, grace expresses God's unconditional love and God's *favor,* which is not conditioned by any achievements of human agency. Furthermore and closely related, grace is therefore also surprising, an unexpected gift, *donum.* Grace is outside the control of the laws of nature, but still works in, with, and under them — sometimes in ways we are not (yet?) able to understand. Therefore, *healing grace* can also be seen as an expression of God's freedom, a freedom that God then in turn also bestows on those who experience his gifts as liberation from the past and as opening up to the future.

The embodied character of healing, exemplified by the laying on of hands, also suggests that healing grace can be realized in, by, with, and under the conditions of human life: it requires the concrete *incarnation* of God's manifestation of grace in nature. This is so not only in the case of Jesus as healer but also in the sacramental elements, and in other embodied human beings, who can display the gifting character of God for other embodied beings. Healing grace is grace experienced as embodied.

Healing and Faith

The relation between healing and faith is sometimes complicated. That healing is integrated into a larger framework of faith recognizes its ambiguity:

24. See Joseph Sittler, *Essays on Nature and Grace* (Philadelphia: Fortress, 1972), pp. 15–16.

it is a phenomenon that needs a wider interpretative framework in order to make sense. Christian faith provides one such framework. However, a Christian understanding of healing should, as we have just seen, avoid basing itself on a metaphysical separation between the natural and supernatural. Such a dualistic basis for the interpretation of healing events is unable to explicate fully a trinitarian doctrine of a God who works in, with, and under the conditions of nature, as well as beyond them.[25]

Although healing events call for an interpretation in faith, this does not mean that faith is a condition for healing to happen. Healing is not based on faith in Jesus as the Son of God or in a specific belief about his atonement for our sins. Nothing indicates unambiguously that this is the case, neither in the New Testament material nor in more recent reports of healing.[26] Although people meet Jesus with faith and with expectations, faith is not a necessary condition for healing to occur. This is most clearly the case in healings where the healees are not present, and there is no indication that they are aware of others intervening on their behalf (see the son of the official in John 4:46, and the servant of the Roman officer in Luke 7:1-10). On the contemporary scene, however, there are ambiguous interpretations of the need for faith: Pavel Hejzlar identifies two distinct paradigms.

> The healing evangelists adhere to the doctrine of healing in the atonement. Since all that was to be done on God's part has been already accomplished once for all, the most urgent task is to take hold of the benefits of the cross by faith. It follows that faith is accentuated by them as an indispensable prerequisite of healing. It is implied, then, or even explicitly stated that those who resort to medical science for help are immature in faith. The alternative paradigm has been developed in reaction to the former. It de-emphasizes faith, points to the complexity of factors involved in sickness and healing, holds a much more positive view of medical science, and understands healing more in terms of the influence of the Holy Spirit over a period of time rather than something to be received in an instant and confessed henceforth, symptoms notwithstanding.[27]

25. See Webster, "Wunder, Dogmatisch," p. 1728.

26. For a thorough summary of how healing is understood in the Bible in relation to Jewish and Christian faith, see in addition to the first part of this book (pp. 75-76) Frederick J. Gaiser, *Healing in the Bible: Theological Insight for Christian Ministry* (Grand Rapids: Baker Academic, 2010), pp. 245ff.

27. Pavel Hejzlar, *Two Paradigms for Divine Healing: Fred F. Bosworth, Kenneth E. Hagin, Agnes Sanford, and Francis MacNutt in Dialogue* (Leiden: Brill, 2010), p. 11.

Although there is sufficient empirical evidence to suggest that healing is not always caused by faith, there is also strong evidence suggesting that faith may have an impact on healing processes. As previously indicated, some of the healings that take place may also be "explained" by the so-called placebo effect, but this is not sufficient to explain all healings that take place in the context of healers — including Jesus.[28] It is also worth noting that even when there is such an effect as the so-called placebo effect, scientists are not totally convinced about what is actually happening — and it is due to this situation that I put the word "explained" in quotation marks here. Accordingly, to describe something as caused by this effect hardly provides us with a full explanation of the phenomenon.[29]

The discussion of placebo in the context of healing and religious faith is nevertheless interesting, as skeptics often reference this phenomenon to claim that nothing spiritual or special takes place when healing occurs. However, as should be clear by now (and especially in light of Schleiermacher's observation that everything is an expression of God's creative power), to claim that nothing divine is taking place because we "know" the cause of a phenomenon is an inference that rests on a false assumption: God works not only through what we do not know but also through what we do know. It is also important to repeat this argument in light of the widespread claim of the so-called new atheists, who say that if we can explain something by natural causes, God as an explanation becomes superfluous. From a strictly theological point of view, God does not explain anything, because explanations refer to detectable systems of causations and effects in the created world, and God is not part of any such system, as that would make God a part of this world. Hence, it appears unwarranted to say that something caused by the placebo effect eliminates the basis for a belief in Jesus as a healer called by God.

An atheist rejection of claims that Jesus heals by divine powers may have some strength, however, if one sees these powers as part of a "supernatural" reality that is different from and set aside from our natural conditions for life and health. Such a claim may be discredited for a number of reasons: First, because it does not seem open to the fact that healing is a widespread phenomenon, although not quite common in everyday life. This makes it

28. For more on this effect, see pp. 147–48 above.

29. A thorough and fairly open-minded study of healing in comparison to alternative medicine and with reference to the placebo effect in both is found T. J. Kaptchuk, "The Placebo Effect in Alternative Medicine: Can the Performance of a Healing Ritual Have Clinical Significance?" *Annals of Internal Medicine* 136, no. 11 (2002): 817–25. See also the discussion of placebo on pp. 147–48 above.

possible to see healing as an expression of capacities or capabilities of the created world, rather than something that is caused by direct supernatural intervention. Second, we may at a later stage learn more about what is going on in extraordinary healing processes — and this may in turn suggest that a mere reference to the "supernatural" does indeed become superfluous. And third, if Jesus heals due to supernatural power, how are we to interpret the healings performed by other people of other faiths — including people who sometimes have practices and beliefs contrary to faith in Jesus?

One way to solve these dilemmas is to see healings within the perspective suggested above: as signs of the kingdom of God, as broken symbols, and not as the true and definite evidence for the reality of the God whom Jesus proclaimed. As symbols, we can liken healings to the elements of the sacraments: they are concrete and visible signs of the reality of the kingdom, although they also consist of natural elements. Faith, however, embraces the elements or the instances of healing as more than the natural, and sees these symbols as manifesting the actual and creative presence of God in the world, as transformations of the concrete created world (from illness to health), as well as bearers of promises for the future. This perspective means that Christian theology need not recognize the supernatural element in healings as their primary theological point. Faith nevertheless constitutes the theological significance of healings as symbols when it allows these events to point toward a reality in which Christians believe, as originating from a source beyond the world in which we live. Thereby these sacramental elements also become something that guides and orients the life of believers in the world.

The observant reader will see that the approach suggested here implies that the discussion about God as interventionist in relation to natural laws is obsolete or problematic. The incarnation itself suggests that we adopt a compatibilist rather than an interventionist model for understanding how God acts (including through Jesus and his healings) in this world. Furthermore, this model indicates that Jesus as healer transforms the concrete and actual world and peoples' experience of it, rather than simply "adding" a supernatural dimension to something that remains natural and unchanged in character. Thus Jesus' healings testify to both the creative and the transforming power of God.

This argument has some advantages when it comes to integrating science and religion, particularly as they address Jesus as healer: both science and religion could and should be able to recognize Jesus as a healer, and as a man who was in fact able to alleviate the suffering of others and to perform extraordinary things. Theology, however, can admit that to see these events as instances of God's work is more significant with respect to the reality that they open up to than to the causes behind them. The latter can in principle be investigated by science, although theology may also claim that these causes are part of God's work as God is the creator of all that is. This interpretation then allows us to see Jesus as a healer who engages with the conditions of creation in order to open up our reality to the kingdom that manifests the salvific grace of God. Jesus as the incarnated God is the God who is part of the natural and created conditions of our reality, and who uses these conditions to open up to a reality that is shaped by more than our ordinary and everyday conditions. Faith recognizes this reality of grace both within and beyond the realities that manifest themselves in his healing ministry.

A final advantage with this approach is that it allows us to recognize the ambiguous character of healing events: they can be interpreted in different ways and from different perspectives; from faith and from medicine. For a believer, healings may be an integral part of how he or she sees God at work and as manifesting God's reality. A nonbeliever may not see this in the same way. But the phenomenon of healing nevertheless calls for both parties to relate to it and integrate it into their respective frameworks of interpretation. Given this way of reasoning, it is advisable to suggest the following: Christians must be aware that their interpretation of the phenomenon of healing is not the only one, despite the fact that they may — even with good reason — see such phenomena as integral to and confirming their faith. Nonbelievers must allow for the existence of such phenomena, and not try to refute or ignore their existence simply because they do not agree with any of the interpretations that are offered for it. In other words, the ambiguous character of the healings calls for caution regarding their status in a scholarly based argument.

To see healings as *miracles* is a common interpretation. However, our previous discussion of miracles, as well as the lines of reasoning suggested here, indicates that the category of "miracles" is fairly imprecise. I would suggest that theology leave this term aside, and instead uses the Johannine term "sign." This is also more in accordance with the use of the notion of symbol I have presented above. The notion of miracle is also problematic from a scientific point of view, especially if it is understood to indicate that something is happening contrary to natural laws. A precise formulation would be that things described as miraculous denote events that are beyond what we presently know as laws of nature. But to define something as miraculous in any other sense would be to suggest that there is something that science in principle cannot investigate — but science itself should not and cannot define what that something is. From a more phenomenological point of view, a miracle denotes that which lies beyond our everyday expectations, and that which is contrary to what we can understand and grasp. Therefore the use of the notion of miracle should be attributed to how things are perceived by us, more than to the scholarly or scientific determination of the ontological status of an event.[30]

That God can work through and by means of faith, as faith includes the attitudes and expectations of those in need of healing, does not exclude phenomena like placebo as a relevant factor to consider as causing such processes. But my point here is to suggest that placebo can hardly function as the only explanation behind instances of healing. Faith may give rise to the effects called placebo, but hardly in all cases or without some reservations.

Faith nevertheless implies a trusting relationship with the one in whom one puts one's faith, and we are aware that the relational character is of importance for healing processes. Accordingly, faith is an important accompanying factor in such processes. But it is not empirically warranted to identify faith as the main factor in causing people's healing, nor is this recommended from a theological point of view: if this were the case, it would place another burden on the one in need of healing, namely, the demand to have enough faith to be healed.

Against the backdrop of the reflections above, it is understandable why the Church of England is reluctant to speak about "faith healing." They argue that the term

> is liable to give rise to dangerous misconceptions. Many who use this phrase mean that healing is in some healing power within, in healing by ambiguous energy source, or simply that the sufferer is going to be healed because of something heard or read. A more subtle error is believing that God has already determined that recovery from a particular disease will

---

30. See Denis Edwards along similar lines when it comes to the interpretation of miracles: Such an approach "suggests that a marvelous manifestation of the Spirit, such as an act of healing, may take us beyond the laws of nature understood in the first sense — as our limited models of reality. But it may not be beyond the laws of nature understood in the second sense — as the relationships and processes that function in reality, which are more than we have fully understood or adequately modeled. And, of course, all of these patterns of relationship and causality that escape our present models are, theologically, secondary causes. This opens up the possibility that miracles may occur through a whole range of secondary causes that our current science cannot yet model or cannot yet model well" (Denis Edwards, *How God Acts: Creation, Redemption, and Special Divine Action* [Minneapolis: Fortress, 2010], p. 87). More extensive ways of reasoning along the lines suggested here, but within a more distinctive Thomistic framework, can be found on pp. 77ff.

happen — that is, when such a belief depends solely on human instincts and not on any authentic word from the Lord. Faith in God is what is traditionally known as a theological virtue necessary to salvation (which is health in the fullest sense of the word), but we cannot dogmatize about the causal connection between personal faith and recovery from particular bodily ailments.[31]

When Jesus recognizes and addresses people's faith when they ask for healing, this must then be seen as an expression of his recognition of their needs and hopes more than as an affirmation that they have what is needed to be healed. Their faith may in turn open up to all dimensions of human experience, so that they can experience the reality of God in its fullness: healing overcomes the restrictions of sin in such a way that one can live more fully in the physical, social, and psychological realm and realize that something spiritual is happening outside one's control and grasp. Furthermore, faith as the overcoming of sin implies that one anticipates and expects something more than what is, and thereby becomes open to healing processes in new ways. Thus faith can alleviate illness, and liberate resources for healing internal to the body, as well as make it receptive to resources that are external to it.

To recognize the possible element of faith in relation to healing means that instances of healing for Christians testify to the unity of the human being: faith embraces the embodied character of healing, and thereby faith itself is strengthened and transformed. Thus not only body but also soul and spirit partake in the transformative processes of healing. The Cartesian divide between mind and body is refuted in the Christian approach to healing, as the body itself is integrated into the wholeness of life that faith opens up to. The joy of becoming whole emerges out of the actual occurrence of healing and health itself. To say that healing only has to do with how the mind perceives things, or with the body and not the soul or mind, is deeply misleading. When Jesus heals, one of the things that becomes most visible is how the humans who relate to him are whole persons who long for wholeness (healing) in all experiential dimensions of life, because these dimensions belong together and are so deeply affected by the illness from which the persons suffer.

In light of the reflections in this section so far, we can now summarize what it means to talk of spiritual healing: What is spiritual in healing? The spiritual part of healing is, from the perspective of Christian theology, how

31. *A Time to Heal: A Contribution to the Ministry of Healing; A Report for the House of Bishops on the Healing Ministry* (London: Church House Publishing, 2000), p. 232.

the Spirit of God works to heal humans and restore their faith and hope in the reality of God, as this is promised and manifested in Jesus' proclamation of the kingdom of God. Because the Spirit is the one who creates life, and life is always embodied life, spiritual healing is healing of the body for the sake of living fully. Spiritual healing is never merely spiritual, and has to do with more than the faith and hope of the mind: it opens up healees to becoming more fully the persons they were created to be. Spiritual healing may nevertheless still be seen as something that works on the conditions of the present world: not everyone is healed, not all are fully healed, and suffering and death are still enduring conditions of life as we know it. Therefore, spiritual healing is also the work of the Spirit in the fact that it creates hope and faith in the reality of the kingdom. Spiritual healing cannot, accordingly, be understood or interpreted in isolation from its eschatological character — just as the sacramental reality of the church cannot be. There is an element of surplus in spiritual healing compared to that of ordinary restorations of health, because of its symbolic character. To see healings as the work of God is to see them as more than repeating and mirroring already existing conditions of life, in that they witness to something beyond this reality called the kingdom of God. It may be a main point here to suggest that the one who is ill is not only ill: the ill person is recognized in the kingdom as a whole person, created in the image of God, and thereby as one who is more than a passive person in need. He or she, even in a condition of illness, is also a witness to the gifts of God, and a receiver of God's caring love and compassion.

To interpret Jesus' healings as signs of the kingdom should nevertheless not lead us to ignore their significance in the present world. To link Jesus' healings to his proclamation of the kingdom of God implies an affirmation of this kingdom as one in which God is already present, and where God offers salvation. However, in the Gospels, what salvation means is quite open: it is not only, as depicted in Protestant theology, the forgiveness of sins, but may also be deliverance from illness. The kingdom of God, as Stephen Parsons interprets it for example, is therefore not only something to be talked about — it is a reality already present. Its presence becomes apparent especially in the concrete healing powers of Jesus. "In short, healings and miracles were signs and pointers for the breakthrough of the kingdom of God in the world. Both healing and forgiveness were a part of the real salvation of God that Jesus proclaimed to the world."[32]

---

32. See Stephen Parsons, *Helhed og Helbred* (Valby Kbh.: Unitas, 1998), pp. 124–25. My translation from Danish.

Finally, healing opens up a framework for interpreting the relationship between the body of Christ and the bodies of the members of the Christian community, because healing can be interpreted as emerging out of the same power that was at work in the resurrection of Christ. In this way, healing may have an effect beyond the immediate and point toward the context of Christian eschatology. As Porterfield notes, Christians throughout history have experienced the vision of eternal life manifested in the resurrection as a vitalizing presence in their present lives.[33] Thus the phenomenon of healing binds together the acts of God in creation, redemption, and renewal, and in the promised future. Healing is an eschatological event that is anticipated in the present.

Healing in the Wider Context of Christology, Christianity, and New Age

In contemporary culture, so-called alternative practices of healing flourish. In what way can the above considerations contribute to a theological understanding of these? Without any claim to being exhaustive, I will here offer some basic and principled considerations that can provide a basis for orientation with regard to this topic.

Modern medicine often seems to ignore the whole person. It also often overlooks resources other than the biological in the processes of healing — including sociological, psychological, and spiritual ones. Furthermore, its emphasis on the biomedical approach has in turn also excluded others who are not trained as medical doctors as legitimate participants in healing processes. The question is whether there are other approaches to healing than the purely medical one, and whether this can be developed as a viable approach from the point of view of theology.

Initially, we can admit that there are many reasons for being skeptical toward religious healing, some of which are rooted in the way healing is actually practiced in some Christian groups: the claims of televangelists that enough faith (and donations) will allow God to intervene in a supernatural way for healing, together with the claim made by the same people that God strikes people with AIDS or Alzheimer's in order to teach them a lesson, is rightly seen as appalling and as a distortion of the healing practice in Jesus' ministry. When Christian spiritual healing is presented in this way, it be-

---

33. Porterfield, *Healing in the History of Christianity,* p. 7.

comes difficult to propose other approaches to and ways of understanding healing. This is because the aforementioned approach engages people in a double-bind from which it is hard to free oneself both emotionally and cognitively. (It is so easy and so tempting to see one's own illness as something for which oneself is responsible, be it for blame or for merit.)

Other reasons for skepticism have to do with how the modern, evidence-based, experiential approach to health and healing that is adopted by many or most Christians in the Western world is at odds with all the diverse and often unsubstantiated methods of healing that are present in the flora of so-called New Age healers. Such practices are also at odds with the metaphysical and rationalistic approach that many Christians have adopted, consciously or not. However, parallel to this feature, many have actually found healing in such practices, whereas others have experienced problematic claims and disturbing relations and interpretations of illness and lack of health.[34]

Furthermore, Bruce Epperly comments that many mainstream Christians today seem to "have been imprisoned by what they do not believe about healing rather than the positive and life-affirming healing possibilities in their midst."[35] Sadly, this also means that their approach to healing is shaped more by negation than by an affirmative faith that may open up to and recognize the importance of healing practices that may also be related to or rooted in religious or spiritual traditions.

In the history of Christianity, health and healing were a religious concern until the dawn of modernity. But they are still religiously relevant. Whereas other religious traditions have maintained practices that affirm this insight, modernized and secularized Christianity has differentiated religious from medical knowledge and has handed over the concerns for health to another sphere than its own — at least to a great extent.[36] The flip side of this development is that healing in a religious context has been neglected, ridiculed, and/or looked on with suspicion — also from the point of view of modern theology. People practicing healing within a religious context have been met with suspicion and accusation of superstition.

Given the many reports of the experience of actual religious healing, there is nevertheless reason to suggest that the biomedical regime should not be considered the only one that cares for people's health. A complementary

---

34. See Bruce Gordon Epperly, *God's Touch: Faith, Wholeness, and the Healing Miracles of Jesus* (Louisville: Westminster John Knox, 2001), p. 12.

35. Epperly, *God's Touch*, p. 14.

36. As indicated, there are some exceptions to this picture, e.g., in the Pentecostal movement and in the healing movement within the Anglican Church.

view, which also allows for and recognizes a more holistic approach to health and healing, is called for. Religious traditions have traditionally been stewards of such holistic approaches. This does not mean that one has to admit that there is truth in every doctrinal claim (or interpretation of their experience) these traditions make, but their experiential basis is hard to dispute. Accordingly, one has to admit that, from a scientific as well as a theological point of view, healing takes place and can contribute to increased health and better lives for many. Furthermore, healing and recovery may take place in many different forms and ways, some caused by medical treatment and some by other means and interactions.

On the contemporary scene, and mostly due to the success of modern medicine in combination with the modernization of Christian theology, religious or spiritual healing has been placed in the shadow. As a consequence, other religious traditions have today gained most of the attention on the "alternative health and healing scene," with the exception of Christian healers who have mostly belonged to the charismatic movement or those in the Christian Science context. There are many ways to heal, and many possibilities for interpreting healing, and Christian theology should not shy away from this fact. Christian healing may also be more than one thing.

To admit that healing takes place in different ways and contexts opens up new possibilities for dialogue among religious traditions regarding their experiences and practices, even without having to enter into more "doctrinal" or theoretical discussions. If healing and the gift of healing is a real phenomenon, it can be discussed as such, apart from different interpretations of it. A Christian view that emphasizes God as the creator of all things would imply that God is also at work as healer in other contexts and traditions than the Christian one. Of course, such an interpretation cannot be developed uncritically, just as Christian theology should not address the concrete practices of Christian healers uncritically with regard to issues of power, the calling forth of unrealistic expectations, abuse, manipulation, requests for money, and so on.

If Christ as a healer is then someone who manifests the capacities and capabilities of what humans can be, and thereby testifies to how God the creator cares for all of God's creatures, this means that other healers can be identified as more or less Christlike in their function as healers, even when they belong to other religious traditions and even when one must conclude that there are elements in their practices or doctrine that are definitely *not* Christlike. However, Christian theology should not simply hand the practice of healing over to other traditions. Instead, it should try to find viable and fruitful ways to complement the medical treatment of suffering with other means that are not accessible to the medical profession. This point has to be seen in connection with the recognition of Jesus as healer. A well-developed theology of Christian healing may in turn also be a basis for engaging with other religious traditions in which healing is practiced, including so-called New Age or alternative modes of healing. However, such a theology needs to affirm that the healing practices of the church exist between two extremes: the omnipotence or impotence of such practices. It is as equally problematic to expect God to do everything one may wish for through such practices as it is to assume that God can do nothing.

Conclusion: The Healing Christ — A Vision for Contemporary Christology

The doctrine of the incarnation has significant relevance for the theological understanding of healing. Not only does it take the embodied character of human life fully into account, but it also suggests that, in becoming incarnate, God acts in order to provide a healing that is only made possible through the concrete, embodied interaction and communication between God and humanity. Healing as a part of Jesus' ministry can thus be summarized along the lines suggested by Ruben Zimmermann: It is — as a series of concrete, embodied, and body-related acts — proof of Jesus' identity as coming from God. Healing events are a display of God's mercy in Christ, a means of creating faith in Jesus as the Son of God and thus also "signs and seals" of his messianic activity, and in all of this, healing is a function of the kingdom of God.[37]

Traditionally, however, Christian theology has interpreted the ministry of Jesus as foreshadowed in different functions that we find already in the Old Testament. In Reformed theology (e.g., Calvin, *Institutes* 2.15.1) this has led to the formulation of the *triplex munus Christi* — his three offices as prophet, priest, and king. It was originally suggested by Eusebius in his *Ecclesiastical History* (1.3.8); there he first described the concept of these threefold offices of Christ. It is striking, however, that none of the sources behind this idea about Christ's offices contain any reference to his healings.

---

37. Ruben Zimmermann, "Grundfragen zu den frühchristlichen Wundererzählungen," in *Kompendium der frühchristlichen Wundererzählungen*, vol. 1, *Die Wunder Jesu*, ed. Ruben Zimmermann et al. (Gütersloh: Gütersloher Verlagshaus, 2013), p. 46.

In fact, the healing Christ is virtually absent in much of the Christian theological tradition.[38] This may have to do with the aforementioned emphasis on the spiritual as opposed to the embodied and material in Calvin's theology. It is nevertheless a feature that we would suggest needs rectification. As we have tried to argue throughout this book, the healing ministry of Jesus is intertwined with the way in which he reveals God as creator and redeemer of the world. As healer, Jesus reveals a God of love and compassion, who does not turn away from the suffering of creation but instead makes possible concrete hope for redemption and fulfillment by acting in, with, and under creaturely conditions in order to reveal the kingdom. The idea that Christ's work can be summed up in the offices of priest, prophet, and king without taking his healing ministry into account should accordingly be rejected as an inadequate description of his work.[39]

This leads naturally to a final approach in the history of doctrine that is relevant for the interpretation of Jesus as healer. It is to be found in the idea that Jesus is true God and true human. This is a far more adequate basis for interpreting his healing ministry than the *triplex munus,* as it allows us to see him acting as a healer by being human while at the same time making manifest the reality of God. In a different context, I have formulated the idea that this understanding of Jesus can be formulated in contemporary terms as follows: as this concrete human being, Jesus is the incarnated God. Jesus is who God is when God is human. With reference to healing, this means that God — as Jesus — engages the powers of creation in his graceful approach to humanity in order to alleviate the suffering of the sick and destitute. Jesus thereby fulfills what it means to be human, that is, to bear full witness to God by realizing the will of God in and for and with creation. In the healings, God recognizes human reality as worthy of healing, while the healings are simultaneously a proclamation of and a calling to faith in God. Thereby God

---

38. There are some notable exceptions. In addition to those we have referred to earlier, we can mention Justin Martyr. However, at some point this topic seems to disappear as theologically interesting. For Justin, see p. 9 above.

39. Similar critiques of this narrowing down of the whole ministry of Christ have been expressed previously, e.g., by the Lutheran theologian Werner Elert, who says that "Angesichts dieser Fülle von Attributen, die Christus im Neuen Testament beigelegt werden, ist es eine recht zweifelhafte Bereicherung der Christologie, wenn man alle von ihm ausgehenden Wirkungen in der Lehre vom dreifachen Amt zusammenfassen will. Diese Lehre bedeutet vielmehr eine unzulässige Verengung, weil sie wichtigste Attribute, wie das des *soter* oder des Erlösers entweder unterschlägt oder auf eins der drei 'Ämter' beschränkt und dadurch verkürzt" (Werner Elert and Ernst Kinder, *Der Christliche Glaube: Grundlinien der Lutherischen Dogmatik,* 5th ed. [Hamburg: Furche-Verlag, 1960], p. 333).

is revealed as the concrete source of love and compassion, which requires recognition of the identity of God from the side of the human.

Rowan Williams has suggested some lines of reflection that sum up well an interpretation of healing based in Christology. Similar to what I have already pointed out, he sees health as overcoming the restrictions and separations of the different realms of human life; or, as he puts it, health has to do with the bridging "of a gulf between flesh and spirit" and overcoming different forms of alienation, including the alienation between God and humanity.[40] Further-more, "God also wants to inhabit the world — he does not only want the world to be inhabited."[41] This is where Christology enters the picture more fully, in a manner relevant for the present considerations and in a way that allows for taking the embodied character of life and health fully into consideration.

> God is already inhabiting what has been made but the task that God un-dertakes in our human history is, you might say, the harder one of inhab-iting the thoughts, the feelings, the reactions, the passions, the grief and the exhilaration of very contingent and messy human beings like you and me. And the pivotal moment is when God fully and unequivocally inhabits that life which is Jesus of Nazareth, that death and the resurrection which belong to Jesus of Nazareth and which make all the difference to your body and mine so that our own inhabitation of the world changes.[42]

Accordingly, Williams stresses "how important it is to link healing, in what can sometimes seem a rather narrowly focused sense, with everything we want to say about the gospel." Not only is the world created by God so that we may inhabit it, but God has, through the gospel and the ministry of Je-sus Christ, "made it possible for us to inhabit the world more fully, more deeply, more joyfully than we could ever have possibly imagined."[43] Healing thus involves all realms of human existence. And it has an eschatological di-mension rooted in the resurrection. This makes an individualistic or merely medical approach to healing contrary to this potential fullness. In Jesus and his healing practice all the experiential realms of human life come together, and accordingly, it is in him that we in glimpses can see revealed the destiny of this world in the future of God.

40. Rowan Williams, "A Theology of Health for Today," in *Wounds That Heal: Theology, Imagination and Health,* ed. Jonathan Baxter (London: SPCK, 2007), p. 6.
41. Williams, "A Theology of Health for Today," p. 10.
42. Williams, "A Theology of Health for Today," p. 11.
43. Williams, "A Theology of Health for Today," p. 11.

Concluding Considerations about the Theological Understanding of Jesus as Healer

In the previous parts of this book we have identified clusters of topics related to the theological understanding of Jesus as healer. We are now in a position to summarize, from a contemporary theological point of view, what we take to be the main implications of our analyses. Understanding Jesus as a healer has implications both for a christologically based theology of healing and for the church's own ministry of healing. This understanding of Jesus as healer is simultaneously informed by both historical material and contemporary anthropological elements. We can start by summarizing our reflections related to the historical findings as follows.

1. Healing is a dominant aspect of how Jesus was remembered. Although this remembrance proceeds from the fact that Jesus was indeed a healer, this does not imply that every single incident reported is authentic.

2. Jesus was not alone in performing healings at his time. The sheer number of his healings makes him a distinct figure among "colleagues." However, it is first and foremost the religious and practical parameters used to make sense of his activity as a healer that make him unique compared to others.

3. The healing stories are reminders that Jesus' ministry addressed human beings holistically, without leaving out bodily concerns. Much research on Jesus' healings has in effect turned these stories into evidence for theological or christological concerns. It is, however, important to see that these stories are primarily about responses to petitions from people suffering from bodily illnesses, even though these could also involve psychological, collective, and even political aspects. Dogmatically speaking, we can say that Jesus as healer testifies to the incarnational dimension of Christian theology, underscoring the embodied and experiential character of Christian faith, as well as God's relation to and taking part in all dimensions of human life with concern, care, mercy, and compassion. Thus healing reveals dimensions

both of who God as triune (incarnated) is and of God's grace. Healing is not only related to the atoning character of Christ's ministry but also to the works of the full Trinity in order to create, restore, redeem, and fulfill the world. Accordingly, there is a gospel for the body.

4. There are three facts taken from the Gospel stories about healing that the New Testament research discussed in our analysis fails to meet. First, the role of the spectators in these stories implies that what happened went beyond having meaning restored to one's life, although meaning is far more than an inward experience. Second, the fact that the healing of "lepers," whatever they suffered from, was to be inspected, likewise suggests that something outward, something visible had taken place. Third, analogies from psychotherapy or placebo may offer partial help in understanding the phenomenon of healing, but both approaches fail to come to terms with the immediacy of Jesus' healings. The analogies are conditioned on time and gradual change; even placebo often relies on a relationship with some continuity.

5. Jesus' raising the dead is to be reckoned among the healings done by Jesus. This certainly stretches our credulity, but the Gospels address them as an integral part of his healing ministry. It is worth noticing, though, that such stories do not abound in the material. This becomes evident when seen against the backdrop of apocryphal acts. A hermeneutical model of "nature and grace" is here left with what a Norwegian idiom labels "white spots on the map," that is, places not fully explored and in need of further investigation. Furthermore, it is also difficult to assess the stories of raising the dead with reference to analogies in the past or present: there are a few such stories, they are hard to inspect in detail, and they are even harder to use in order to develop a full-fledged contemporary theology of Jesus as healer. What can be said, however, is that these stories somehow testify to the power Jesus was able to use in order to save people from the distress caused by illness. They serve to amplify the experiences of this power in a striking and extraordinary way, although they hardly add anything significantly new to what can be incorporated into a contemporary theology of healing.

6. Jesus' healing ministry continues after his death. In the New Testament this is witnessed to in the commission texts, in Paul, and in the book of Acts, and is embodied in the statement found in the latter book, namely, "Christ heals you." Furthermore, the healing activity of Jesus is also continued by his disciples according to other sources from the first centuries. The present book has sketched this primarily in order to make precisely this point. However, the healing of Jesus performed through his followers

receives less attention and significance than in the earlier tradition. When the healing incidents from Jesus' ministry are told of and passed on to people who were not there, these texts function to keep alive this aspect for future readers. This is in line with Jesus' last words according to Matthew: "I am with you always, to the end of the age." Already here we see, then, how the healings of Jesus point to the ministry of the church as well as toward the eschatological future.

7. The healings Jesus performed brought about something unexpected and unpredictable. It is the same way with the continuous ministry of Jesus as a healer. In the biblical stories, healing and faith occur in tandem. Faith is manifested in petitions and prayers in various forms, for restoring health in all aspects. From this follows that healing is gift-like; it is grace. Hence healing cannot be preconditioned on faith, as witnessed to, for example, in the distance healings of Jesus. Healing may well be awaited in expectations and hope, but in making theology out of these stories, we should not turn healing into regularities and normalities. As Ruben Zimmermann points out, Jesus' healings bring irritation because they oppose easy systematization. This irritation may, however, be turned into wonder and hope.

8. The healing tradition in Christian theologies, and the New Testament in particular, portrays God in a way that challenges narrow positivism (or rationalism) and envisages possibilities beyond normal experiences but that are nevertheless not beyond possibility. A rejection of narrow positivism does not mean, however, that we should not also approach stories about healing with the same ideals as the ones that direct other critical scholarly work. It is as a result of examining existing data along such lines that we find evidence for a more fully developed understanding of and theology about Jesus as healer.

9. Any healing attributed to Jesus claims to represent a restoration of life as God intended it to be, albeit both incomplete and anticipatory. This makes such healing "prophetic" in terms of being partial and provisional images of what God has in store for the people. Thus Jesus as healer belongs firmly within a theology of the restoration of creation *(recapitulatio)*. From this perspective, it becomes questionable to make divine interventions "contrary to nature" the most important element of the healings Jesus performed, be they in the past or the present. Instead, we can see healings as events that reveal who God is as Creator, Redeemer, and Fulfiller of this world.

10. Augustine distinguishes between "knowledge found or discovered" and "knowledge introduced by human beings." The first refers to what God has made available through his creation and that is therefore, in principle,

attainable everywhere. Augustine places contemporary medicine in this category. This knowledge is a means whereby God maintains his creation, and it is not exclusive to the church and Christians. This militates against any view claiming exclusivism on the part of Jesus as healer. This aspect of Augustine's thought thus develops somewhat the idea of "the gold and silver of Egypt," which from early on was a slogan for finding helpful and relevant knowledge even in paganism. Such ideas do not favor exclusivism, but rather invite attempts at seeing Jesus as a healer in a wider context, without neglecting the ways in which he really is distinct and even unique.

From the viewpoint of contemporary systematic theology, we can elaborate the above considerations further along the following lines.

1. That Jesus was a healer is a testimony to his full humanity: as a healer he reveals how the powers of God can become manifest in humans in ways that allow them to take fuller part in the goal that God has set for creation. Thus his healings testify to both the creational, redemptive, and fulfilling intentions of God, and allow for seeing these different dimensions of God's work as integrated with each other. Christian healing is accordingly not a mere spiritual concept. It is about the wholeness and fullness of all dimensions of human life coming to fulfillment in the symbol "the kingdom of God." This understanding of the kingdom implies, to state it again, that there is a gospel for the body.

2. As incarnational, healing can also be interpreted along sacramental lines as concrete, felt, sensual, and bodily experienced instances that God works in, with, and under, in order to create or sustain faith in God's generosity, grace, and mercy. We do not, however, propose to see healing as a sacrament, but we suggest that it is possible to detect a sacramental aspect to healing events, when they are interpreted as sensual signs of the grace of God. Against this backdrop, then, the healings may be seen as broken symbols, or signs of the eschatological reality of the kingdom of God. This kingdom is already provisionally present in the present age.

3. Jesus' practice as a healer means that the gospel for the body is at the basis of his ministry: the incarnation of Jesus Christ not only is about the spiritual dimension of human life but also demonstrates that the gospel addresses all aspects of human life, including the body. Against theological traditions that see Jesus as healer as mainly a pedagogical practice or as signs with spiritual significance, we affirm that the ministry of Jesus as healer must be read as a revelation of a gospel for the body. This means that Christianity can acknowledge the embodied character of human life as part of God's concern for humanity.

4. Jesus as healer reveals that human life in its fullness is dependent on both nature and grace: as grace has no meaning without nature, nature cannot be fully realized without the grace that is present in his healings, and that anticipates the eschatological fulfillment of all that is.

5. Healing then — both in the ministry of Jesus and now — anticipates the future and is a sign of how we may not be fully determined by our past, and of God's power to overcome the limitations of the past in God's work for creation and redemption.

6. Healing is no solution to the problem of evil and suffering, but a sign that points to a future reality that works on other conditions than the present in order to overcome the negative aspects of created and fallen reality. Healing opens up hope and faith more than a final solution to suffering in the here and now.

7. Why healing sometimes happens and sometimes does not cannot be explained by any theology. It is recommendable to leave phenomena like healing unexplained and to see them as uncontrolled and surprising events that call attention to the graceful freedom of God as God acts in reality. Instances of healing testify to the open character of a theology that allows for God's free work in creation in order to instigate faith, hope, and love.

8. Healing calls to faith. As already indicated, healing is not dependent on prior faith, but dependent only on the grace of God. And as it is solely dependent on God's free action, it is not something humans should take on as a burden of responsibility to bring about. This being said, though, all humans have a responsibility for providing good conditions for health and restoration. But when healing happens in ways outside our realm of knowledge, we cannot hold humans or their faith (or lack of such) responsible for it.

9. That God works healing in all of creation suggests that God's care is not restricted to Christian believers and a Christian context. Furthermore, healing is not only one thing, but may be used as a concept to describe how God allows human life to be renewed and fulfilled in a multitude of new ways that overcome the limitations and impediments previously experienced by humans.

10. Anything that happens to the body is in need of interpretation. It can be interpreted from different perspectives and is, accordingly, ambiguous. All experiences of healing thus fall within the category of the ambiguous. A Christian theology of healing should recognize the ambiguity of healing and claims of healing, while simultaneously seeing experiences of healing as a call to faith in a God who can restore life in unexpected and hitherto unexplained ways.

11. Healing is preferably not to be described in terms of "miracle" or as "supernatural," because it has to do with the realization and fulfillment of the natural conditions of human life. Furthermore, it is advisable to employ an "open" notion of healing that allows for it to take place in different ways and different modes, and not to restrict it. Only on this basis can we then see healings as instances of the reality that will be renewed and fulfilled in the final consummation that is manifested and anticipated in the resurrection of Christ. Thus healing links past, present, and future and signifies that all times are in the hands of God, the Almighty.

Bibliography

Aasgaard, Reidar. *The Childhood of Jesus: Decoding the Apocryphal Infancy Gospel of Thomas.* Eugene, OR: Cascade, 2009.

Alkier, Stefan, and David Moffitt. "Miracles Revisited: A Short Theological and Historical Survey." In *Miracles Revisited: New Testament Miracle Stories and Their Concepts of Reality,* edited by Stefan Alkier and Annette Weissenrieder, pp. 315–36. Studies of the Bible and Its Reception 2. Berlin: De Gruyter, 2013.

Allen, Joel Stevens. *The Despoliation of Egypt in Pre-rabbinic, Rabbinic and Patristic Sources.* Supplements to Vigiliae Christianae 92. Leiden: Brill, 2008.

Amundsen, Darrel W., and Gary B. Ferngren. "The Perception of Disease and Disease Causality in the New Testament." In *ANRW* 37.3, pp. 2934–56. Berlin: De Gruyter, 1996.

Avalos, Hector. *Health Care and the Rise of Christianity.* Peabody, MA: Hendrickson, 1999.

Barr, James. *The Semantics of Biblical Language.* Oxford: Oxford University Press, 1961.

Barth, Karl. *Church Dogmatics* IV/2. Edited by Geoffrey W. Bromiley and T. F. Torrance. Translated by Geoffrey W. Bromiley. London: T&T Clark, 2010.

Bauckham, Richard. "The Acts of Paul as a Sequel to Acts." In *The Book of Acts in Its First Century Setting,* vol. 1, *The Book of Acts in Its Ancient Literary Setting,* edited by Bruce W. Winter and Andrew D. Clarke, pp. 105–52. Grand Rapids: Eerdmans, 1993.

Berger, Klaus. *Identity and Experience in the New Testament.* Translated by Charles Muenchow. Minneapolis: Fortress, 2003.

Berry, R. J. "Divine Action: Expected and Unexpected." *Zygon: Journal of Religion and Science* 37, no. 3 (2002): 717–28.

Betcher, Sharon V. "Disability and the Terror of the Miracle Tradition." In *Miracles Revisited: New Testament Miracle Stories and Their Concepts of Reality,* edited by Stefan Alkier and Annette Weissenrieder, pp. 161–81. Studies of the Bible and Its Reception 2. Berlin: De Gruyter, 2013.

Betz, Hans Dieter, ed. *The Greek Magical Papyri in Translation, Including the Demotic Spells.* Chicago: University of Chicago Press, 1992.

Bourne, Charles, and Fraser Watts. "Conceptualizations of Spiritual Healing: Christian and Secular." In *Spiritual Healing: Scientific and Religious Perspectives,* edited by Fraser Watts, pp. 77–89. Cambridge: Cambridge University Press, 2011.

Bovon, François. *Luke 1: A Commentary.* Translated by Christine M. Thomas. Hermeneia. Minneapolis: Fortress, 2002.

Brant, Jo-Ann A. *John.* Paideia: Commentaries on the New Testament. Grand Rapids: Baker Academic, 2011.

Brodie, Thomas L. "Towards Unravelling Luke's Use of the Old Testament: Luke 7:11–17 as an Imitatio of 1 Kings 17:17–24." *New Testament Studies* 32 (1986): 247–67.

Brody, Howard. "Ritual, Medicine, and the Placebo Response." In *The Problem of Ritual Efficacy,* edited by William S. Sax, Johannes Quack, and Jan Weinhold, pp. 151–67. Oxford Ritual Studies. Oxford: Oxford University Press, 2010.

Brown, Michael L. *Israel's Divine Healer.* Grand Rapids: Zondervan, 1995.

Bultmann, Rudolf. *Glauben und Verstehen.* Tübingen: Mohr, 1952. ET: *Faith and Understanding.* New York: Harper & Row, 1969.

———. *Rudolf Bultmann: Interpreting Faith for the Modern Era.* Edited by Roger A. Johnson. London: Collins, 1987.

Capps, Donald. *Jesus the Village Psychiatrist.* Louisville: Westminster John Knox, 2008.

Chilton, Bruce D. *The Isaiah Targum: Introduction, Translation, Apparatus and Notes.* The Aramaic Bible 11. Edinburgh: T&T Clark, 1987.

Chrysovergi, Maria. "Attitudes towards the Use of Medicine in Jewish Literature from the Third and Second Centuries B.C.E." Ph.D. diss., Durham University, 2011. http://etheses.dur.ac.uk/3568.

———. "Contrasting Views on Physicians in Tobit and Sirach." *Journal for the Study of Pseudepigrapha* 21 (2011): 37–54.

Clarke, Andrew C. *Parallel Lives: The Relation of Paul to the Apostles in the Lucan Perspective.* Paternoster Biblical Monographs. Milton Keynes, UK: Paternoster, 2001.

Clayton, Philip. "The Theology of Spiritual Healing." In *Spiritual Healing: Scientific and Religious Perspectives,* edited by Fraser Watts, pp. 44–63. Cambridge: Cambridge University Press, 2011.

Colle, Ralph Del. "Miracles in Christianity." In *The Cambridge Companion to Miracles,* edited by Graham Twelftree, pp. 235–53. Cambridge: Cambridge University Press, 2011.

Cook, John Granger. *The Interpretation of the New Testament in Greco-Roman Paganism.* Peabody, MA: Hendrickson, 2002.

Cotter, Wendy J. *The Christ of the Miracle Stories: Portrait through Encounter.* Grand Rapids: Baker Academic, 2010.

Craffert, Pieter F. "Crossan's Historical Jesus as Healer, Exorcist and Miracle Worker." *Religion & Theology* 10 (2003): 243–66.

———. *The Life of a Galilean Shaman: Jesus of Nazareth in Anthropological-Historical Perspective.* Eugene, OR: Cascade, 2008.

———. "Medical Anthropology as an Antidote for Ethnocentrism in Jesus Research? Putting the Illness-Disease Distinction into Perspective." *Harvard Theological*

Studies 67, no. 1 (2011): 1–14. http://www.hts.org.za/index.php/HTS/article/viewFile/970/1549.

———. Review of *Jesus the Village Psychiatrist*, by Donald Capps. *Review of Biblical Literature* 10 (2008). http://www.bookreviews.org/bookdetail.asp?TitleId=6392.

Crawford, Robert. "A Cultural Account of Health: Control, Release and the Social Body." In *Issues in the Political Economy of Health Care,* edited by John B. McKinley, pp. 60–103. New York: Tavistock, 1984.

Crossan, John Dominic. *The Historical Jesus: The Life of a Mediterranean Jewish Peasant.* San Francisco: HarperSanFrancisco, 1991.

———. *Jesus: A Revolutionary Biography.* San Francisco: HarperSanFrancisco, 1994.

———. "Jesus and the Challenge of Collaborative Eschatology." In *The Historical Jesus: Five Views,* edited by James K. Beilby and Paul Rhodes Eddy, pp. 105–52. Downers Grove, IL: IVP Academic, 2009.

Csordas, Thomas J. *Body/Meaning/Healing.* Contemporary Anthropology of Religion. New York: Palgrave Macmillan, 2002.

———. *The Sacred Self: A Cultural Phenomenology of Charismatic Healing.* Berkeley: University of California Press, 1994.

Darling, Frank C. *Biblical Healing: Hebrew and Christian Roots.* Boulder, CO: Vista Publications, 1989.

———. *Christian Healing in the Middle Ages and Beyond.* Boulder, CO: Vista Publications, 1990.

Daunton-Fear, Andrew. *Healing in the Early Church: The Church's Ministry of Healing and Exorcism from the First to the Fifth Century.* Studies in Christian History and Thought. Milton Keynes, UK: Paternoster, 2009.

Davies, Stevan L. *Jesus the Healer: Possession, Trance and the Origins of Christianity.* London: SCM, 1995.

Dunn, James D. G. *Jesus Remembered.* Christianity in the Making 1. Grand Rapids: Eerdmans, 2003.

Edwards, Denis. *How God Acts: Creation, Redemption, and Special Divine Action.* Theology and the Sciences. Minneapolis: Fortress, 2010.

Ehrman, Bart D., ed. *After the New Testament: A Reader in Early Christianity.* New York: Oxford University Press, 1999.

Elert, Werner, and Ernst Kinder. *Der Christliche Glaube: Grundlinien der Lutherischen Dogmatik.* 5th ed. Hamburg: Furche-Verlag, 1960.

Elliott, John H. "Paul, Galatians, and the Evil Eye." In *The Social World of the New Testament: Insights and Models,* edited by Jerome H. Neyrey and Eric C. Stewart, pp. 221–34. Peabody, MA: Hendrickson, 2008.

Epperly, Bruce Gordon. *God's Touch: Faith, Wholeness, and the Healing Miracles of Jesus.* Louisville: Westminster John Knox, 2001.

Evans, Craig A. *Mark 8:27–16:20.* Word Biblical Commentary 34B. Nashville: Thomas Nelson, 2001.

Evans, Dylan. *Placebo: Mind over Matter in Modern Medicine.* London: HarperCollins, 2003.

Eve, Eric. *The Healer from Nazareth: Jesus' Miracles in Historical Context.* London: SPCK, 2009.

Fee, Gordon D. *God's Empowering Spirit: The Holy Spirit in the Letters of Paul.* Peabody, MA: Hendrickson, 1994.

Ferngren, Gary B. *Medicine and Health Care in Early Christianity.* Baltimore: Johns Hopkins University Press, 2009.

Ford, Lewis S. "The Three Strands of Tillich's Theory of Religious Symbols." *Journal of Religion* 46, no. 1 (1966): 104–30.

Frank, Jerome. *Persuasion and Healing: A Comparative Study of Psychotherapy.* Baltimore: Johns Hopkins University Press, 1974.

Gaiser, Frederick J. *Healing in the Bible: Theological Insight for Christian Ministry.* Grand Rapids: Baker Academic, 2010.

Gnilka, Christian. *CHRÊSIS: Die Methode der Kirchenväter im Umgang mit der Antiken Kultur,* vol. 1, *Der Begriff des "rechten Gebrauchs."* Basel: Schwabe, 1984.

Gnilka, Joachim. *Jesus of Nazareth: Message and History.* Translated by Siegfried S. Schatzmann. Peabody, MA: Hendrickson, 1997.

Goppelt, Leonhard. *Typos: Die typologische Deutung des Alten Testaments im Neuen.* Gütersloh: Gerd Mohn, 1939.

Grabner, Wolf-Jürgen, Hanna Kasparick, and Gabriele Metzner. "Über Wundererzählungen heute predigen (Homiletik der Wundererzählungen)." In *Kompendium der frühchristlichen Wundererzählungen,* vol. 1, *Die Wunder Jesu,* edited by Ruben Zimmermann et al., pp. 156–62. Gütersloh: Gütersloher Verlagshaus, 2013.

Gregersen, N. H. "Deep Incarnation: Why Evolutionary Continuity Matters in Christology." *Toronto Journal of Theology* 26, no. 2 (2010): 173–88.

———. "Special Divine Action and the Quilt of Laws." In *Scientific Perspectives on Divine Action: Twenty Years of Challenge and Progress,* edited by Robert J. Russell, Nancey C. Murphy, and William R. Stoeger. Scientific Perspectives on Divine Action 6. Vatican City: Vatican Observatory; Berkeley, CA: Center for Theology and the Natural Sciences; Notre Dame: University of Notre Dame Press, 2008.

Grimm, Werner. *Die Verkündigung Jesu und Deuterojesaja.* Frankfurt am Main: Peter Lang, 1981.

Guelich, Robert A. *Mark 1–8:26.* Word Biblical Commentary 34A. Nashville: Thomas Nelson, 1989.

Gunkel, Hermann. *The Influence of the Holy Spirit: The Popular View of the Apostolic Age and the Teaching of the Apostle Paul.* Translated by Roy A. Harrisville and Philip A. Quanbeck II. Philadelphia: Fortress, 1979.

Hagner, Donald. *Matthew 14–28.* Word Biblical Commentary 33B. Dallas: Word, 1995.

Harnack, Adolf von. *Die Mission und Ausbreitung des Christentums in den ersten drei Jahrhunderten.* 4th ed. Wiesbaden: VMA-Verlag, 1924.

Harrington, Anne. "Placebo: Conversations at the Disciplinary Borders." In *The Placebo Effect: An Interdisciplinary Exploration,* edited by Anne Harrington, pp. 338–73. Cambridge: Harvard University Press, 1997.

———. "The Placebo Effect: What Is Interesting for Scholars of Religion." *Zygon: Journal of Religion and Science* 46, no. 2 (2011): 265–80.

Haught, John F. *God after Darwin: A Theology of Evolution.* 2nd ed. Boulder: Westview, 2008.

Hejzlar, Pavel. *Two Paradigms for Divine Healing: Fred F. Bosworth, Kenneth E. Hagin, Agnes Sanford, and Francis MacNutt in Dialogue.* Global Pentecostal and Charismatic Studies. Leiden: Brill, 2010.

Hengel, Rudolf, and Martin Hengel. "Die Heilungen Jesu und medizinisches Denken." In *Der Wunderbegriff im Neuen Testament,* edited by Alfred Suhl, pp. 338–73. Wege der Forschung 195. Darmstadt: Wissenschaftliche Buchgesellschaft, 1980.

Henriksen, Jan-Olav. *Life, Love, and Hope: God and Human Experience.* Grand Rapids: Eerdmans, 2014.

Hooker, Morna D. *The Signs of a Prophet: The Prophetic Actions of Jesus.* London: SCM, 1997.

Horst, Pieter W. van der. "Peter's Shadow: The Religio-Historical Background of Acts v. 15." *New Testament Studies* 23, no. 2 (1977): 204–12.

Hultgren, Arland J. *Paul's Letter to the Romans: A Commentary.* Grand Rapids: Eerdmans, 2011.

Hvalvik, Reidar. "In Word and Deed: The Expansion of the Church in the Pre-Constantinian Era." In *The Mission of the Early Church to Jews and Gentiles,* edited by Jostein Ådna and Hans Kvalbein, pp. 265–87. WUNT 127. Tübingen: Mohr Siebeck, 2000.

Jervell, Jacob. "Der schwache Charismatiker." In *Rechtfertigung: Festschrift für Ernst Käsemann zum 70. Geburtstag,* edited by Johannes Friedrich, Wolfgang Pöhlmann, and Peter Stuhlmacher, pp. 185–98. Tübingen: Mohr Siebeck, 1976.

———. *The Theology of the Acts of the Apostles.* New Testament Theology. Cambridge: Cambridge University Press, 1996.

———. *The Unknown Paul: Essays on Luke-Acts and Early Christian History.* Minneapolis: Augsburg, 1984.

Kaiser, Sigurd. *Krankenheilung. Untersuchungen zu Form, Sprache, traditionsgeschichtlichem Hintergrund und Aussage zu Jak 5,13–18.* Wissenschaftliche Monographien zum Alten und Neuen Testament 112. Neukirchen-Vluyn: Neukirchener Verlag, 2006.

Kaptchuk, T. J. "The Placebo Effect in Alternative Medicine: Can the Performance of a Healing Ritual Have Clinical Significance?" *Annals of Internal Medicine* 136, no. 11 (2002): 817–25.

Keener, Craig S. *Miracles: The Credibility of the New Testament Accounts.* 2 vols. Grand Rapids: Baker Academic, 2011.

Keith, Chris. "Memory and Authenticity: Jesus Tradition and What Really Happened." *Zeitschrift für die Neutestamentliche Wissenschaft und die Kunde der älteren Kirche* 102 (2011): 155–77.

Kelhoffer, James A. *Miracle and Mission: The Authentication of Missionaries and Their Message in the Longer Ending of Mark.* WUNT 2/112. Tübingen: Mohr Siebeck, 2000.

Klauck, Hans-Josef. *The Apocryphal Acts of the Apostles: An Introduction.* Translated by Brian J. MacNeil. Waco: Baylor University Press, 2008.

————. *The Religious Context of Early Christianity. A Guide to Graeco-Roman Religions.* Translated by Brian J. MacNeil. London: T&T Clark, 2003.

Kleinmann, Arthur. *Patients and Healers in the Context of Culture: An Exploration of the Borderland between Anthropology, Medicine and Psychiatry.* Berkeley: University of California Press, 1980.

Kollmann, Bernd. "Krankheitsbilder und soziale Folgen: Blindheit, Lähmung, Aussatz, Taubheit oder Taubstummheit." In *Kompendium der frühchristlichen Wundererzählungen,* vol. 1, *Die Wunder Jesu,* edited by Ruben Zimmermann et al., pp. 87–93. Gütersloh: Gütersloher Verlagshaus, 2013.

————. *Neutestamentliche Wundergeschichten: Biblisch-theologische Zugänge und Impulse für die Praxis.* Stuttgart: Kohlhammer, 2002.

Köster, Helmut. "Σπλάγχνον, κτλ." *Theological Dictionary of the New Testament,* edited by Gerhard Kittel and Gerhard Friedrich, translated by Geoffrey W. Bromiley, 7:548–59. Grand Rapids: Eerdmans, 1972.

Krieger, Dolores. *Therapeutic Touch as Transpersonal Healing.* New York: Lantern, 2002.

Kvalbein, Hans. *Jesus: Hva ville han? Hvem var han? En innføring i de tre første evangelienes budskap.* Oslo: Luther, 2008.

————. "The Wonders of the End-Time: Metaphoric Language in 4Q 521 and the Interpretation of Matthew 11.5 Par." *Journal for the Study of the Pseudepigrapha* 18 (1998): 87–110.

Labahn, Michael, and Bert Jan Lietaert Peerbolte, eds. *Wonders Never Cease: The Purpose of Narrating Miracle Stories in the New Testament and Its Religious Environment.* Library of New Testament Studies 288. London: T&T Clark, 2006.

Le Donne, Anthony. *Historical Jesus: What Can We Know and How Can We Know It?* Grand Rapids: Eerdmans, 2011.

LeShan, Lawrence. *The Medium, the Mystic, and the Physicist: Toward a General Theory of the Paranormal.* New York: Viking, 1974.

Lindström, Lars G. *Christian Spiritual Healing: A Psychological Study: Ideology and Experience in the British Healing Movement.* Acta Universitatis Upsaliensis Psychologia et Sociologia Religionum. Uppsala: Academiae Ubsaliensis, 1992.

Loos, Hendrik van der. *The Miracles of Jesus.* Supplements to Novum Testamentum 9. Leiden: Brill, 1965.

Lüdemann, Gerd. *Early Christianity according to the Tradition in Acts: A Commentary.* Translated by John Bowden. Minneapolis: Fortress, 1989.

Luz, Ulrich. *Matthew 8–20.* Translated by James E. Crouch. Hermeneia. Minneapolis: Fortress, 2001.

————. *Matthew 21–28.* Translated by James E. Crouch. Hermeneia. Minneapolis: Fortress, 2005.

————. *Studies in Matthew.* Translated by Rosemary Selle. Grand Rapids: Eerdmans, 2005.

MacDonald, Margaret Y. *Early Christian Women and Pagan Opinion: The Power of the Hysterical Woman.* Cambridge: Cambridge University Press, 1996.

MacMullen, Ramsay. *Christianizing the Roman Empire A.D. 100–400.* New Haven: Yale University Press, 1984.

MacNutt, Francis. *Healing.* Notre Dame: Ave Maria Press, 2006.

Maddocks, Morris. *The Christian Healing Ministry.* 3rd ed. London: SPCK, 1995.

McGuire, Meredith B. *Lived Religion: Faith and Practice in Everyday Life.* Oxford: Oxford University Press, 2008.

McGuire, Meredith B., and Debra Kantor. *Ritual Healing in Suburban America.* New Brunswick, NJ: Rutgers University Press, 1988.

Meggitt, Justin. "The Historical Jesus and Healing: Jesus' Miracles in Psychosocial Context." In *Spiritual Healing: Scientific and Religious Perspectives,* edited by Fraser Watts, pp. 17–43. Cambridge: Cambridge University Press, 2011.

Merz, Annette. "Der historische Jesus als Wundertäter in Spektrum antiker Wundertäter." In *Kompendium der frühchristlichen Wundererzählungen,* vol. 1, *Die Wunder Jesu,* edited by Ruben Zimmermann et al., pp. 108–23. Gütersloh: Gütersloher Verlagshaus, 2013.

Milgrom, Jacob. *Leviticus: A Book of Rituals and Ethics.* Continental Commentary. Minneapolis: Fortress, 2004.

Moerman, Daniel. *Meaning, Medicine and "Placebo Effect."* Cambridge: Cambridge University Press, 2002.

Moltmann, Jürgen. *Der Weg Jesu Christi: Christologie in Messianischen Dimensionen.* Munich: Kaiser, 1989.

———. *The Spirit of Life: A Universal Affirmation.* Translated by Margaret Kohl. Minneapolis: Fortress, 1992.

Murdock, G. P. *Theories of Illness: A World Survey.* Pittsburgh: University of Pittsburgh Press, 1980.

Neville, Robert Cummings. *The Truth of Broken Symbols.* Albany: State University of New York Press, 1996.

Nichols, Terrence. "Miracles in Science and Theology." *Zygon: Journal of Religion and Science* 37, no. 3 (2002): 703–16.

Nolland, John. *The Gospel of Matthew.* New International Greek Testament Commentary. Grand Rapids: Eerdmans, 2005.

Paget, James Carleton. "Miracles in Early Christianity." In *The Cambridge Companion to Miracles,* edited by Graham Twelftree, pp. 131–48. Cambridge: Cambridge University Press, 2011.

Pannenberg, Wolfhart. *Basic Questions in Theology: Collected Essays.* 2 vols. Translated by George H. Kehm. Philadelphia: Fortress, 1970.

———. "The Concept of Miracle." *Zygon: Journal of Religion and Science* 37, no. 3 (2002): 759–62.

Parsons, Stephen. *The Challenge of Christian Healing.* London: SPCK, 1986.

———. *Helhed Og Helbred.* Valby Kbh.: Unitas, 1998.

Pattison, Stephen. *Alive and Kicking: Towards a Practical Theology of Illness and Healing.* London: SCM, 1989.

———. *The Challenge of Practical Theology: Selected Essays.* London and Philadelphia: Jessica Kingsley Publishers, 2007.

Percy, Martyn. "Christ the Healer: Modern Healing Movements and the Imperative of Praxis for the Poor." *Studies in World Christianity* 1, no. 2 (1995): 111–30.

Pilch, John J. *Healing in the New Testament: Insights from Medical and Mediterranean Anthropology.* Minneapolis: Fortress, 2000.

———. "Jesus' Healing Activity: Political Acts?" In *Understanding the Social World of the New Testament,* edited by Dietmar Neufeld and Richard E. DeMaris, pp. 147–55. London: Routledge, 2010.

———. *Visions and Healing in the Acts of the Apostles: How the Early Believers Experienced God.* Collegeville: Liturgical Press, 2004.

Polkinghorne, John C. "The Credibility of the Miraculous." *Zygon: Journal of Religion and Science* 37, no. 3 (2002): 751–58.

Porterfield, Amanda. *Healing in the History of Christianity.* Oxford: Oxford University Press, 2005.

Pyysiäinen, Illka. "Mind and Miracles." *Zygon: Journal of Religion and Science* 37, no. 3 (2002): 729–40.

Reed, Jonathan L. *Archaeology and the Galilean Jesus: A Re-Examination of the Evidence.* Harrisburg, PA: Trinity Press International, 2000.

Remus, Harold. *Jesus as Healer.* Understanding Jesus Today. Cambridge: Cambridge University Press, 1997.

Robinson, Andrew. *God and the World of Signs: Trinity, Evolution, and the Metaphysical Semiotics of C. S. Peirce.* Philosophical Studies in Science and Religion. Leiden: Brill, 2010.

Sandnes, Karl Olav. "Beyond 'Love Language': A Critical Examination of Krister Stendahl's Exegesis of Acts 4:12." *Studia Theologica* 52 (1998): 43–56.

———. *The Challenge of Homer: School, Pagan Poets, and Early Christianity.* Library of New Testament Studies 400. London: T&T Clark, 2009.

———. "Imitatio Homeri? An Appraisal of Dennis R. MacDonald's 'Mimesis Criticism.'" *Journal of Biblical Literature* 124 (2005): 715–32.

———. "Markus — en allegorisk biografi?" *Dansk Teologisk Tidsskrift* 69 (2006): 275–97.

———. "Whence and Whither: A Narrative Perspective on Birth *Anōthen* (John 3,3–8)." *Biblica* 86 (2005): 153–73.

Schleiermacher, Friedrich. *The Christian Faith.* Edited by H. R. Mackintosh and J. S. Stewart. Edinburgh: T&T Clark, 1999.

Schlier, H. "Ἔλαιον." In *Theological Dictionary of the New Testament,* edited by Gerhard Kittel and Gerhard Friedrich, translated by Geoffrey W. Bromiley, 2:470–73. Grand Rapids: Eerdmans, 1964.

Schlitz, Marilyn. "Spirituality and Health: Assessing the Evidence." In *Spiritual Healing: Scientific and Religious Perspectives,* edited by Fraser Watts, pp. 140–52. Cambridge: Cambridge University Press, 2011.

Schneemelcher, Wilhelm, and R. McL. Wilson, eds. *New Testament Apocrypha.* 2 vols. Louisville: Westminster John Knox, 1991–1992.

Schnelle, Udo. *Theology of the New Testament.* Translated by M. Eugene Boring. Grand Rapids: Baker Academic, 2007.

Sittler, Joseph. *Essays on Nature and Grace*. Philadelphia: Fortress, 1972.

Sloan, Robert Bryan. *The Favorable Year of the Lord: A Study of Jubilary Theology in the Gospel of Luke*. Austin, TX: Scholars Press, 1977.

Stark, Rodney. *The Rise of Christianity: A Sociologist Reconsiders History*. Princeton: Princeton University Press, 1996.

Stenmark, Mikael. *Scientism: Science, Ethics, and Religion*. Ashgate Science and Religion Series. Aldershot, UK: Ashgate, 2001.

Strelan, Rick. "Acts 19:12: Paul's 'Aprons' Again." *Journal of Theological Studies* 54 (2003): 154–57.

Talbert, Charles H. *Reading Acts: A Literary and Theological Commentary*. Rev. ed. Macon, GA: Smyth & Helwys, 2005.

Taylor, Charles. *A Secular Age*. Cambridge: Harvard University Press, 2007.

Theissen, Gerd. "Jesus and His Followers as Healers: Symbolic Healing in Early Christianity." In *The Problem of Ritual Efficacy,* edited by William S. Sax, Johannes Quack, and Jan Weinhold, pp. 45–65. Oxford Ritual Studies. Oxford: Oxford University Press, 2010.

———. *Miracle Stories of the Early Christian Tradition*. Translated by Francis Mcdonagh. Edinburgh: T&T Clark, 1983 (German version 1974).

———. *The Shadow of the Galilean: The Quest for the Historical Jesus in Narrative Form*. Translated by John Bowden. London: SCM, 1987.

Theissen, Gerd, and Annette Merz. *The Historical Jesus: A Comprehensive Guide*. Translated by John Bowden. London: SCM, 1998.

Tillich, Paul. *Systematic Theology*. Vol. 1. Chicago: University of Chicago Press, 1967.

A Time to Heal: A Contribution to the Ministry of Healing; A Report for the House of Bishops on the Healing Ministry. London: Church House Publishing, 2000.

Twelftree, Graham H. *Jesus the Miracle Worker: A Historical and Theological Study*. Downers Grove, IL: InterVarsity, 1999.

———. *Paul and the Miraculous: A Historical Reconstruction*. Grand Rapids: Baker Academic, 2013.

Twelftree, Graham H., ed. *The Cambridge Companion to Miracles*. Cambridge: Cambridge University Press, 2011.

Van Huyssteen, J. Wentzel. *Alone in the World? Human Uniqueness in Science and Theology*. Grand Rapids: Eerdmans, 2006.

Van Voorst, Robert E. *Jesus outside the New Testament: An Introduction to the Ancient Evidence*. Grand Rapids: Eerdmans, 2000.

Ward, Keith. "Believing in Miracles." *Zygon: Journal of Religion and Science* 37, no. 3 (2002): 741–50.

Warrington, Keith. *Jesus the Healer: Paradigm or Unique Phenomenon?* Carlisle, UK: Paternoster, 2000.

Watts, Fraser N. "Conceptual Issues in Spiritual Healing." In *Spiritual Healing: Scientific and Religious Perspectives,* edited by Fraser Watts, pp. 1–16. Cambridge: Cambridge University Press, 2011.

Webster, John: "Wunder, Dogmatisch." In *Die Religion in Geschichte und Gegenwart:*

Handwörterbuch für Theologie und Religionswissenschaft, edited by Hans Dieter Betz et al., vol. 8, cols. 1055–59, 1727–29. Tübingen: Mohr Siebeck, 2005.

Weissenrider, Annette. "Stories Just under the Skin: Lepra in the Gospel of Luke." In *Miracles Revisited: New Testament Miracle Stories and Their Concepts of Reality,* edited by Stefan Alkier and Annette Weissenrieder, pp. 73–100. Studies of the Bible and Its Reception 2. Berlin: De Gruyter, 2013.

Wells, Louise. *The Greek Language of Healing from Homer to New Testament Times.* Beihefte zur Zeitschrift für die neutestamentliche Wissenschaft 83. Berlin: De Gruyter, 1998.

Wilkinson, John. *The Bible and Healing: A Medical and Theological Commentary.* Edinburgh: Handsel Press; Grand Rapids: Eerdmans, 1998.

———. *Health and Healing: Studies in New Testament Principles and Practice.* Edinburgh: Handsel Press, 1980.

Williams, Rowan. "A Theology of Health for Today." In *Wounds That Heal: Theology, Imagination and Health,* edited by Jonathan Baxter, pp. 3–14. London: SPCK, 2007.

Witherington, Ben, III. *The Acts of the Apostles: A Socio-Rhetorical Commentary.* Grand Rapids: Eerdmans, 1998.

———. "Salvation and Health in Christian Antiquity: The Soteriology of Luke-Acts in Its First-Century Setting." In *Witness to the Gospel: The Theology of Acts,* edited by I. Howard Marshall and David Peterson, pp. 145–66. Grand Rapids: Eerdmans, 1998.

Wright, David P., and Richard N Jones. "Leprosy." In *The Anchor Bible Dictionary,* edited by David Noel Freeman, 4:277–82. New York: Doubleday, 1992.

Index of Names

Index of Subjects

Index of Scripture and Other Ancient Texts